NARROW BOAT

'Narrow Boat'

NARROW BOAT

L.T.C. ROLT

This seventieth anniversary edition is supported
by the Canal & River Trust, in grateful thanks to
the countless enthusiasts, past, present and future,
who keep our waterways alive

Dedicated to the Vanishing Company of
'Number Ones'

First published 1944
Second revised edition 1948
Published by Methuen London Ltd in 1984
Published by Mandarin Paperbacks in 1991
Published by Alan Sutton Publishing Ltd in 1994, in association with
The Inland Waterways Association

First published by The History Press in 2009
This anniversary edition published in 2014

Reprinted 2017, 2020, 2024

The History Press
97 St George's Place, Cheltenham, Gloucestershire, GL50 3QB
www.thehistorypress.co.uk

British Library Cataloguing in Publication Data.
A catalogue record for this book is available from the British Library.

ISBN 978 0 7509 6061 8

Printed by TJ Books Limited, Padstow, Cornwall

FOREWORD TO THE SEVENTIETH ANNIVERSARY EDITION

Welcome to the book that, more than any other, made the modern canal possible. *Narrow Boat* is a slow travelogue; a joyous and sensual celebration of life afloat; a long, delicious hymn to the waterways. It is a reminder that life can be lived fully – perhaps most fully – in a small space. It is, above all, a description of life on and around the British canals, full of human and natural history, and much of what it describes is still there.

Narrow Boat is a great book by a prolific author. It is full of love and respect; it tells a true story in a strong voice. It is driven by a compulsion to explain the canals to those who don't yet know them. Rolt was a missionary for the canals – he wants you, the reader, to feel the connection between land and water, between then and now, between the people of water and bank.

Its first publication, seventy years ago this year, focused the attention of a post-war generation on the waterways. These men and women rolled up their sleeves and began the work – political and physical – of restoring, maintaining and publicising the network of once-working water. Now in the custody of the Canal & River Trust, the inland waterways are transformed from their declining and sleepy status of 1944.

The live-aboard boating community, of which I am one moving part, has changed immensely since Rolt's day. Born-and-bred boat people can be counted in the dozens, and most working boats survive only as living relics. But there is a new floating population – a small town's worth of 15,000, caterpillaring around the waterways, meeting each other at Honeystreet or Red Bull. Some things remain unchanged – the White Swan at Fradley, the Greyhound at Sutton Stop and any pub called the Navigation remain landmarks for the boat community and the holiday boaters who swell our ranks each year. It is still true amongst us that 'there is no distinction but that of capability' – so long as you can fit a bilge pump, we have no interest in what you do for a living. And Rolt might be surprised to know that a handful of 'Number Ones' – the owner-skippers who carry coal and other cargo – still exist, serving the needs of the floating village.

Boaters are not the only custodians of the water. Is it still true that 'most people know no more of the canals than they do of the old green roads which the pack-horse trains once travelled'? Perhaps not. The towpaths are populated not with children in hobnail boots, but with steely-bottomed cyclists in Lycra and young parents with pushchairs. Cities like Birmingham and Manchester have rediscovered the canal as a location for lively pubs and city walks. Engineering marvels like the Caen Hill Locks or the Anderton Boat Lift are tourist attractions and educational centres. Wildlife thrives in 2,000 miles of clean post-industrial water: otters in the middle of Bath, kingfishers in Wolverhampton!

If you know *Narrow Boat* already, this new edition will remind you of its pleasures. If you haven't read it before – beware. This book may change your life, as it did mine. At the very least, it will change your view of the canals that run just a few miles from you, wherever you are reading it.

The canal is a place of small miracles – a heron in the housing estate, a family working a holiday boat slowly through a lock. I write this in the living room of my boat *Tinker*, as Rolt wrote his aboard *Cressy*, and I write it half a mile from the dry dock in Stone, where *Cressy* saw out her days. I'm using a word processor, not a fountain pen. Much has changed in seventy years but it may still be true, as Tom Rolt reports in the words of old boatman Jack, 'If no-one went faster than what I do, there'd be a sight less trouble in this world'.

Jo Bell
Canal & River Trust's Canal Laureate
Spring 2014

FOREWORD

BY CHARLES HADFIELD

MY copy of *Narrow Boat* is on my desk. Published in 1944, Eyre
& Spottiswoode, London, price 12s 6d, Book Production War
Economy Standard. Inside the front cover is stuck the label of
The Ken Bookshop, 84 Victoria Street, S.W.1.

I was then working at neighbouring Horseferry House, writing instructional manuals as a member of the staff of the
National Fire Service, and had walked to Victoria Street for a
pub lunch, one ear cocked for the sound of a flying bomb. The
book's title and Herbert Tooley's richly coloured swag of canal
roses on the jacket caught my eye. I went in and bought it.

I knew nothing of L.T.C. Rolt. I had, however, already developed an interest in waterways from schooldays beside the
Grand Western Canal. Later I had spent the first three war
years on the fireboats of the London Fire Service, with leave
days given mostly to building up a canal-book collection from
the bomb-threatened shelves of the Charing Cross Road (including No. 84) and Museum Street, beginning canal-history
research behind the sandbagged library windows of the Institution of Civil Engineers, and with a fellow river-man planning
to buy a narrow boat, convert it, and then achieve splendid
canal cruises, all worked out from *Bradshaw*. Later, on the
Staff, I had opportunities to glimpse (seldom more than when
on duty) most of the country's canals and fix them in my mind,
and to research and write an instructional chapter on 'Fireboats
and Ship Fires'.

Frank Eyre was a colleague on the Staff. A yachtsman and
wild-water canoeist, our interests were close enough to colla-
borate in writing *English Rivers and Canals* (1945) for the
'Britain in Pictures' series published by Collins. It was almost
done when *Narrow Boat* appeared in time to be included in our
bibliography.

I read it through at a sitting, and felt like Stanley meeting
Livingstone. Here was a man who had done the voyaging, made
the discoveries, that I had planned. I wrote, he replied, I wrote
again, as seemingly a little earlier had another romantic, Robert

Aickman. From us three, with Frank Eyre as fourth, came the Inland Waterways Association.

I came to know Tom very well. We wrote, we visited, I spent a weekend with him and Angela on *Cressy*; he stayed with my wife and family in London. We soon realised that, about waterways as much else, we had quite different outlooks. But we always backed each other, stuck to each other, teased each other, gave each other copies of our books, exasperated each other, until that dreadful day when I left him, hardly able to lift his hand, in his Stanley Pontlarge garden a few weeks before he died.

In the whole post-war canal revival and flowering, *Narrow Boat* gave Tom Rolt a unique place, for by 1944 he had already done it. He knew, he understood how canal people lived and what they did, how canals worked. Aickman didn't, Hadfield didn't, Eyre didn't. None of us had ever steered a narrow boat, though Eyre was an experienced yachtsman and canoeist, and I could take a twin-screw fireboat on the tides of London River in the blackout. Today one has only to turn the pages of *Waterways World*, visit a canal bookshop, attend a boat rally, to realise Tom's achievement.

Since those long-ago days, I have become well-known in the canal world: a shelf-ful of books, four-year member of the British Waterways Board, founder or part-founder of several waterway organisations, president or vice-president of enthusiast bodies. As a product of mainly spare-time activity, it's not a bad record. Yet little of it, except maybe one or two canal histories, would have happened had *Narrow Boat* not been written. The time, the need and the man came together to produce the book. Here it is once more, triumphantly alive, almost fifty years after our first meeting.

February, 1991.

PREFACE TO THE SECOND EDITION

OVER eight years have now passed since the journey described in this book began—eight years which, in days more stable and assured than ours, would have seemed but a brief span. But in this age of dissolution that spring day in 1939 when I first stepped aboard 'Cressy' at Banbury seems to have receded into a past as remote as the first memories of my childhood. Truly I have sailed into another age.

Last summer 'Cressy' voyaged again over the greater part of the route which is here described, and it was an interesting, though, alas, generally melancholy experience to note the changes which had taken place in the years between. They make a sorry catalogue. Of that gallant company of master-men, the 'Number Ones' of the Oxford Canal, one alone, Mr. Joseph Skinner of the 'Friendship', survives. The rest have either sold their boats and their labour to Carrying Companies or, disheartened by the continuing deterioration of the waterway and the difficulties of this bureaucratic age, they have given up boating and taken jobs ashore. Yet often I have seen them on the drawbridge at Banbury gazing wistfully at the waterway they know so well, for their hearts are on 'the cut'.

The old post-mill on the green crown of Burton Dassett Hill is no longer a distant landmark for the boatmen who still traverse that winding summit-level from Marston Doles to Claydon, and they can no longer slake their thirst in the friendly bar of the 'Bull and Butcher' at Napton. The mill was reduced to splintered wreckage by a violent summer gale in 1946, while the licence of the 'Bull and Butcher' has been transferred to some street-corner house in Leamington.

In 1939, when we passed through Junction Lock on the River Soar below Leicester, an old lady came out of the lock cottage and showed us a cherished framed photograph of 'Cressy' taken some years before. Remembering this in 1947, as we worked our way up from the Trent, we resolved to moor for the night at Junction Lock. But when we reached our destination in the dusk of a fine summer's evening we could not believe our eyes. The cottage had vanished without trace; not a brick remained, and the trim garden had become a wilderness.

On the Shropshire Union Canal a once-sheltered mooring had been laid waste by an aerodrome; the trees hacked down, the fields a desert of tarmac runways and rusty hangars. When we attempted to come alongside Victoria Wharf at Market Drayton, as we had done before, we found we could not get within six feet of the quay wall for the mud which choked the waterway. There was still coal on the wharf, but it came by lorry, and not by boat. Not Cheshire cheese, but an imported substance euphemistically so called now fills the canal-side warehouse at Nantwich, while down in the town, Churche's Mansion, where we had taken tea in the candle-lit panelled hall, stands empty and fast falling to complete ruin. These are but a few examples out of many.

When this book first appeared I was accused by certain left-wing reviewers of waxing sentimental and nostalgic over a vanished and largely mythical past, and of ignoring that bright 'progressive' future which, according to their philosophy, lies always just round the next corner. But the portents of this future which I saw in the course of my 1947 voyage were fungus-like outcroppings of those tin huts called 'pre-fabs'; new factories in the fields while the land's fertility was squandered in the smoke of straw fires and woodlands were clear-felled. I was not impressed.

To the devotees of this brave new world, to talk of master-men, of mills or village pubs, oak trees or English cheese is merely to be sentimental and reactionary. Yet I believe now, as I believed when I wrote this book, that these things do not belong merely to the past. They are timeless because they represent certain qualities and standards of value which, in the words of Mr. H. J. Massingham in his Foreword, are immortal and cannot altogether die. If they did so, the soul of England would go with them. As a result of the most pathetic fallacy that ever be-devilled the mind of man, that soul is threatened to-day as it has never been threatened before, yet it will not perish.

It is a strange comment on our age to reflect that the custodians of what remains of the England of the spirit are no longer her appointed governors, but a number of voluntary Societies and private bodies engaged in a ceaseless struggle against that collectivist bureaucracy which has now inherited the illusions of industrialism. The Council for the Preservation of Rural England; the National Trust; the Society for the Preservation of Ancient Buildings; the Footpaths Preservation Society—these and many others have done and are doing much excellent work. Yet the canals and rivers of England, threatened as they are by neglect, maltreatment and pollution, have hitherto had no organised body specifically devoted to championing their cause. Perhaps this is because that cause is so complex, our waterways being at once a transport system, a source of water supply and land drainage, a sporting amenity as well as a characteristic feature of our countryside. It is pleasant, therefore, to be able to say that, partly as a result of the interest aroused by this book, an Inland Waterways Association has been formed for the purpose of safeguarding this particular part of our heritage. Already it has done much useful work. If you find pleasure in the pages which follow you could not register your appreciation in a more practical manner than by giving your support to the Association's efforts.

11, *Gower Street,*
*London, W.C.*1
November, 1947.

CONTENTS

PART 1

PART 2

CONTENTS

PART 3

Grateful acknowledgements are due to Messrs. Sidgwick and Jackson for permission to quote the stanzas opposite from a poem by Rupert Brooke; and to Messrs. Methuen and the Executors of the late Sir Arthur Quiller-Couch for part of the latter's poem "Upon Eckington Bridge".

" I shall desire and I shall find
         The best of my desires;
The Autumn road, the mellow wind
That soothes the darkening shires,
         And laughter, and inn-fires.

" White mist about the black hedgerows,
         The slumbering Midland plain,
The silence where the clover grows,
And the dead leaves in the lane,
         Certainly, these remain."

RUPERT BROOKE

WATERWAYS
OF THE
MIDLANDS
▪▪
CRESSY'S ROUTE ▭
OTHER CANALS ▬

E.S. Morton

PART ONE

PART ONE

Chapter I

INTRODUCTION TO THE CANALS

MOST people know no more of the canals than they do of the old green roads which the pack-horse trains once travelled. Of all the authors who have written of their journeyings about England, only Mr. Temple Thurston chose to travel by water, and his delightful book 'The Flower of Gloster', published nearly thirty years ago, stands on the one small shelf in my library which is sufficient to contain all that has been written about the canals. For they have lapsed into the neglected obscurity which overtook the turnpikes when the railway deposed the stage-coach and ruined the great posting-houses along Watling Street and the North Road. Now the motor-car has brought the road into its own again, but the canals have withdrawn still farther into the shadows. Knowledge of them is confined to the narrow hump-backed bridges which trap the incautious motorist, or to an occasional glimpse from the train of a ribbon of still water winding through the meadows to some unknown destination.

I was equally ignorant myself until, ten years ago, a relative of mine purchased 'Cressy', an old horse-drawn barge, installed an engine, and converted her into a 'pleasure boat'. I was fortunate enough to be a member of the crew on her maiden voyage, and there and then acquired a passion for canal travel which has increased with the passing of years. It seemed to me to fulfil in the fullest sense the meaning of travel as opposed to a mere blind hurrying from place to place, and I felt certain that there could be no better way of approaching what is left to us of that older England of tradition which is fast disappearing.

To step down from some busy thoroughfare on to the quiet tow-path of a canal, even in the heart of a town, is to step backward a hundred years or more and to see things in a different, and perhaps more balanced perspective. The rush of traffic on the road above seems to become the purposeless scurrying of an overturned anthill beside the unruffled calm of the water, which even the slow passage of the boats does not disturb.

Because they have been outpaced and forgotten in the headlong flight of modern progress, many old traditions and customs survive on the canals. Their people are still a highly individual community who have so far escaped the levelling influence of standardised urban thought and education. They rarely marry 'off the land', for they have a strong clannish pride, and the boatman's roving life allows him little time for courtship. Moreover, few girls not born in a boat cabin can stand the hard conditions of cramped quarters and exposure to all weathers. On still summer days this peaceful gliding through the green heart of the country may seem idyllic, but it is a different tale to stand for hours at the tiller or work a boat through endless locks when cold winter rains come sheeting down, or when a bitter north-easter numbs the fingers, ruffles the water into little breaking waves and makes locksides treacherous with ice.

Few boatmen can either read or write, and, like many country folk, they often appear surly and taciturn to strangers from the towns. But beneath this natural reserve there shines a bright intelligence whose great charm lies in the fact that it has not been acquired from Council schools and newspapers, but is in part traditional and in part evolved during many slow journeyings with only heron and plover for company. Their inborn gipsy love of colour and polished metal finds expression in the gaily painted cabins of their boats and in the wealth of glittering brass ornaments which adorn them. These gay, vividly contrasting colours have become as naturally a part of the canal scene as the bright plumage of the kingfisher, because they are the product of an artistic instinct which is entirely unselfconscious.

The canals have their own inns and their own shops, and because they follow their own independent, tortuous routes about England, often seeming purposely to avoid towns, the places whose names are household words to the boatman mean nothing to the landsman. And what attractive names they are! Cowroast, last of the fifty-seven locks by which the Grand Union Canal climbs out of London over the Chiltern ridge; Stoke Bruerne, a canal village by the southern portal of Blisworth Tunnel in Northamptonshire; Great Haywood in Staffordshire, where the canal from the Severn meets the Grand Trunk waterway from east to west. Cowroast is only a cottage by a lock, and the other two are quiet villages, yet their names are as significant to the boatman as are those of Crewe or Swindon to the railwayman.

As one would expect, such an exclusive community possesses a traditional language of its own. For instance, there is no 'port' or 'starboard' on the canal, the boat captain calling to the 'steerer', 'Hold in!' (*i.e.*, towards the towing path) or 'Hold out!' The canal itself is invariably referred to as the 'cut', owing to its artificial character as distinct from the natural channel of a river, while 'Cressy', the craft which gave me my first experience of canal travel, was not, in correct parlance, a barge at all, but a 'narrow boat', built to pass the locks of 'narrow cuts'. To become still more technical, she was a 'Shroppie fly-boat', which, being interpreted, means that she was built by the Shropshire Union Canal Company, and worked for them 'fly'—that is, she travelled night and day, using relays of horses, like the old fliers of the roads. For this reason she was of slightly finer build than the slower craft, being intended for lighter and more perishable cargoes.

When the Shropshire Union Company ceased carrying with their own boats, 'Cressy' was sold to a miller at Maesbury on the Welsh Canal, for whom she carried coal until she changed hands once more and was converted.

For ten years I kept track of her vagrant wanderings about England, for I had made a resolve that one day I would acquire, if not 'Cressy' herself, then a boat like her, and use her not merely as a holiday craft, but as a permanent home. I felt convinced that it would be possible to live both comfortably and economically in the space available.

During this long period of waiting I snatched a few all-too-brief trips aboard her, walked many miles along canal towing-paths, and spent long winter evenings planning the arrangements of a floating home down to the smallest detail. A large-scale map of the canal system hung on the wall of my bedroom, and I would lie abed planning imaginary journeys.

I had also acquired a second-hand copy of a book which is indispensable to any canal traveller, 'Bradshaw's Guide to the Canals and Navigable Rivers of England and Wales', by the late Mr. Rodolph de Salis. This may sound dry reading, but I pored over it by the hour. Perhaps it was the names which appeared in the distance tables which fascinated me most and made the pages live. Sheepwash Staunch, Maids Moreton Mill and Wainlode; Honeystreet, Rushey Lock, Freewarrens and Stoke Bardolph; Foxhangers, Sexton's Lode, Offord D'Arcy and Withybed Green— these names had for me the power of poetry to conjure beauty in my imagination. Others stirred me no less by their oddity: Bumble-hole Bridge, Popes Corner and Nip Square; Plucks Gutter, Stew-poney Wharf and Blunder Lock; Old Man's Footbridge and Guthram Gout; Baitsbite Sluice, Dog-in-a-Doublet, Twentypence Ferry and Totterdown. What a wealth of history and legend spoke here and clamoured to be explored! Honeystreet and Wainlode had all the languorous scents and sounds of summer in them, while surely foxes barked in the dark coverts of Foxhangers under the harvest moon. Did fishermen flock to Baitsbite Sluice? Who was Guthram, and did they brew strong ale at Totterdown? I was resolved to find out.

Meanwhile each year brought tidings of declining canal traffic, of once-thriving waterways becoming choked with weeds and mud and, worse still, of some closed forever. Maesbury Mill closed down, and the little boatyard at Frankton on the Welsh Marches, where 'Cressy' was converted, soon followed. It was a significant comment on the times that the boat-builder went to work as a carpenter at a nearby aerodrome on what, a year or two before, had been open fields.

Next came the news of a 'burst'. Part of the canal bank blew out on the western section of the Welsh Canal just below its junction with the arm that runs north to Llangollen over Telford's great aqueducts at Chirk and Pont-Cysyllte. It was not a serious matter, for canal lengthmen have since told me that it would have taken only a few days' work to restore the canal to navigable condition, but this was not to be. For the Railway Company it was a welcome pretext to abandon a liability, and so thirty-five miles of canal up the lovely valley of the Severn between the Long Mynd

and the Mountains of Montgomery as far as Newtown was left to
fall to ruin. One horse-boat, trading to Welshpool with coal, was
caught on the wrong side of the breach, and there, presumably,
she will lie until her gay paintwork is weathered away and her
timbers rot, for there is no way out.

In a few years the Welsh Canal will doubtless become no more
than a dry ditch, like the old Wilts and Berks Canal or the waterway connecting the Thames with the Severn, which look as
though they had lain idle for a century, although there are boatmen still living who have worked over them.

There is something indescribably forlorn about these abandoned
waterways; like old ruined houses or silent mills, they are haunted
by the bygone life and toil which has left its deathless, eloquent
mark upon them. Just as in old houses the worn stone steps are
the memorial of many vanished feet, so on the canals it is the
grooves worn by the towing-lines in the rotting wooden lockbeams
or the crumbling brickwork of bridges that bring the past to life.

Most beautiful and most tragic of all is the old Thames and
Severn Canal, climbing up the Golden Valley between great hills
that wear their beechwoods like a mane. At the summit at Sapperton it pierces the spine of the Cotswold scarp by a tunnel two and
a quarter miles in length, and thereafter winds across the open
wolds to join the young Thames at Inglesham above Lechlade. At
Daneway, a tiny village clinging to the steep slope by the western
portal of the tunnel, there is an old inn of Cotswold stone where
they still remember the boats. The wide windows under their
carved drip-stones have seen them moored in what is now a grassy
hollow, and they have watched the smoke of cabin fires soar upward on still evenings against the dark background of the hanging
beechwoods. The 'Flower of Gloster' was one of the last boats to
travel from the Severn to the Thames by this route, and I shall
never cease to envy Mr. Temple Thurston his good fortune. Perhaps
it is because I have a particular regard for the Cotswold country
that I regret most the passing of this, the only Cotswold canal.

These waterways were gone, but how many more would fall to
ruin before I got my boat? I knew of two that were in danger: the
Kennet and Avon Canal from Reading, which crosses the Wiltshire
downs to Bath, and the Stratford-on-Avon Canal, which joins the
Avon at Stratford by way of Lowson Ford and Preston Bagot in
Arden. If I did not take to the water soon, these, and perhaps
many more, might be lost to me.

Then I was lucky enough to meet a companion who found the prospect of a roving life on a canal boat equally attractive. What were the alternatives? An unsettled existence in some urban flat, or the uneasy isolation of a country cottage menaced by the ever-present threats of new aerodromes, by-pass roads or 'desirable' building sites. These prospects did not please us, and we resolved to find a suitable boat and get married the following year.

I knew that 'Cressy' had been laid up for some time past at a boatyard on the Oxford Canal at Banbury, so I went over and saw her. Her cabin-work stood in need of repair and she badly wanted repainting, but her hull was still sound, so I took the plunge and bought her. She had been fitted out as a holiday craft to accommodate a party of eight, and my biggest job would be to convert her interior into comfortable permanent quarters for a crew of two. An engineer by profession, I knew not the first thing about carpentry, but I determined to tackle this job myself, not only to ease the strain on my slender resources, but to obtain that added satisfaction which only one's own handiwork can give.

Thus it came about that ten years of waiting and planning came to an end one April day when I loaded my old car with luggage, blankets and provisions and headed for Banbury. At last I was the captain of the 'Cressy', and I could hardly believe my good fortune.

THE BOATYARD, BANBURY

Chapter II

TO BANBURY CROSS

IT was a sunny, boisterous day, and my road lay over the northern Cotswolds. Most motorists choose the tarmac highway which scorns the villages and cuts straight across the bare uplands through Stow-on-the-Wold and Chipping Norton. This is the route indicated by those motoring maps which depict the face of England covered by a network of thick red lines as ugly as the roads themselves. They are a useful diagram of roads to be avoided, but that is all. My guide has always been the inch-to-the-mile Ordnance Survey Map, which is a mine of information about the country, and the unfailing philosopher and friend of the true traveller.

The route I had chosen took me straight and steeply on to the hills above Winchcombe by way of Sudeley, and from their lofty summit the old town appeared as a small cluster of smoke-shrouded grey roofs sheltering under the great shoulders of Langley and Cleeve Common. This brought me to the old hill road to Campden, which follows the majestic, wave-like lift and fall of the Wolds by Lynes Barn and Stumps Cross. It was the turn of the year, and although the wind which swept across these great uplands had not yet lost its winter keenness, the sun shone with a brave new warmth. Buds, though unbroken, had already softened the starkness of trees and hedgerows, so that as I dropped down into Campden they gave to the view across the Vale of the Red Horse that particular misty quality which is so characteristic of early spring.

There is a great charm about the broken country between Camp-

den and Banbury. The lias of the Warwickshire Plain thrusts a
deep bay between the northernmost outposts of Cotswold and the
Edge Hills, where the limestone appears once more, but of that
more ochreous hue which is due to the presence of iron. The little
towns and villages along the road faithfully reflect the swift transition from one geological district to another because they are old,
and therefore true to local tradition and environment. Thus the
grey houses of Campden, with their roofs of stone slats from the
hill quars, are as much a part of the Cotswolds as the hills themselves, while Shipston-on-Stour, seven miles on, is built of that
rose-red brick which is so much in harmony with the softer landscape of the vale. The villages of Upper and Lower Brailes, though
under the shadow of the hills, are also of brick, but journey a little
farther and the thatched cottages of Swalcliffe, Tadmarton and
Broughton are all built of the tawny Edge Hill limestone.

After such a journey the outskirts of Banbury were a sorry sight,
for the sturdy stone heart of this old market town by the Cherwell
is besieged on all sides by semi-detached monstrosities whose
growth has recently received fresh impetus from new industrial
expansion. Doubtless it is for this reason that Banbury has received scant treatment from such authors as have visited her in
search of the 'picturesque', for as long ago as 1911 one wrote:
'There is little of the old aspect of Banbury left now'. Yet the
worth and the character of places cannot always be accurately
judged by first impressions. The beautiful 'show village', on
deeper investigation, often turns out to be as lifeless as a stuffed
bird in a museum, the cottages week-end dormitories for jaded
business men, and the great barns riding-schools or Road Houses.
'All for the eye', as an old Gloucestershire farmer I know once
said of them, 'and nothen for the belly'. On the other hand, towns
and villages which have a more workaday appearance often conceal, beneath an exterior that may seem positively drab, a character and charm which are no less than the old vigorous life of the
place. This was what I discovered in Banbury during my three
months stay. Had I only stayed as many weeks I might have
missed it.

The Oxford Canal is typically secretive in its passage through
the town, and, although there is a large wharf which handles a substantial trade in coal, a stranger would have difficulty in finding
any trace of it. Even some of the inhabitants of Banbury seem to
be unaware of its existence, as I discovered later when my state-

ment that I was living on a boat was accepted by local tradesmen as a sally of Münchausen humour. I do not blame them, for I paid several visits to the boatyard where 'Cressy' was moored before I became certain of finding my way without error. It lay down an extremely narrow street opening unobtrusively out of a corner of the Market Square. The name 'Factory Street' was almost illegible with age, and the best clue to its identity was a sign over a small shop on the corner which proclaimed 'Tripe, Ox Heels and Neats-foot Oil for Sale'. The street ended at a wooden drawbridge over the canal, to the left of which was the boatyard where 'Cressy' lay between two derelict narrow boats.

When I had shipped my belongings aboard I hurried back into the town to obtain the additional stores I needed before the shops closed: a loaf of bread and a pint of milk; sausages for supper and bacon for breakfast; paraffin for the lamps and a sack of coke from the gasworks for the saloon stove, since the nights were still cold.

On the opposite side of the drawbridge from the boatyard there was a lock, and on the lockside stood a toll office. There all the boats southward bound for Oxford with their cargoes of coal were checked and gauged. At eight o'clock every week-day evening the toll clerk locked the bridge in the closed position and swung a heavy door across the towing path, so that any late-comers had to tie up until the following morning. There can be no mistaking this hour of closing, for they still ring the curfew in Banbury. I heard the measured tolling of the bell very distinctly that evening as I was cooking my first meal in the galley, for the wind had fallen with the going down of the sun, and the air was still and very clear. It struck me as singularly appropriate that, on this lane of still water which was like a road that had fallen asleep, it should be this tranquil, ancient voice of the town, and not the roar of traffic, that I should hear.

I had selected the most promising of an elderly and rather dubious assortment of Li-Lo mattresses and was making my bed when the creak of tackle and the slow clip-clop of hooves on the towing-path opposite heralded the arrival of a belated horse-boat. I looked out. The boatman was walking beside his horse, and when they drew abreast of my window they halted, dim shapes in the darkness. The tow-line fell slack as the boat, low laden in the water, slid into view, and the scarcely perceptible ripples round her bluff bows died as she was checked and drawn into the side.

Golden lamplight streaming from the open aft doors of the cabin illumined the weather-beaten face of the woman at the tiller, and glinted on her gold earrings. These were my unknown neighbours on my first night afloat. Though they must have cast away soon after sunrise, they did not disturb me, for I slept soundly, despite the fact that the mattress I had so laboriously blown up deflated overnight, so that I awoke to find myself on the hard boards.

PAINTING THE CAN

Chapter III

THE BOAT BUILDERS

WHEN I awoke, the sunlight, reflected by the breeze-ruffled water, was weaving patterns of shifting light on the cabin roof, and from without came sounds of manifold activity. There was a clinking of hammer on anvil, the creak and sigh of forge bellows and the clatter of caulking mallets, while a lusty male voice was singing 'Bonnie Mary'. Presumably this songster was the blacksmith, for occasionally there came a stamping of hooves and the song would be interrupted by shouts of 'Whoa!' or 'Hold up, will you!' I looked out to see two cart-horses outside the door of the smithy, awaiting their turn to be shod, and men at work on the narrow boat in the dry dock.

The Banbury Boatyard was a typical example of the small, skilled family business which is having such a bitter struggle for existence in these days when the demand is for quantity and not quality. This demand expects extended credit and cut prices, two conditions which the craftsman cannot fulfil, since he lacks the necessary capital reserve, and is unwilling and unable to compete against the inferior mass-produced article.

Old Mr. Tooley had been a boatman like his father until he went into the boat-building business many years ago. He was a little, bent old man with drooping white moustaches, and a most engaging smile that sent fans of wrinkles spreading from the corners of his remarkably bright eyes. He wore a battered bowler hat whose austere black had mellowed with age to a rusty brown, and the combination was so inseparable that the eye soon grew to accept the ancient headgear as a natural part of the man. He was getting too old for heavy work, and, as he himself admitted, he 'couldn't get his breath like he used'. But, like the old blacksmith next door, who, although nearly blind, still pottered down to the forge to blow the fire for his son, Mr. Tooley could not leave the scene of his life's work. It was gratifying indeed to find that his two sons were carrying on their father's craft.

Time was when they built the long wooden boats at Tooley's yard, but now, owing to the decline of canal traffic and the introduction of the steel boat, their work was confined to repairs. The average wooden narrow boat requires docking about once every three years, so that this work was spasmodic and, despite the fact that the family were prepared to tackle any job in the way of joinery or wheelwrighting that would tide them over, there were times when the yard fell slack. Because of this, George, the elder son, had been forced to take a job at the new factory on the outskirts of the town. This is a typical instance of the way in which the craftsman is being compelled to forfeit the birthright of his hereditary craft and lose himself in the modern industrial system, where the skill of hands is subordinate to the rapidity of the machine. Perhaps one day we shall awaken from the spell of the machine and realise how much natural art and skill we have lost in this sorry process.

One of the most damaging effects of modern mechanised industry is the intensive specialisation it involves. The so-called skilled operative acquires such a mechanical dexterity by performing a single repetition job that he becomes as helpless as a raw apprentice when confronted with a strange task, or if he is deprived of his costly jigs and tools. Your true craftsman, on the other hand, is infinitely versatile, because he relies primarily upon the hand and the eye, the finest and most adaptable tools in the world. The Tooley family demonstrated this versatility in the way they had adapted themselves to meet changing conditions by acquiring a considerable mechanical skill which was entirely self-taught. When the crude-oil engine began to supersede the horse on the Oxford Canal they fitted several motors in horse-boats with

great success. They installed their own generating plant to light
the workshop and charge the boatmen's wireless batteries. Most
remarkable of all, when this engine broke a piston, they did not, as
you would suppose, send an urgent order to the manufacturer for
a spare, but set to work to make another. This meant making a
wooden pattern, core and mould-box, constructing the mould in
sand, melting the iron in a crucible over their small open hearth,
pouring the mould and turning the casting to size. All this was
done as though the task was of every-day occurrence, and the
engine has run perfectly ever since.

Nevertheless it was their work of repairing and furbishing the
wooden boats that most delighted me, for it was no less than the
last miraculous survival of a craft centuries old. In the thirteenth-
century Sainte-Chapelle, of Pierre de Montereau, in Paris there is a
carving upon a door which represents the building of the Ark.
Three mediaeval boat-builders are at work; one is swinging his
mallet as he caulks the seams between the timbers, which a second
is tarring from a pot with the aid of a long-handled brush; a third,
standing inside the hull, is using the adze. I saw these tools used
in precisely the same manner at Tooley's Yard. The adze has become almost extinct among the tools of the country carpenter,
who once used it extensively for squaring beams and roof-timbers,
but among canal boat-builders this rural bygone still survives. The
seams of the narrow boats are caulked with strands of oakum, and
the noise of the mallets which I heard so often was that same
sound which must have echoed through the woods by Beaulieu
River when they were building the 'Agamemnon' and the 'Eury-
alus' on the slips at Buckler's Hard. The tall rudder-post of the
canal boat suggests an association even older, for the boatmen call
it a 'ram's head', and so recall the carved fighting ships of the
Norsemen. On the inside of the hull the timbers are plastered with
hot 'chalico', a time-honoured mixture of tar, cow-hair and horse-
dung. Then a layer of felt or brown paper is applied, and finally
the thin vertical oak planks, or 'shearing', are nailed into position.
Sometimes the main timbers, or 'strakes', at the bow or stern have
to be renewed. These have a double curvature to conform to the
graceful inward and upward sweep of the hull. A single curve can
be obtained by the conventional method of steaming, but it was
explained to me that if both curves were obtained by this method
in a piece of straight-grained oak, it would sooner or later crack
and split. The craftsman's solution is to obtain a timber having one

correct curve already in the grain, so that it need be bent only in one direction. Mr. Tooley must have carried this natural curve in his mind's eye, for he related how, years ago, he had spotted a suitable oak tree growing on the outskirts of the town, and when at last he heard that it was to be felled to make way for housing development, he bought it. Now it lay in the yard sawn into timbers ready for use, and I can think of no better fate that could befall an English oak.

When the heavier jobs on the hull have been completed, the boat-builder's next task is the re-decoration, and I was lucky enough to see this work carried out on the boat 'Florence', which was on the dock at the time of my arrival. Each member of the family played his especial part. George began in his spare time from the factory; he was the lettering expert, and painted the owner's name and port of origin in elaborate cream lettering, shaded with blue, on the large vermilion centre panel of the cabin side. Then it was the old man's turn to embellish his son's work with little garlands of bright flowers in the four corners and between the lettering. Finally it was left to Herbert, the younger son, to paint his castles on the four small side panels. Apart from striking a line with a chalked string to keep the lettering level, they did no preliminary sketching or spacing out whatever, but worked straight out of their heads with wonderful rapidity and skill. I watched fascinated while Herbert painted the four castles in the space of one afternoon. Dipping first into one and then another of the small tins of oil paint of his own grinding and mixing, he blended together the green, the blue and the sepia until a typical scene, dear to generations of canal folk, suddenly took shape under his hand. Here it would be a castle with a single battlemented turret, rising against a background of rolling blue hills and red sunset; there a more monastic structure, twin towered, and backed by woods, a stream flowing improbably through an arch in the base of one tower and spreading into a lake in the foreground. Each panel differed from its neighbour, yet all were true to that traditional form which appears so strangely foreign in its conception. Who first established this convention of tall stuccoed towers and wide-eaved red roofs? Perhaps it was some old wandering Romany who exchanged his caravan for a narrow boat when the canals were young, and adorned the walls of his new home with his memories of fairy-tale castles in the Carpathians. Whatever the origin, its influence is still strong, for this was by no means the end of the decorative work. Castles were also painted on the inside of the cabin doors and in the cabin itself, while the 'ram's head', the tiller bar and the 'stands' and 'cratches' which support the gangplanks all had to be picked out with bright geometrical patterns of colour before the boatman's exacting eye was satisfied.

When all the work had been accomplished, and the 'Florence' was floated out, her captain stood beside old Mr. Tooley on the dock side. After an unhurried, critical scrutiny, 'Well, George,' he said, 'I reckon she looks well.' This remark, coming from a boatman, was high praise, and to my mind it was certainly well merited. A modern economist would have pointed out quite truthfully that she would have been just as serviceable had she been painted battleship grey throughout at a great saving of labour. But because the men of the canals are not economists, and have a standard of values which is not based upon paper money, the 'Florence' bore a coat of many colours, and lay resplendent in the morning sun.

Each boat carries two water-cans, one an open 'dipper' which, as its name implies, is dipped into the canal and used for a hundred and one domestic uses, from peeling potatoes to washing the captain's wool vest; the other is a tall can with handle, spout and lid, like a mammoth hot-water jug, in which drinking-water is stored. Both are elaborately decorated with flowers, and often carry the owner's name in white letters on a red circumferential band. The boatmen brought these cans to Mr. Tooley when they needed a repaint, for the old man excelled at this work. To behold him, as I did, when he sat before the bench in his narrow workshop, the battered bowler firmly planted on the back of his head and a tray of many-coloured paints at his elbow, was to see the past miraculously living in the present. Not a past preserved in a museum or spuriously recreated in an Art and Craft shop, but a vital tradition. Handling his fine camel-hair brushes with wonderful sureness and delicacy, he first of all painted little shaded discs of sepia, ochre and pink on the green ground of the can and surrounded them with at garland of pale green leaves. These were the centres of the roses. When they were dry, the petals, red on sepia, yellow on ochre and white on pink, were superimposed so simply and swiftly that only in the way a mere blob of paint seemed suddenly to blossom forth was the skill revealed. The bright work was completed when the veining of the leaves had been painted in with a very fine brush and a coat of varnish applied to preserve it.

Mr. Tooley was once asked by a London store to teach their

employees how to paint these flowers. I am glad that he refused, for his must surely be the only surviving natural art in this country which has not been commercially exploited and debased. I obtained a promise from him that, when my own work on 'Cressy' had reached the decorating stage, he would paint for me a bunch of roses on each of the four panels in the sleeping-cabin. Later I feared that he would never be able to keep this promise, for the old man was taken seriously ill with pneumonia and spent some time in the local hospital. When he was at length discharged he was still far from well, but he had not forgotten, and insisted upon painting them. The work tired him exceedingly, he rested frequently on the stool I provided for him, but his hand was still sure. He has painted no flowers since.*

Now, I do not envy the art collector his masterpieces of the past, for they, though great, are dead. These simple paintings are rarer, because they still live. They are unique survivals of the days when beauty was implicit in the work of hands, and was made manifest by those hands in an infinite variety of form and pattern which transformed the simplest object that they wrought into a thing of inspiration and delight.

* It is with sorrow that I have to record the death of Mr. George Tooley soon after this book was written.

Chapter IV

FITTING OUT

The company of such craftsmen as the Tooley family inevitably acted as a stimulus to my own amateurish activities, and I set to work with a will. I was given the freedom of their workshop and tools—a great privilege which I hope I respected as much as I appreciated it. If ever I should attain their degree of skill, which is unlikely, I hope that I shall be equally tolerant of the bungling efforts of beginners. I had set myself to complete an ambitious task in a very short space of time, for Angela and I had planned to marry in July, and were determined to set forth on our first cruise before the end of the summer. This inevitably induced a fatal temptation to hurry over the job which had to be most firmly suppressed. It would be out of place here to describe the work in minute detail, or enter into the technics of 'Cressy's' arrangement, but those who are interested will find a short description and a plan of the boat in the appendix at the end of this book.

As I have already mentioned, 'Cressy' had been fitted out as a holiday craft, and her accommodation, aft of a for'ard well deck, consisted of a large saloon twenty feet in length, containing two berths, an anthracite stove and built-in cupboards; a small galley with cooking-stove and sink, and three twin-berth sleeping cabins. The arrangement which I planned was to consist of a small dining saloon convertible into a spare sleeping cabin, a galley, a roomy sitting-cabin, a state-room, bathroom and, right aft, a small workshop. This scheme involved moving every existing bulkhead to a new position; installing a bath with hot-water system and sundry tanks; moving the sink and putting in a new stove, not to mention constructing innumerable lockers, cupboards and shelves. Meanwhile I commissioned the Tooleys to caulk and tar the hull, renew part of the cabin work, and repaint externally from stem to stern.

My long-thought-out plan of campaign was to establish myself as comfortably as possible in the fore-end of the boat, and tackle first what in a house would be described as 'the usual offices', before aspiring to more ambitious work in the new living-cabins. I began humbly enough by removing the chemical closet from its embarrassing position amidships and re-erecting it at the stern. Emboldened by this successful accomplishment, the workshop, with its bench and shelves, rapidly took shape. The bathroom came next, a far more formidable task, and here the first serious snag cropped up. In planning the interior of a boat every inch of space is vital, and we had decided to instal what is known as a 'short bath', a species which Angela had discovered in London. It was deeper than most, the occupant sitting with his feet in a trough, and its advantage was a considerable saving in overall length. Unfortunately we had entirely overlooked the fact that it was much too wide to pass through either fore or aft doors, whose maximum width was only eighteen and a half inches. Nothing daunted, I armed myself with a two-foot rule and set forth in search of another. Luckily, like most market towns, Banbury possessed several excellent ironmongers, and I found one only a minute's walk from the boatyard. Here I was led into a warehouse, where I clambered about among baths of every size and shape, a veritable labyrinth of cold white porcelain, at last unearthing one which measured exactly eighteen and a half inches in depth without its feet. I made a rapid mental reconstruction of my projected bathroom to allow for its extra length, and decided that it would do.

In the homes of the poor a fitted bath is still a rare luxury, but on a canal boat it was a phenomenon as fabulous as the alabaster swimming-pool of a millionaire. It was not surprising, therefore, that the arrival of my bath the following morning, borne upon a handcart in all its nakedness, and escorted by three men, should cause something of a stir in the boatyard. By dint of considerable effort on the part of the three custodians it was manoeuvred on board and lowered into position through the aft doors without accident. My next job was to mount it upon blocks of sufficient height to allow the waste to flow overside above water level, for I was anxious to avoid the tedious labour of pumping out, which, on so many craft, detracts from the pleasure of a hot bath. When this had been done the bath presented rather an odd appearance, there being a considerable space beneath, and I conceived the idea of enclosing it to make a couple of roomy cupboards. It was a more ambitious project than any I had tackled so far, and when I had carried it out successfully my carpentering confidence had grown to such an extent that I set about making the berth, dressing-table and hanging cupboard for the state room without more ado. In this fashion I steadily worked my way through the boat, tackling more elaborate work as I went on: a set of bookshelves covering one bulkhead of the sitting-cabin, with a writing-desk incorporated; two berths in the dining saloon with linen-chests below; a folding table; a wardrobe for guests and a dresser for china. Meanwhile my living and cooking space retreated before the rising tide of alterations, and I existed permanently in a resinous atmosphere of sawdust. In winter this state of affairs would have been most uncomfortable, but by this time spring had turned to summer.

At last the structural work was finished, and the next problem was the original one of decoration. Previously the boat had been painted throughout in the canal style of bright colours, but after much thought I decided not to repeat this. It struck me that the adoption of this style to such an unnatural extent and purpose savoured of the 'precious', a suggestion I was most anxious to avoid. Such an overwhelming assortment of colour was also distracting to the eye, which soon tired of its originality. On the other hand, I did not want 'Cressy' to resemble a chromium-plated Maidenhead cruiser. Somehow I had to steer a middle course between these two extremes, and the best plan seemed to be to abandon any set precedent, merely following the dictates of personal taste for better or worse. As a result, the small dining saloon and the galley were finished in the style of the boats, except that the walls had cream panelling to give more light. Berths and cupboards were painted and grained with scratch-combs in light oak with dark blue interiors in the traditional style. Doors, window surrounds, roof-beams and gunwale were all picked out in bright colours, and one of Herbert Tooley's castles adorned a wall panel. The workshop was treated in the same way, and as all three cabins were small, while the area of light paintwork was relatively large, the effect of the colours did not seem unnatural or overwhelming. The sitting-cabin was treated entirely with a flat cream paint to exaggerate its roominess and still further to enhance the light from the six windows. The desired effect of space was achieved most successfully, and in such a light, undistracting setting the bindings of the books in their shelves, a single bowl of flowers, or the map of the canals which occupies one panel of the wall, make adequate and satisfying focal points of colour. I know nothing of the art of interior decoration, yet I believe that it should never be assertive, aiming rather to provide a sympathetic background for a few well-chosen possessions. In the state-room Mr. Tooley's roses provided the colour, otherwise the scheme was the same, except that the roof-beams were painted apple-green to soften the transition between it and the bathroom, which was painted entirely in that shade.

Finally the question of curtains and coverings had to be settled, and Angela paid a flying visit from London with a host of patterns which we hung in windows and surveyed critically from every angle. Obviously we needed a very small-patterned material which would not overpower the diminutive windows. We eventually decided upon two designs: one a sateen with a minute sprigged pattern of roses on a cream ground, for use in the bathroom and state-room; the other a linen fabric having a small varied pattern of bright flowers which blended well with the colours of the galley and the dining saloon, but was not too bold for the sitting-cabin. We also used this material for cushion covers. We chose a serviceable dark brown linen for covering the mattress tops of the spare berths, and a carpet of the same shade for the sitting-cabin floor. All the other floors were stained only. Our two easy chairs were covered in plain buff linen. These last nearly shared the fate of the 'short bath', for once again we had chosen them in London with more enthusiasm than forethought. Angela was on board when they arrived, and when we saw them standing on the canal bank beside the boat, our hearts sank, they appeared so impossibly bulky. Obviously they would not pass through either doorway, and I almost fell to sawing the ends off the legs there and then. As a last resort we decided to try pushing them through the

large double windows of the sitting cabin, and after a prodigious amount of twisting, turning and struggling, we succeeded in getting them aboard. I do not think we shall ever wish
to move house, but if we do I am sure our chairs will never leave
the boat.

Chapter V

THE PEOPLE OF THE BOATS

DURING the weeks I was working on the boat I became familiar with all the boatmen who traded regularly along the canal. We would exchange greetings as they drifted by on their slow journeyings back and forth between Atherstone and Oxford, and, when they moored for the night by Banbury Stop, they evinced a lively interest in my progress, asking when I hoped to be ready and whither I was bound. There was ' Four-Boat Joe', so called because he and his companions worked between them no less than four horse-boats and always travelled in close company. One of them, the fattest man I have ever seen, habitually sat at the tiller of the hindmost boat, and was never seen ashore. His appearances were sometimes infrequent, because they occasionally loaded coal as far north as Langley Mill on the Cromford Canal in Derbyshire. This journey over half the length of England included three tunnels, which they had to negotiate by the old system of 'legging'. This meant lying on boards called 'wings' out-rigged from the boat sides and pushing with their feet against the tunnel walls. Then there were crudely painted boats from Moira on the Ashby-de-la-Zouch Canal, and black Warwickshire Canal motor boats from Nuneaton, but most interesting of all were the 'Number Ones'.

A 'Number One' is the canal term for a boat owned by her captain, as distinct from those owned by the canal carrying companies, which are worked by paid crews. In the past the bulk of the canal traffic was handled by these independents, the carrying company being a comparatively recent development, but modern conditions are all against the old race of owner-boatmen. Possessing no capital reserve to see them through a slack spell, and unable to draw dole allowance, they cannot survive the cut-throat com-

'A Long Horse's Tail Floated from the "Ram's Head" of the
"White City"'

petition of the modern haulage business. Many have given up the
unequal struggle by selling their boats and their labours to one or
other of the companies, and so—more is the pity—there are few
'Number Ones' left on the canals now, and certainly none finer
than those surviving on the Oxford Canal. Old John Harwood,
captain of the 'Searchlight'; Joseph Skinner of the 'Friendship';
Townsend of Abingdon and Beauchamp of Oxford; the Hones of
Banbury, father and son—these were fine men of the old school
who still kept their own boats. Three generations of Hones
worked three boats between them, Alfred Hone senior and his wife
the 'Cylgate', his son and daughter-in-law the 'White City', and his
granddaughters the 'Rose and Betty', which was named after
them. These boats were kept in spotless condition, as was only to
be expected, for an owner naturally has more pride in his boat
than a paid crew. All the paintwork was mopped down and the
brasswork polished at every available opportunity, and on one
boat there were canvas sheets which could be let down to protect
the varnish on the cabin sides from the sun. In addition to the
customary binding of pipe-clayed turk's heads, there floated from
the 'rams head' of the 'White City' a long horse's tail. I have tried
in vain to discover the origin of this custom, which I have since
seen on a few other boats, but, whatever the tradition, it has been
lost in the past. The brass bands and safety chains of the stove
chimneys always glittered like gold, and through the cabin doors
I would catch glimpses of the beloved rows of brass knobs glim-
mering and winking in the light, of the prized openwork plates
hanging on the walls, of immaculate lace curtains and gleaming
pans. Beside the resplendent water-cans on the cabin roof stood
green-painted flower-boxes planted out with pink and white
bachelors-buttons. Often there would be jam-jars also, filled with
great bunches of wild flowers gathered on the wayside—primroses,
cowslips, hyacinths or dog-daisies in their season.

Nearly every canal boat carries a pet. I once saw an old lady at
Brentford who had a great tabby cat, wearing a collar, which was
stalking round the cabin roof with mincing step and flaunting tail
while she stood at the tiller. A dog is a far more common companion, however, and most boatmen seem to find room for a
kennel somewhere in the cargo space. Often, too, a linnet or
canary in a cage swings from the cabin roof or flutters in the sun
on the deck. 'White City' carried two dogs and a coop of chickens,
while grand-daughter Betty kept a pair of rabbits on her boat.

When the boats are empty there is plenty of room for children and animals to play, and on one occasion I watched a boat pass the yard with three diminutive children having the time of their lives on improvised swings hung from the cross stretchers. When the boats are loaded it is a very different story; animals must find a precarious niche amongst the cargo, while the children are confined to the cabin.

The mere landsman, sitting in one of these narrow-boat cabins, only 8 ft. long by 7 ft. wide, cannot help but marvel that this is the boatman's home; that within this tiny compass all the manifold needs of a large family are administered, and that it has been a witness of all the comedy, drama and tragedy of many lifetimes. When the cabin doors are closed the only daylight comes from a small 'bull-eye' in the roof and a lookout forward, only a foot square, which is often obscured when the boat is loaded. Light at night is provided by a large three-cornered paraffin lantern hung in an angle of the wall. Immediately to the left of the doorway is the coal-fired cooking and heating stove, the space around it occupied by saucepans. On the stove-top tea is forever brewing, for the boat people are inveterate tea-drinkers. Their teapots, like their water-cans, are usually of an original and traditional design— a brown salt glaze stoneware ornamented with a band of coloured flowers in relief and a white plaque bearing in blue letters some simple motto such as 'Love at Home'. Their manufacture is now extinct, as I found when I tried to obtain one. They were last made especially for an old lady who kept a shop on the Ashby Canal, or the 'Moira Cut', as the boatmen call it. The supply failed with her death and the closing of her shop.

The boat wife keeps her provisions in two cupboards, one in the tapering stern aft of the deck, and the other beneath the deck floor. Next to the stove is another tall cupboard, set at an angle of forty-five degrees to the wall, the door of which, elaborately decorated with castle and flowers, is hinged at the base, and when opened forms a table for meals. When it is folded back after use any crumbs fall into a shallow drawer beneath, which is specially provided for this purpose. A wide bench along the opposite wall is the only sitting accommodation, and does duty at night as a side-bed for the children. A second and wider cross-bed, with cupboards above it and a folding centre portion, lies athwart the fore end of the cabin. It is usually screened by a pair of lace curtains. This is the boatman's marriage bed; here, in this little space, he was born and will one day die. No simpler existence can be imagined. The boatman's life is stripped of all the complex comforts with which we have surrounded ourselves at the price of contentment. He works and lives hard, but he has not heard of hire-purchase agreements, while the collectors of light and telephone accounts, rates and taxes, know him not.

Cleanliness in such cramped quarters means unremitting labour; there can be no half measures, and the canal folk are either scrupulously clean or unbelievably squalid. On investigation the latter class usually turn out to be a family 'off the land', the new poor without pride who are the product of industrial cities. Of recent years they have been extensively employed by the larger canal carrying companies, who are finding it difficult to recruit sufficient crews from the dwindling ranks of the old proud stock of independent boatmen. Soon they will be an extinct race. Their traditional and graceful dress is fast disappearing, a shoddy, shameless poverty is taking its place. Not so very long ago the boat captain wore trousers of buff corduroy or dark mock-moleskin, tight fitting, but belling from the knee. These he kept in place by a broad belt, woven of such bright colours that it resembled a vivid sash. His waistcoat, too, was of corduroy or moleskin, and he wore a coat of distinctive cut with high, old-fashioned lapels. I have seen one or other of these garments in use, but never the complete outfit, and only once, ten years ago, the gay belt. The captain's wife wore a tight-waisted cotton dress of checked or sprigged pattern, the bodice most elaborately ornamented with tucks or smocking, and the ankle-length skirt very full with pleats. Her feet were protected by black boots lacing to the calf. In cold weather she would drape a shawl about her shoulders or over her head, but in summer she would don a most wondrous black sub-bonnet, more closely resembling the mantillas of Spain than the simple bonnet of the English countrywomen. Man is usually the conservative of fashion, but curiously enough on the canals the position seems to be reversed, for it is the women who cling more tenaciously to their traditional dress. I have seen many wearing their distinctive dresses and shawls, and even the sun-bonnet is not quite extinct. I had thought that this was another item on the list of old and gracious things which had gone forever until, one warm summer evening when I was working on 'Cressy', an unfamiliar Warwickshire Canal boat passed by. The woman who stood at the tiller might have floated serenely through a century. She had on the typical tight-waisted dress, the full skirt swinging gracefully to her every movement and, to my wonder and delight, she was wearing her black bonnet. Rows of tucks made a dark halo over her head, and from the gathered crown a broad frilled wimple fell wide and low over her shoulders. Her vital, gipsy face and gold earrings could have found no more fitting frame. A little group of women from the cottages on Factory Street stood gossiping by the drawbridge, undistinguished and drab in their cheap, mass-produced clothes. She was poorer than they, yet possessed a grace and dignity that seemed almost regal.

The ubiquitous wireless set has become almost universal in the boat cabins, and is the boatman's only link with the modern world. He cannot read the newspapers, which is small loss to him, and he seldom has time or inclination for the cinema. Like our rural ancestors with their country songs, festivals and dances, he has to provide his own amusement, than which there is no healthier stimulant for talent. As a result many boatmen are self-taught musicians, and I found that nearly every boat on the Oxford Canal carried a melodeon, a concertina or an accordion. Often of a night time I would hear the familiar strains of 'Daisy Bell' or 'Two Lovely Black Eyes' floating over the water from the cabin of a moored boat. Needless to say, Herbert Tooley had become proficient in repairing these instruments, and I looked on one evening while he dexterously fitted a new key spring to a melodeon belonging to John Harwood of the 'Searchlight'. While he worked, the old boatman talked, his unhurried, rhythmical speech as soothing as a Gregorian chant. He described graphically his only journey in 'one o' they moty cars', whose speed struck him as being out of all reason, so great that it 'fair took the breath out of him'. He then went on to relate an encounter he had had with a local policeman, a story I shall never forget because it was such a perfect example of the boatman's simple yet shrewd philosophy. It happened early one morning that the policeman was crossing the Brackley Road bridge as the 'Searchlight' passed beneath bound for Oxford. He was a very young policeman, and seeing the old man placidly ensconced at the tiller of his slow-moving boat, he leant over the parapet and called sarcastically, 'Now then, don't you be in too much of a hurry'. He had not reckoned with old Jack, however. 'If no one went no faster than what I do,' came the sonorous reply from the canal, 'there'd be a sight less trouble in this world, and what's more, young man, you'd be out of a job like as not.' Even old Jack, wise though he is, cannot realise what a volume of truth lay in those few words.

Chapter VI

BELLS AND BEER

WHEN my work was unavoidably held up, or the boatyard workshop was shut down at week-ends, I found time to explore Banbury and the country district around it, discovering beneath a workaday surface the old life of the town which has survived the combined onslaughts of the Civil War and the Industrial Revolution. Cromwell and his Puritans ravaged the town with exceptional severity, pillaging the beautiful Gothic church so effectively that it was afterwards demolished. An engraving of it hangs in the vestry of the present church, a pompous structure in the Palladian style designed by a contemporary of Wren, a style that commemorates the birth of that self-conscious intellectualism which first scorned tradition. The local stone does not respond to this conceit, as it did to the simple but inspired hands of the Gothic craftsmen, and the church is as empty of feeling and faith as a mausoleum.

I climbed to the top of the tower with the young churchwarden, and together we leant over the balustrade while he pointed out various landmarks and we discussed the architectural merits of old buildings which we both knew. On this subject he was remarkably well informed, and it was gratifying to discover, in so young a man, an interest in the past so rare and so sincere. Below us lay the town, sprawling untidily across the broad valley of the Cherwell, and it was easy to trace its growth, from the nucleus of old buildings clustered about the market square, to the red rash of modern suburbia which had broken out on the western slopes along the Oxford road. From this high vantage point the canal assumed a more important place; for it was possible to follow its course—a broad silver ribbon winding through the meadows by the river—long after the roads out of the town had been lost to sight.

Meanwhile, inside the tower two perspiring individuals from a local firm of watchmakers were busily engaged in winding the church clock. This was no mean task, for no less than four great weights had to be raised from the base of the tower. These operated the movement, the quarter chime, the strike and the carillon. This last was installed in commemoration of Victoria's Jubilee, and interested me greatly, because although I had heard the carillons of Dursley, in the South Cotswolds, and of the bell tower of Evesham, I had never before seen the mechanism. The movement was similar to that of a child's musical box, being operated by a revolving fibre drum studded with brass pins which tripped the spring-and-cam-returned bell-cranks that were connected to the bell clappers by cables. When it was desired to change the tune, the drum could be moved laterally along its spindle so that another set of pegs was brought into action. Unfortunately the Banbury carillon was in a sorry state of repair, many of the pegs being worn or broken, so that only two of the original six tunes were still playable. I was lucky to see it at work, for in order to conserve its failing energies it was only set to play twice during the day. We watched and waited until the clock, ponderously ticking, crept to the hour and tripped the release. Then the old machine came to life with a most prodigious whirring and jangling of cables, and, high overhead, the bells rang out. There is a great serenity in the sound of a carillon, especially if it be heard distantly on a windless evening of high summer, or upon the hills. Then this measured repetition of simple notes voicing the passing of time seems also to express that unhurried, unshakeable continuity which is the very essence of country life. I hope that the Banbury carillon will not fall silent, but it will be an even sorrier day if that tradition which it voices, albeit brokenly, should perish.

The bells of Banbury were cast by successive generations of rural craftsmen at a long-vanished foundry in the neighbouring village of Chacombe. One can imagine what an undertaking the casting of the big tenor must have been, how all the villagers were agog for news that the cast had been successful, and eager to hear the bell's first deep, sonorous note. The Banbury men are great bell-ringers, and the records of past ringings of 'Grandsire Triples' hang round the belfry walls, together with a very perfect set of hand-bells.

The vandalism of the Puritans was inspired by misguided idealism and an understandable revolt against the autocracy of the Church. The second revolution is the more tragic because it lacks any ideal whatever. The brewers who have despoiled the old inns of Banbury, and the chain-store mongers who have defaced the ancient houses with their chromium and plate-glass shop fronts have been actuated solely by the aim of money-making. The English inn holds a place in the life of the village or country town as important as that of the church. For generations it has been the hub about which the vigorous life of the rural community revolved; it has been the poor man's parliament and platform, his playground, and his solace after labour. It is an institution which the milk-bar, the cinema and the social club can never replace, but the brewers have transformed it into a sordid drink-shop as characterless as their liquor. The Banbury inns were a particularly unhappy example. Old gables had been covered with drab pebble-dash or stucco and further disfigured by glaring signs which proclaimed the beer, not the house, while their interiors either displayed a featureless modernity or, more frequently, languished in the chill bleakness of pretentious Victorian mahogany and fly-blown aspidistras. Only at one a magnificent pair of oak doors beneath the courtyard archway remain to speak eloquently of the past. If, in some more enlightened future time, the havoc wrought by our commercialised age comes to be assessed, the brewers will face a heavy charge.

The shops have not suffered so hardly. A number still retain their old bow windows, especially in the bewildering maze of alleyways between High Street and Parsons Street, while above many an example of modern shop fitting the original upper windows of the fifteenth-century houses gaze down upon the busy streets like wise old eyes, their carved drip-stones like placid brows above them.

Banbury is at its best on Market Day, especially on a winter's evening, when the square is filled with stalls, each with its flickering naphtha flare, which casts such a magical leaping light upon the pyramids of oranges and apples that they glow like enchanted fruits of the Hesperides. I was glad to find that they still held open market, for too many have been banished from streets and squares that have seen their booths for centuries, and been condemned to gloomy market halls where they lose their vagabond charm, to become a species of multiple store where the kerb-side pedlar and the vociferous cheap-jack find no place. Two markets a week supply the old and the new life of the town. The first, held on a Thursday, is the larger, and caters, as it has always done, for the rural district of North Oxfordshire. Brightly painted mowers, ploughs and reapers are pushed on to the kerb-side before the ironmongers' shops, the better to catch the eyes of likely buyers; in one corner of the square protesting chickens, great baskets of eggs and golden farm butter are sold to the highest bidder by a voluble auctioneer. Around him stand groups of gaitered farmers and their plump, bustling wives, filling the air with the murmur of their rich country dialect. The Saturday market is very different. Here come the wives of the men from the factories with the contents of Friday night's pay envelopes, and theirs is the discordant, clipped speech of Birmingham. They crowd round the Jew vendors of shoddy clothing and gawdy ornaments, clutching their string bags and shrilly admonishing their grubby children.

One day I watched a kerb-side pedlar who, with the aid of a very second-hand aluminium saucepan, was demonstrating the infallibility of a cold solder he was hawking. He was a spare, grey-haired figure in the sixties, dressed in cloth cap and shabby blue raincoat. His harangue drew little attention, so that he presently fell to packing his wares into a dog-eared suitcase, muttering bitterly to himself on the inconstancy of customers. He had been 'in the game' all his life, he said, adding morosely that the markets were not what they had been, particularly in the South and West of England. He only 'ran' one line at a time, and had been hawking his solder for the past nine years with enough success to earn a living. Time was when he had roamed the whole of England for twelve months of the year, but now he was growing old. He had settled down in Northampton with 'the best wife a man could have', and there he spent the winter months, only visiting local markets 'just to keep his hand in'. When the warm days came round he confessed that he still felt the urge to wander, and in a fortnight, he said, he would be away once more, travelling the market towns of Yorkshire and Durham before crossing the moors to Cumberland. I have never used the tube of solder which was the price of this conversation, but I consider that sixpence was small fee for a talk with a travelling tinker.

COMPTON WYNIATES

Chapter VII

FOUR HOUSES

IN my wanderings farther afield I came upon four magnificent examples of the English country house. They made a striking contrast, not merely of architectural style and type, but of the typical vicissitudes of fortune that had overtaken them of recent years.

The first was Compton Wyniates, surely one of the most perfect specimens of Tudor domestic architecture in the country. Possessing the added advantage of a secluded and flawless setting in a natural cup of the Edgehill scarp, it looks out over the Warwickshire Vale to westward, and is sheltered upon the other three sides by slopes of verdant parkland studded with great trees. It was on a fine spring evening that I came along the narrow road which skirts the southern rim of this natural amphitheatre, and it was with almost incredulous wonder that I first saw the great house glowing below me like a rosy jewel laid upon green velvet. For the trees were casting long fingers of shadow across the grass, and the walls of the house, the many turrets, gables and tall twisted chimneys absorbed the light of the westering sun as only old Warwickshire brickwork can. It was evident that Compton Wyniates was fortunate in its owner, for not only was the fabric in excellent repair, but it was surrounded by a sea of smooth-shaven lawns, while the terraced garden on the south front was a marvel of topiary work. The small stone church in one corner of the grounds was the only other evidence of man's handiwork visible, so that this still, sequestered place seems to have become an island outside time. I should not have felt surprised if an Elizabethan gallant in gay hose and slashed doublet had suddenly appeared in the yew walk, or a cavalier in cloak and plume ridden out through the great doorway from the central court.

Gracious Compton Wyniates resembles a court favourite of ready charm, a long, low building slumbering amidst gardens with no thought but beauty and peace. Broughton Castle, on the other hand, is a grim old warrior with little time for airs and graces. It has always been a Protestant stronghold, and it was here, in a secluded upper room, that the Cromwellians hatched the plot which plunged England in civil war. As I walked over the moat bridge and through the forbidding stone gatehouse which guards the only approach, I thought that they could have chosen no more fitting place in which to plan violence and the overthrow of kings. The stone of which the house is built is a sterner medium than the warm brick, and has been employed to more austere purpose on the site of an older fortified dwelling whose ruins are still visible. From the edge of the encircling moat the tall gables soar upward in a compact, powerful mass, their stone-mullioned windows looking down sombrely at their reflections in the dark water where swans float among the lilies. After the polished elegance of Compton Wyniates there seemed to be an atmosphere of neglect about Broughton; the lawn before the house was untrimmed, and the only guardian of the gate was an elderly gander who regarded me askance out of the corner of a bright blue eye, and hissed suspiciously. One would make a perfect setting for Shakespearean comedy, but the other is an incarnation of Poe's 'House of Usher', particularly when the tall, rook-haunted trees beside the moat are bare of leaf and the dead water lies still under a darkling winter sky.

Sulgrave, some miles east of Banbury in the direction of Northampton, came next. It is typical of the smaller Northamptonshire Manor House, simply and graciously built of stone in a style closely akin to the Cotswold, though lacking the latter's finer graces. Today it might have been an obscure farmhouse, had it not cradled the Washington family. For this reason greatness has been thrust upon it, the Stars and Stripes floats from a flag-pole on the lawn, and the whole interior has been turned into a museum of the period with a thoroughness and good sense of showmanship which are characteristically American. Sulgrave is fortunate in possessing a custodian who combines great enthusiasm and sympathy with exceptional knowledge and good taste, for the house is a treasury of all those naturally lovely things that were once a part of every-day life to the self-sufficient rural community which Sulgrave once housed. It was with a curious blend of wonder and sadness that I went from room to room: wonder at the beauty that crowded upon the eye at every turn; sadness because that beauty, for all the consummate showmanship, was only the hollow image of its former self, because the hands and the spirit which once breathed life into it had gone, perhaps never to return. I was reminded of Yeats's golden bird:

'Such a form as Grecian goldsmiths make
Of hammered gold and gold enamelling
To keep a drowsy Emperor awake;
Or set upon a golden bough to sing
To lords and ladies of Byzantium
Of what is past, or passing, or to come. . . .'

I had rather see one simple painted can in Mr. Tooley's workshop than all the wealth of Sulgrave. One is a poor spark of still-living tradition, the other an embalmed splendour.

In search of the last house I came to Wroxton, and I have yet to find a comelier village east of the Cotswolds. It hangs on the slope of a little valley, and though the main road from Banbury to Stratford-on-Avon touches the fringe of it at the top of the slope, the village has suffered little harm. The old main street runs along the valley bottom, an uneven rank of thatched stone cottages whose gardens were a riot of blossom when I walked down it on a drowsy afternoon in early summer. At the end of it was the gateway to Wroxton Abbey, and passing through it I came upon tragedy in the midst of peace. The great house of ochreous stone lay empty, the shuttered windows staring blindly at a fussy scarlet tractor which was hauling timber from the park across the drive, and at the man who was mowing with a scythe what had once been the rose garden. One bush of crimson roses still bloomed in wild unpruned profusion, and here the bees were busy. Their humming mingled with the whirr of a mowing machine from a nearby paddock, and lapped about by these soft summer sounds, it was easy to believe that Wroxton was not dead, but sleeping. Yet, walking round the flagged terrace where dandelions and docks were sprouting, I felt that the tide of life had left it, just as it had left the butter-patters, the wool-comb and the spit in Sulgrave kitchen.

Chapter VIII

THE UPPER AVON

"Piping Pebworth, Dancing Marston,
Haunted Hillborough, Hungry Grafton,
Dodging Exhall, Papist Wixford,
Beggarly Broom, and Drunken Bidford."

IT was among these villages immortalised by Shakespeare that we spent the first few days after our marriage, and the last for many months on land. I know of no better place in which to spend a summer's day than this green heart of England, the Vale of Avon. The windows of our room in the inn at 'Drunken Bidford' looked out over willow-bordered meadows towards the village of Barton and the slope of Marcliff. In the foreground the river, a broad spate of rippling shallows, flowed under King John's bridge, which has carried the wayfarers of Buckle Street for four hundred and fifty years. Below the bridge the water tumbled over a weir, and in the night-time, when house and street were silent, the slumbrous murmur of the falling water so filled the room that it was easy to believe that we were afloat.

I had hoped that 'Cressy' would have been ready, so that we might have set out on our long-awaited cruise immediately, but although my own work was finished, Mr. Tooley's illness had delayed the work on the hull, which required three more days to complete. We had therefore decided to spend this time explor-ing a river which, alas, 'Cressy' could never visit, for the Upper

Avon Navigation has lain derelict since 1873. Only traces of the ruined locks remain, while the channel is in places so shallow, in others so beset by dangerous currents, that to attempt such a journey even in a canoe would be to court disaster.

On the first morning of our stay we followed the course of the river downstream from Bidford, crossing the tributary Arrow at Salford Priors, and continuing through that pleasant village until we caught sight of the tall, ogee-curved gable heads of Abbots Salford Hall upreared among the trees. This is a house that is not easily passed by at any time, and as we had all the day before us, we turned beneath the arch of the gatehouse and over the weed-grown flagstones to the door. Our knock was answered by the old lady who looks after the Catholic chapel, which, unlike the rest of the building, is still in use.

'Will you be pleased to come in', said she, and ushered us into a lofty hall floored with stone, as bare and chill as an empty coal-cellar.

If it be true that a house can be haunted by the past, then every room at Abbots Salford must harbour some sad spectre. As at Wroxton, life has gone from it, but gone so great a while ago that wind and weather have taken heavy toll. We wandered through a labyrinth of forsaken rooms, some utterly bare, others containing a few pathetic sticks of Victorian furniture, a cheap veneer wash-stand or a jangling truckle bed. Layers of faded paper hung in tatters from the walls or bellied from the ceiling, stained with damp and stirred to an uncanny rustling by unsuspected draughts. As we climbed to the second storey this tale of ruin became more tragic still, for floors had rotted into gaping holes and laths protruded through plaster like broken bones. In one of these rooms was the entrance to that not uncommon provision in old Catholic houses, a secret hiding-place for the concealment of priests in the period of persecution. This hide is so ingeniously constructed that, although there is no record of its history, it may well have been the work of that master builder of hides, Nicholas Owen, alias 'Little John'. I could visualise him, ostensibly a journeyman mason, coming with his pack of tools to do general repairs during the day, but at night, unsuspected even by the servants, setting about this secret work. The hide itself is cunningly concealed in an angle of the roof, the entrance a seemingly sub-stantial recessed cupboard lined with oak. The whole back of this cupboard with its two shelves swings inwards upon hidden hinges, and could then be bolted upon the inside. If an accomplice were at hand to place a few articles upon the shelves, the result would elude the most practised pursuivant. Who knows who may have sought shelter here?—perhaps one or both of those erstwhile notorious recusants, Father Garnet and Father John Gerrard.

The old Hall is called 'The Nunnery' locally, because it once gave brief shelter to a certain French order, and I thought the most pleasant room in the house was the great garret under the roof which is reputed to have been their dormitory. It is an airy place of whitewashed plaster walls and fine high windows which look out over the tree-tops to the river. Nevertheless we were glad to be out in the bright sunlight again with the scent of warm grass about us, for the whole house struck cold as a vault, even on this summer day, and over all there lay a heavy, mouldering smell of damp and decay. As we left the staring windows of the old Hall behind, walking over Worcester meadows towards the river, there came into my head those lines from Hood's 'Haunted House':

> 'O'er all there hung the shadow of a fear;
> A sense of mystery the spirit daunted;
> And said, as plain as whisper in the ear,
> The place is haunted.'

We had thought to cross the river at Cleeve Mill and so climb the farther bank to Cleeve Prior, but the floods of early spring had made a yawning breach in the weir sill, carrying with it the wooden footbridge. No doubt it was the violence of these annual floods which led to the abandonment of the old navigation, for they must have inflicted serious damage to the locks. Beyond the weir stood the old mill, beautifully placed under the steep shoulder of Cleeve Hill, but it had become a tea-house for Birmingham anglers, the wheels silent forever.

Determined to cross the river somehow, we walked two miles farther downstream to Harvington Mill. This, too, was abandoned and stood in the grounds of a substantial Georgian farmhouse of a type that is frequently met with in the Vale of Evesham. It was a secluded place far removed from the road, and our approach set dogs a-barking, while fantail pigeons rose from the roof-ridge like wind-blown white cloths as we went to the door. Certainly we might cross the river, we were told, but there was no bridge; we would have to wade across the head of the weir. Determined not to be intimidated, although the noise of falling water seemed alarmingly loud, we were led along a narrow, mown pathway

through a jungle of reeds and withies past the mill to the weir brink.
The mill-race and the old navigable channel by the ruined lock
made two little islets so lost and so densely overgrown with
nettles, old rotting willows and gnarled apple trees, that a fugitive
could have lain hidden there for a twelve-month. The Avon
looked perilously swift and deep, but we took off our shoes and
stockings and set forth as mediaeval pilgrims must have done when
they journeyed to the Holy Blood of Hayles, or to pluck a twig
from the Holy Thorn at Glastonbury. By keeping to the weir
sill, the water did not come above our calves, and ten minutes'
walk through the meadows on the farther side brought us to
'The Fish and Anchor', a solitary inn, where we celebrated our
crossing. Our frugal lunch of bread and cheese and beer would
not have been so welcome had there been a bridge across the river
at Harvington.

On our return by the same route we were welcomed by the
mother and daughter of the farm, simple and most kindly people,
who showed us their garden, gracious lawns sloping to the water's
edge and half-wild flower-beds crowded with marigolds, canterbury
bells and sweet william. They took an unfeigned and unaffected
delight in displaying their flowers and fruit, dogs and cats, each
of which had its story. The most interesting of these concerned
the fine house plant, or house leek as it is sometimes called, which
grew on the roof of an outbuilding.

One day, we were told, a family of gipsies had encamped near by,
as they are wont to do in this neighbourhood for the pea-picking.
Their youngest child was taken ill with pneumonia—so ill that her
life was despaired of until by some means the parents discovered
the existence of this house plant. They were permitted to take away
some of the thick, cactus-like leaves, from which they made an
infusion, and the child rapidly recovered when this primitive
medicine had been administered. The sceptic will say 'in spite of'
rather than 'because', but is it unduly credulous to credit the
wandering gipsy with shreds of ancient wisdom which the more
civilised have lost? In this quiet, remote place by the dreaming
river stranger things would have seemed literal truth.

*　　*　　*　　*　　*

That evening we motored to the Memorial Theatre at Stratford-
on-Avon, a pilgrimage every good Shakespearean makes at least
once in a lifetime. I like Stratford despite the fact that it has become a factory of Shakespeare and an apotheosis of all that is

Artful and Crafty. I can find it in my heart to forgive all the Birmingham brass knick-knacks, the bus-loads of sightseers, and the pseudo-Tudor frontages when I see Hugh of Clopton's Bridge, or the spire of Trinity Church soaring above the lime trees by the river's margin. Between these two stands the theatre, and I admire this also, though a fierce controversy rages ceaselessly about it. Many maintain that it resembles an electric power-station, but when asked what they would set in its place, can only mutter vaguely: 'Something more appropriate', by which they mean, presumably, a Tudor plagiarism as empty of inspiration as Victorian Gothic. What a travesty, and what a condemnation of our impoverished age such a building would have been! The brickwork of the New Theatre harmonises gracefully with Clopton Bridge, otherwise it rightly belongs to our own age, and is one of the very rare examples of modern architecture wherein a crystallised style seems actually to have emerged from a bewildering confliction of form, of pretentious vulgarity or commercial degradation. There is a suggestion of permanence and power in the bold proportion of masses culminating in the squat tower, a stark cleanliness of line that speaks a certain passionate austerity fitting to the play-house of so noble a poet. I think great William would approve his memorial.

The Stratford-on-Avon Canal has been broadened into an ornamental lake where it passes through the grounds before the Theatre, and this is well enough, but whoever was responsible for laying out the gardens has committed the unforgivable crime of throwing an ugly horizontal bridge across the centre of the lock by which the canal joins the Avon. The lock, otherwise complete, is thus not only made impassable, to the great inconvenience of the owners of the small pleasure-boats on the river who had been accustomed to move their craft onto the canal in times of flood, but it is entirely robbed of its naturally practical and pleasing appearance, and looks, surrounded by flower-beds, as incongruous as a rick staddle stone in a suburban garden. An arched bridge of traditional canal style built just above or below the lock would have made a world of difference at little extra cost, but the imagination of the designers of municipal gardens seldom seems to rise above litter baskets, cast-iron seats and strictly regimented flowerborders.

Under the wall in the corner of the gardens near Clopton Bridge there rests a relic which most visitors to Stratford miss

because it has nothing to do with Shakespeare. This is no less than
one of the wagons which once ran on the ancient horse tramway
between Stratford and Shipston-on-Stour. Standing on a short
length of the original fish-bellied cast-iron rail, it looks strangely
out of place amid these lawns and poplars, as though it had been
shunted there and forgotten long years before there was a theatre
at Stratford. After a surfeit of the pseudo in the streets of the town,
it is a refreshing sight and an interesting one, for it is a significant
symbol of our early transition from the agricultural to the industrial,
being no more than a farm tumbril set upon primitive flanged wheels,
the brake an oak block fixed to a pivoted wooden lever.

By the time we had finished examining this grandfather among
railway wagons the square before the theatre was packed with
cars and it was time to take our seats. The play at Stratford certainly
attracts a varied audience, of whom the most surprising element
is the prosaic Birmingham business man who, one feels, would
be more at home in the stalls at a musical comedy. He sits there,
stolid and imperturbable in his sober chamber-of-commerce
suit, rubbing shoulders on the one hand with a supercilious
member of the local county, who loudly discourses on a recent
run with the Grafton, to the detriment of the delightful prelude
of Elizabethan music, and on the other with an intellectual poseur
from Bloomsbury or Chelsea. Add to these a leavening of the inevitable Americans, a number of adolescent school-girls cherishing
their first naïve eroticisms over Romeo, and you have a fairly
representative cross section of an average audience at the Memorial
Theatre. Mixed though it may be, it is appreciative, perhaps
because most of its members have travelled a considerable distance
to attend. Many people hold that the place of the theatre is in the
heart of a big city, and that when it is removed to the country the
drama tends to stagnate and become tainted with the affectations
of an unrepresentative coterie. I do not believe this, nor do I
think it true of Stratford. Admittedly there is a tendency, particularly in the production of the comedies, towards extravagance
of décor at the expense of the play itself, and a speeding up to
a tempo approaching that of the modern farce, but London
productions have exhibited the same faults. Certain it is that I
would rather leave the play for the dark quiet of the Avon flowing
beneath her bridges than for the discordant clamour of some city
street.

As we drove back from the play through the warm summer night to Bidford, with white moths dancing in the beam of the headlamps and moonlit mist smoking from the hayfields, we resolved that one day we would bring 'Cressy' by the canal to Stratford and enjoy a week of play-going.

It was with this idea still in mind that we set forth the next morning through winding lanes by Temple Grafton and Billesley to find the Stratford Canal at Old Stratford Locks. So secretive is it that we should, I think, have searched in vain without the aid of the ordnance survey map. We came upon it in a narrow, tree-shaded cutting, and, leaving the car on the bridge above, clambered down onto the overgrown towing-path. The water where it was not shadowed by great, fern-like masses of weed growing up from the bottom, was crystal clear, but there appeared to be disturbingly little depth. A flotilla of plump Aylesbury ducks which swam purposefully by seemed to be the only traffic, but we walked in the direction of Stratford to have a look at the locks, and found them, to our surprise, in excellent order. We encountered also a most original type of over-bridge. It was of extremely short span, there being no towing-path beneath, and the space between the brick abutments being only a boat's width. This would have meant that the boatman must unhitch his tow-line save for a most ingenious provision. The arch consisted of two massive cast-iron brackets set in the brickwork, and these failed to meet by the space of about an inch at the crown. The balustrade was similarly divided, so that as the boat slid under, and the horse walked round, the tow-line could be dropped through the slot. This curious ' divided bridge' is a unique regional type as peculiar to the Stratford Canal as are the wooden drawbridges to the Oxford.

Just below the first two locks we met an old man mowing the long grass on the banks, and of him I enquired whether any boats ever passed through. He was not only very old, but very deaf also, for I had to repeat my question as he leant upon the hand-pin of his scythe and cupped an ear. This time a light of comprehension dawned in his old eyes and he nodded in a most encouraging fashion, 'Oh, ah', he affirmed, 'there comes one sometimes', but when I asked how long it was since he had seen the last he confessed that it was ''bout four years back'. He went on to explain how the railway company who owned the canal had killed the traffic by raising the tolls but were forced to maintain it in theoretically navigable order. 'If you wants to come along this a-way,' he concluded, 'they can't stop you, and what's more they be bound to

give you the water to see as you do get through, but you'd best
come afore the weed be up.' Warming to us, the old man related
bitterly how, after a lifetime spent on the canal here and 'Preston
Bagot way', he was to be dismissed the following year with a
meagre pension, and turned out of his lock cottage. 'But,' he
concluded, with a malicious twinkle in his eye, 'there be'ant no
road to 'en; all my belongings was brought there by boat, and by
boat they'll have to go, whether they likes it or no.' He turned once
more to his mowing, handling his scythe with the effortless grace
of the countryman born, and we left him, pondering the manifold
sins of railway companies, but more than ever determined to make
an assault upon the canal in the not-far-distant future.

The sight of this forgotten canal idling through these quiet
fields, combined with the brilliant weather of high summer, made
us doubly anxious to embark on our voyage, so the following
morning we took the road by Sunrising Hill back to Banbury.
We arrived at the boatyard to see 'Cressy' still on the dock but
complete at last, her cabin-work resplendent in a coat of fresh
blue paint bordered with scarlet, a tiller painted in bands of many
colours like a barber's pole, and a knot of roses on her bow. These
last had been painted by Herbert Tooley in fair imitation of his
father's work. An hour later Herbert raised the stop-planks from
the mouth of the dry dock, the water thundered in, and in a little
while our painted boat floated slowly and majestically out into
the afternoon sunlight. We had only to take in stores, unpack our
numerous belongings and we should be away.

PART TWO

CLAYDON TOP LOCK

PART TWO

Chapter IX

BANBURY TO BRAUNSTON

ON an afternoon of the last week in July the great moment arrived when we slipped 'Cressy's' mooring lines and drew slowly away from the boatyard, heading northwards. Only Herbert Tooley on the bank and the blacksmith at the smithy door watched our un-ostentatious departure. Beside us on the aft deck stood Mr. Tooley senior in his Sunday suit and best bowler. He had suggested 'giving us a hand' as far as Cropredy, such a childlike eagerness lurking beneath his deliberately casual offer that we had not the heart to refuse the old man. As we rounded the bend in the canal that had been the tempting limit of my view for so long, I looked back over the churning wake of our screw for a last glimpse of the familiar yard before the tall hedgerow beside the tow-path hid it from sight.

For a quarter of a mile the canal ran close beside the main road to Coventry, a dreary stretch of tarmac made hideous by hoardings, and along which cars and lorries were buzzing fretfully. But soon we veered away to the east towards open country and entered Salmon's Lock, the first on our journey. Because we were locking uphill the lock chamber was empty, and the cavernous walls of dripping brick rose high above our deck with only a few inches to spare on either side. When we had closed the bottom gate behind us and raised the top sluices or 'paddles', the pent-up water thundered into the lock, foaming about 'Cressy's' bow like a mill race, so that the bright paintwork glistened with spray. This is the spectacular and satisfying reward for the labour of lifting the heavy paddles, a sight I have never tired of watching, seated on the lock beam as the boat lifts gently upward. As the lock fills, calm slowly returns to the water, until only flecks of foam and little eddying whirlpools remain, and the one sound is the gentle scraping of the rope bow fender against the lock gates. We always made this labour of lockage a leisurely affair unless we were holding up another boat, but the boatmen who have their living to earn work their way through with deceptive speed and send a member of the crew hot foot along the tow-path to prepare the locks in advance.

When we moved out of the lock into the 'pound' above we soon left all trace of Banbury's outskirts behind, and found ourselves winding through deserted water-meadows beside the Cherwell, our only spectators the cattle on the banks, who looked up from their grazing to gaze in mild curiosity, wisps of lush grass protruding from the corners of their mouths. No one who has not experienced it can fully appreciate the unfailing fascination of this tranquil voyaging. The movement of the narrow boat is like nothing else in the world; as Temple Thurston so aptly wrote, 'it is no motion, or it is motion asleep'. Stand on 'Cressy's' fore deck with eyes closed, and no sense of motion is left, open them and you see the bluff bows gliding over the still water, while the ever-changing scene of trees and hills, fields and farms drifts past at so measured a pace that the eye has full time to ponder every detail. These spells of idleness are made more pleasurable because they alternate with the labour at the locks, and we passed through three more before we came to Cropredy at five o'clock that evening. Here we bade farewell to Mr. Tooley, watching his bent figure hurrying over the bridge and up the village street to catch the Banbury bus until his familiar bowler hat bobbed out of sight.

Cropredy is not a canal village. The fine church, with its beacon tower, and the street of thatched stone cottages that slopes down to the canal bridge were old in 1644, when they watched the plumed cavaliers sweep by in brave array to do battle for King Charles in the meadows by the Cherwell. Yet the gulf of years narrows with age, so that Cropredy has come to accept the canal, dreaming beneath its old brick bridge, as a part of itself, for it is a hundred and sixty years since the first boat passed by.

Later that evening we walked to the sign of 'The Red Lion' half-way up the street, and found a village inn of the best type which has escaped both stuffy Victorianism and the olde-worlde reconstruction of our own age. The bar parlour was as simple and unpretentious as it had always been: a stone-flagged floor, benches and tables of wood whitened by constant scouring, and a great open fireplace with its crane and ratchet hooks, sunken ash-pit and snug seats beneath the yawning chimney breast. Our beer was drawn straight from the wood in the cellar, so cool that mist formed on the glass. We sat drinking contentedly in this quiet place, listening to the leisurely quarter chime of the church clock and trying to decipher one of the old puzzle cards, once so popular in country inns, which hung on the wall opposite, yellowed by years of exposure to shag-tobacco smoke.

> ' Here's to Pa!' it ran, 'nds Pen Da S
> O CI alh OURin ha? R.M.
> Les Smi rT Ha! ND Fu nle T fr;
> i E nds HIPRE ign B eju, St. an
> d KIn, dan Devil sPe,Ak of N One.'

The moral sentiment is excellent, but beyond this I can give no clue, for beneath it in heavy type was the clause: 'N.B. NO TEACHING ONE ANOTHER TO READ THE ABOVE UNDER FORFEITURE OF A QUART OF THE LAND-LORD'S BEST ALE.' A translation in print would therefore be unpardonable, and render me liable for at least a barrel should I visit 'The Red Lion' again.

We returned to a hot dinner on board which would have been an excellent meal in any place, but was a veritable banquet in such circumstances and surroundings. Banbury and the familiar boat-yard seemed already far away, although we had journeyed only five and a half miles. Yet herein lies the value of canal travel, and the deep core of truth in old Jack Harwood's reply to the cocksure policeman: for if man had never discovered the mechanical arts by which he annihilates space and time he might never have acquired that tragic contempt for local environment, custom and tradition which has led him to break faith with the land. Man has built himself wings before he has fully learned how to walk.

The canal veers away from the river beyond Cropredy, climbing out of the valley in leisurely fashion through Broadmoor, Varney's and Elkington's locks, then more steeply through a flight of five near the village of Claydon. When we left Claydon top lock the next morning we entered the highest section of the Oxford canal, or the 'summit level', as it is called, which cuts across the limestone ridge at its lowest and narrowest point between Mill Hill and Shirne Hill near the villages of Fenny Compton and Worm-leighton. The deep cutting through this high ground was originally a tunnel, and although it was opened out many years ago, it is still so called by the boatmen who have long memories. When we emerged from 'the tunnel' and swung right-handed to follow the slope of the edge, the view opened out with Burton Dassett post-mill on its bare hill standing sentinel above the broad upper valley of the Itchen. The canal leaves the village of Fenny Compton a mile to westward, and the boatmen's 'Fenny' consists solely of a disused wharf and 'The George and Dragon' Inn, a large white-washed building which, though it stands on the very edge of the canal, has no water supply, drinking-water being supplied in jars by the brewers. Here we stopped for tea, as by this time it was late afternoon, and we finally moored for the night by Griffin's Bridge under the arc of Wormleighton Hill. Through a screen of trees on the hill-top we could just discern the roofs of the village, and resolved to walk up to it the following morning.

Lost in woodland away from main roads, the centuries have passed lightly over Wormleighton with no more stir than a flight of birds. Villages such as this—a cluster of cottages of brick, stone and thatch, a manor house and a farm or two—are the simple roots of England. The manor, which is now a farm, sleeps under the tall elms, dreaming of more spacious days.

> 'Like some last courtier at a gipsy camping place
> Babbling of fallen majesty, records what's gone.'

Its magnificent detached gatehouse of stone bears proudly the arms of England and the escutcheon of the Spencers, but the grass grows long about it. In the old church not far distant there is a tablet to the memory of a son of Earl Spencer who died at Blois in 1619. The words look so newly graven, and so ageless is the spirit of the place, that three hundred years seemed but a little span.

On the crest of the long, narrow promontory which Worm-leighton Hill thrusts out into the valley of the Itchen there stands a solitary farmhouse which must be a very familiar landmark to Oxford Canal boatmen. As we left Griffin's bridge it lay dead ahead of us, but we presently turned westward and passed it on the right hand. When we reached the point of the headland the canal made another turn so sharp that 'Cressy' swung round in her own length, and we passed the farm once more, this time on the other side of the hill. As the now familiar buildings fell astern we thought we had surely seen the last of them, but no, they presently reappeared for the third time, now once more ahead of us. We had completed a full circle of nearly three miles and come within half a mile of our starting point. For mile after mile we wound about in this fashion, following the irregular contour of the land, the way so tortuous that we lost all sense of direction. A canal bridge would appear surprisingly in a most improbable position only one field away, and half an hour later we would pass under it, or dis-cover that we had done so some time before. Figures prove that this is no exaggeration, for the summit level from Claydon to Marston Doles is eleven miles long, and yet it is only four and a half as the crow flies, or six by road. It has been said that the roll-ing English drunkard made the rolling English road, but there is not a wandering lane that can vie with the canals in this respect, and this meandering is a great part of their charm. Like the old roads, they were built before the age of hurry, and the way in which they follow the lie of the land is particularly characteristic of the earlier waterways built or surveyed by James Brindley, the father of the English canals. Samuel Smiles in his biography of this pioneer says: 'He would rather go *round* an obstacle in the shape of an elevated range of country, than go *through* it. Although the length of canal to be worked was longer, yet the cost of tun-nelling and lockage was avoided. Besides, the population of the district was fully accommodated.' The italics are in the original.

No road could be so solitary as this canal, for in the whole day's journey we met only one fellow traveller, Alfred Hone, on his weekly journey to Banbury with coal. We exchanged greet-ings and news as we came abreast, continuing in rising voices as our boats slowly drew apart. Doubtless he would pass on the information to other boatmen that he had met 'Cressy' 'up eleven-mile pound'. In this way news travels with surprising swiftness over hundreds of miles of canal.

Not another soul did we see until a carroty-haired boy came out of a cottage by the waterside at Marston Doles to set the lock for us. This was 'Napton Top', the first of a flight of nine, their gates so decrepit and weatherworn that it seemed a push would send them toppling into the water. The process now was reversed, 'Cressy' coming into a full lock and slowly sinking downwards as the water rushed into the pound below. Nine locks take some

'We Met only One Fellow-Traveller'

time to negotiate, so that it was evening by the time we reached the bottom to moor by the village of Napton-on-the-Hill.

This must surely be the strangest village in all Warwickshire, a translation in brick of the stone villages of the South Cotswold valleys. The church stands on the top of the hill, and the cottages, connected by breakneck lanes or cobbled paths, look as though they were struggling to climb the steep slope towards it, seeking salvation. A derelict tower mill also crowns the hill, looking across to its fellow at Burton Dassett, and the canal curved so closely beneath the slope that our moorings were almost in the shadow of the gaunt sails.

It was here that we found our first canal inn.

Approached by a rough track, it stood in the fields on the side of the canal away from the village, and, with outbuildings grouped around the house, it looked like a small farm, except for the faded sign of 'The Bull and Butcher' over the door. Inns such as this fulfil the same purpose as the great posting-houses of coaching days, for they are recognized 'stages' on the water roads where many generations of boatmen have been accustomed to tie up and stable their horses for the night. Today they are fast going the way of their great predecessors, for the motor-boat is emptying their stables and bar parlours. Though the motor travels little faster than the horse, it does not tire, so that once-familiar moorings become filled up with mud, the rings rusty from long disuse, while far into the night the boats pass by.

Thanks to the survival of horse-drawn traffic on the Oxford Canal, 'The Bull and Butcher' has been more fortunate than many inns we encountered subsequently, and we had not been long at our moorings before the first wayfarer arrived and led his horse over the bridge to the stable. By the time dusk fell there were half a dozen boats moored beside us, the womenfolk standing at their cabin doors exchanging gossip while they polished brasses, mopped paintwork or peeled potatoes. Children called shrilly to each other and dogs padded eagerly to and fro along the gang-planks, whining to get ashore. There was a pervasive odour from some simmering stew-pot, and the smoke from the brass-bound stove chimneys rose straight in the windless evening air.

It was dark and there was a thin cry of bats when we walked down to 'The Bull and Butcher' after dinner. By the light of a paraffin lamp the landlord was pouring beer out of a tall enamelled jug. He was more of a farmer than a publican, big-boned and swarthy, his shirt sleeves leaving his bronzed forearms bare to the elbow. Two boat captains in dark corduroys were playing a game of five-O-one on the dartboard. Each wore a gold ring in one ear, which gleamed in the lamplight and lent them an appearance that was strangely foreign. They were joined presently by their wives, who sat on a bench apart, drinking stout and conversing in subdued undertones. There was no interchange of conversation between the two groups, for mixed drinking is not a principle of the canal folk. Here it was permitted on sufferance because there was only one licensed room.

Beside the fireplace there stood a skittle table which appeared to have been ousted from popular favour by the dartboard. This game is played in the same manner as the better-known alley game, its advantage being that it requires little space. The nine-pins are set upon the table, which is protected by a padded back and a suspended net. The oval wooden 'cheese', measuring approximately four inches in diameter by two inches thick, is then thrown at them from a distance of about eight feet. There is considerable skill and sleight of wrist in the way a good local exponent flings the curiously shaped missile and often scores a 'floorer' by striking the leading pin at precisely the right angle and strength. The game has a definite regional character, for I doubt whether it will be found outside a radius of twenty miles of Northampton.

The subject of these old country games is of great interest, and one about which little has been written. Soon many of them will be forgotten, for the dartboard is rapidly becoming ubiquitous, aided and abetted by elaborate electrical pin tables. Some districts still staunchly support their local skittle alleys, while in others the old games of quoits and shove-halfpenny are still popular. I know of one village in Cheshire where they favour an original bagatelle board, while in certain parts of Shropshire they play dominoes with a double set of chips ranging up to double-twelve. In the low-ceilinged bar of an inn at Burbage, a Wiltshire village in Savernake Forest, they still play 'Ringing the Bull'; a copper bull ring hangs suspended by a cord from a hook in the rafters and has to be swung over a peg on the wall. This simple game is said to be the oldest survivor of all, a contemporary perhaps of the 'Nine Men's Morris'. The decline of these games is contemporaneous with that of all the other rural arts, a decline that had begun even in Shakespeare's day:

'The Nine Men's Morris is filled up with mud,
And the quaint mazes of the wanton green
For lack of tread are undistinguishable.'

Just before we left 'The Bull and Butcher' a newcomer entered the bar bearing the largest mushroom we had ever seen. There was great controversy as to its size, which was eventually settled when a ruler was produced and it was found to measure just over a foot in diameter. Such giants are not uncommon, we were told, in the meadows below Napton Hill, and as we rose to go we were presented with two which were only slightly smaller. Next day Angela stewed them, as we had been directed—not without misgivings, it must be admitted, although we found them excellent eating.

We heard the patter of rain on our cabin roof that night, but when we climbed up Napton Hill in the morning the sun was shining brightly and a fresh breeze was blowing a white fleece of clouds overhead, which patterned the green slopes with their swiftly chasing shadows. The climb was well repaid. Immediately below us the canal swept round the base of the hill in a horseshoe curve like a moat about a castle mound, and beyond lay the Warwickshire Plain, a grand expanse of rolling country so richly set with great trees that from this vantage it was easy to believe that there was still a forest in Arden. The wind drummed in our ears as only a wind can that blows unchecked over leagues of open country; it hissed through the bending summer grasses and set the bare sails of the mill creaking and straining impotently. Inside the tower of the mill was a sorry sight, the staunch wooden gearing and the drive-shafts, thick as a stout tree, were still in place, but the stones were gone and the floor had become no more than a rubbish dump and a roost for chickens. Pigeons had made their cote in the cupola, and their murmuring mingled with the whistle of the wind to make a plaintive duet most fitting to this airy ruin. There is no more eerie or more desolate place than a disused wind- or water-mill, especially when the old machinery remains to speak of past activity. Seeing them, so simple in construction and operation, and yet so lastingly wrought, one marvels that man has seen fit to abandon their tireless elemental powers in favour of the intricate, short-lived internal-combustion engine, which is dependant upon a fuel destined one day to become exhausted. Napton Mill is at once a symbol and an epitaph: a symbol of broken faith with the soil, an epitaph to the golden corn which once waved in the neglected pastures below.

Journeying on that afternoon, we passed the brickfield which is eating its way into the western slope of the hill, and presently came to the junction of the Warwick and Napton Canal. This waterway and the five miles of the Oxford Canal to Braunston have become a part of the Grand Union Company's through route between London and Birmingham. It was obvious that we had emerged from a by-way on to a main road, for the channel was wider and deeper, while instead of reedy margins the banks were set with concrete piling to resist the wash of many motor-boats. Although something of the charm of the less-frequented canal was lacking, we found moorings that could not have been bettered, in a belt of tall elm trees by the village of Lower Shuckburgh. The village itself was an undistinguished row of brick cottages strung along a main road, but of this we were out of sight and sound, separated by the trees and the breadth of a paddock.

Having swept the sky clear of clouds, the wind had dropped, as it so often does at the going down of the sun, and it was a perfect summer's evening. We dined on the fore deck, watched with mild, wide-eyed curiosity by two young bullocks who thrust their wet muzzles through the fence, almost touching 'Cressy's' bow, while high overhead a thrush made music for us, pouring out a tireless cascade of song. I have often listened to nightingales in Hampshire coverts, yet I still consider the thrush and the blackbird better songsters. Beside theirs, the nightingale's song lacks depth and feeling, so that I doubt if it would have won such renown did it not sing when other birds are silent.

Till now I had found it difficult to realise fully that the years of waiting and planning had at last come to an end, and that we were actually established in a floating home with hundreds of miles of water before us upon which to roam at will. I began to appreciate this fact that night as I lay in the mellowing influence of a hot bath. The fresh smell of dew-laden grass drifted in through the open window at my side, and a low, large moon silvered the water. The night was so still that every leaf of the dark trees hung in motionless silhouette, like stage scenery against an immense starry horizon. How else, I reflected, could we have approached so near the heart of the country? At times like this the discomforts of camping are bathos, the motor-car a most monstrous anachronism, and a hotel bedroom a stuffy prison. 'Cressy', on the other hand, seemed to become so at one with her peaceful surroundings that even in the dark of our sleeping-cabin the summer night was close about us. The end of the day brought no anti-climax, no closing of doors.

THE LONG BUCKBY CAN

Chapter X

THE GRAND UNION CANAL

BRAUNSTON, with its single street of great length strung along the crest of a low hill ridge above the canal, is typical of the large villages in this part of the world. At the end of the ridge stands the church, whose tall spire is a landmark for many miles westward; beside it an old tower mill bereft of sails. But it was at the opposite end of the village that we found what struck me as the most curious feature of the place. Here the even rank of houses, some of brick, others of Northamptonshire stone, was broken in a most surprising and irrelevant manner by a single diminutive cottage perched upon the strip of greensward flanking the road. A small patch of the common had been enclosed about it, and it had been planted so impudently before its neighbour's doors that only the narrowest of cobbled alleyways separated them. Surely this up-start must be a product of that ancient custom, rooted in the granting of land to bowmen in recognition of their war services, by which a man might claim a holding on common land provided he had one chimney smoking between sunset and sunrise. Whether true or not, it was easy here to visualise dark figures feverishly and furtively at work upon the green at dead of night, and to picture the chagrin of the villagers on looking out the next morning to see a crazy shack sprung up before their doors, its rickety chimney smoking derisively.

We left the Oxford Canal for the Grand Union at Braunston Junction, passed by Nurser's Boatyard, where a new wooden boat lay partially completed on the stocks, and so came to the first of the six locks by which the canal ascends to Braunston Tunnel. These were heavier and more complicated to work than those on the Oxford Canal, being wide locks capable of passing two narrow boats at a time. The gates are therefore more massive, and, in addition, some are equipped with what are called 'side-ponds' to economise water. One of these 'ponds' is constructed beside each lock at a level midway between the upper and lower pounds of the canal, and by means of the 'side-pond paddle', half the contents of a full lock can be discharged into it. The paddle is then dropped, so that this water is stored in the pond, and can subsequently be used again to half-fill the empty lock. In this way half a lock of water is saved, an economy which is worth the additional outlay involved, for each lock holds no less than 56,000 gallons, all of which would otherwise have to be supplied by the summit level of the canal each time a boat passed through.

When we reached the top lock we could see the black mouth of the tunnel ahead of us. It is over a mile in length, and, like the majority of canal tunnels, has no towing path. To relieve horse-boat captains of the tedious and heavy task of 'legging' their way through, the Company used to run a service of steam tugs which plied to a regular time-table, but these were withdrawn from service four years ago, owing to the decline of horse-drawn traffic, the little that remains having to rely on obtaining a tow from a friendly motor-boat. The tunnel is straight, and occasionally in clear weather it is just possible to discern in the dark depths the pinpoint of light which is the opposite mouth; more often, however, it is obscured by the hazy atmosphere and the smoke of cabin fires.

Navigating a canal tunnel is an odd experience, the first difficulty being to keep a straight course. Anyone who has experienced a temporary blindness on entering a dark cinema from broad daylight will be able to appreciate this. The stern of the boat is lit by the light streaming in through the mouth of the tunnel, but the bow, seventy feet ahead, is swallowed up in an impenetrable darkness which the eye strains in vain to pierce. Sense of direction is temporarily lost, and by a curious illusion the boat appears to be swinging rapidly in a circle. The secret is to hold a straight course until the eye becomes accustomed to the dark, for if one obeys the instinctive urge to correct these imaginary gyrations, the boat starts to 'weave', the bow cannoning from one wall to the other with a series of frightening, echoing thuds. This unpleasant proceeding becomes positively dangerous if another boat happens to be approaching, for there is only just passing room. In order to overcome this difficulty as far as possible, I had equipped 'Cressy' with a wide beam electric headlamp which could be quickly mounted on a suitable bracket on the fore end of the cabin top, and plugged in to a convenient socket. Even so, the first few hundred yards were difficult going, until I managed to pick out the arch of the roof illumined by the lamp. Meanwhile the sound of our engine and churning screw, normally almost unnoticeable, was prodigiously magnified by the hollow reverberations from the walls, and ice-cold showers of water fell at intervals from the mouldering bricks overhead, which were festooned with stalactites. Most of these miniature waterfalls seemed to find their way with unerring accuracy down the back of my neck, so on entering subsequent tunnels I always took care to put on a mackintosh. At intervals there were ventilation shafts, the wan beams of light which rayed downwards from them through the murky atmosphere making lonely luminous pools in the darkness. By imperceptible degrees the tiny speck of light ahead became a vivid miniature of green banks and sunlit water, until we finally emerged from the southern portal by Welton Wharf after twenty minutes underground.

A further half-hour brought us within sight of Norton Junction, near Long Buckby, where our short journey over England's busiest inland waterway came to an end. Here we moored 'Cressy' by the toll office at the Junction, and walked on down the tow-path of the main canal to Buckby Wharf, where I knew that we should find a canal shop with painted water-cans for sale.

This insignificant little shop standing beside Buckby top lock has customers all over England; there is scarcely a boat trading down to Brentford or Paddington Basin that does not carry a Buckby can, and I have recognised their distinctive style on boat-decks in every county in the Midlands. For many of the boatmen they are the only outlet left for their instinctive love of colour, because the large canal-carrying companies who handle the bulk of the London–Birmingham traffic no longer budget for castles and flowers, but paint their boats in uniform colours of blue and maroon or red and green. The cans are expensive, but it would never occur to the boatman that a galvanised bucket would answer the purpose equally well, because he has a different and truer sense of values. So he buys his painted can by instalments, paying a shilling or two each time he passes by, the agreement being one of mutual trust.

The old shopkeeper shuffled out of the back regions in response to the clang of the doorbell. It was obvious that he had been a broad, powerfully built man before age had bent him, also, from the way he peered at us, that he was almost blind. At first he was inclined to be surly, but when we explained that we wished to purchase a water-can and dipper, and had duly admired them, he unbent towards us, seating himself on a stool behind the counter. He used to paint the cans himself, he told us, but he confessed sadly that his sight no longer enabled him to do such fine work, and now they were painted for him at Braunston. He went on to deplore the modern conditions which compelled the boatmen to work all hours seven days a week, to the detriment of his trade, recalling wistfully the more leisured days when they were 'steady fellows, and tied up of a Sunday'. Cans were not his only speciality, for he presently produced a cup and saucer for our inspection. It was modern, cheap-quality earthenware, but decorated with an interesting and possibly traditional Chinese design, of a type common to very early 'China'. He explained proudly that this was his special pattern, made for him, and obtainable nowhere else.

'You'll see plenty of them London way,' he declared, as if to say that no visitor to London could escape seeing a specimen, and we felt that Long Buckby had set London firmly in its place. All the while he was talking he fiddled with a small brush, brushing his ears and his bushy moustache, a curious mannerism which attracted us with an awful, hypnotic fascination. When eventually we took leave of him he showed us to the door, still talking volubly, and by this time brushing his shaggy eyebrows.

Interesting and unique though the Buckby shop undoubtedly is, it does not compare in attraction or variety of stock with another canal shop I knew of at Stoke Bruerne, sixteen miles south. It was one of a row of thatched stone cottages along the tow path, and its cool, stone-flagged interior boasted so varied a stock as to call to mind the proud boast of Flecker's Merchant Grocer at the Gate of the Moon:

> 'We have rose-candy, we have spikenard,
> Mastic and Terebinth and oil and spice
> And such sweet jams meticulously jarred
> As God's own prophet eats in paradise.'

This shop specialised in ropes and lines. Coils of every thickness and quality, from coarsest manilla to finest white cotton, lay piled on the floor or hung from the low, whitewashed rafters of the ceiling. Yet this was only the principal item of a stock that catered for the boat family's every need. Here was a great basket full of crusty cottage loaves, there shelves of tea, jams and other groceries were crowded between piles of crockery, fat earthenware teapots and pendant festoons of hurricane lamps, kettles and saucepans. For the ailing there were herbal remedies, salves, liniments and pills a-plenty; clay pipes, shag tobacco, braces and boots for the menfolk; aprons, buttons, hairpins and combs for their wives; while for the children there were liquorice bootlaces, sherbert suckers and great glass jars filled with enticing, gaudy-coloured sweets, bulls-eyes, aniseed balls and gob-stoppers. In the heyday of the horse-boat the shop was well placed, for the southern entrance of Blisworth Tunnel was visible from the threshold, and the tunnel tug had a well-chosen mooring before the door of the inn opposite. Here the north-bound boats would wait for the tug, and when it appeared the south-bound boats in its train would in turn wait until the string of horses came over the hill. Now all that is changed. Like the deserted inns, the canal shop is another victim of the time-saving mania, and two years ago Stoke Bruerne's magic store closed its doors forever. Before very long the shop at Buckby will follow it, because the boatman no longer has the time to stand and stare.

That night at Norton, long after darkness had fallen, the motor-boats passed by the mouth of the junction. We could hear the penetrating and unmistakable beat of their diesel engines, the rattle of paddle ratchets at the lock, and watch their lights creeping along the lip of the embankment. A Grand Union boat southward bound with a cargo of coal; a pair of Fellows Mortons going North, perhaps with fifty tons of sugar from the Pool of London—'Fly-boats', most of them, making the journey of a hundred and thirty-six miles and one hundred and sixty-one locks in fifty-seven hours. No idle journey this, with two boats to handle—the motor and the towed 'butty boat'—under every condition of wind and weather. We fell asleep with the sound of the boats in our ears.

THE STAIRCASE, FOXTON

Chapter XI

THE 'LEICESTER CUT'

THOSE who imagine that the Midlands of England have become no more than a vast built-up area should desert the familiar roads and railways, and take a canal boat over the Leicester Section of the Grand Union Canal from Norton Junction to Market Harborough. In all these twenty-nine winding miles the 'Leicester Cut', as the boatmen call it, passes through only one village, so sparsely populated is the country traversed, and so deliberately does the canal seem to avoid the haunts of men. Traffic, though it has increased slightly of recent years, is very light, and we did not meet a single boat on the three days' journey.

Two miles from Norton we passed under Watling Street and the main line of the L.M.S. Railway, coming presently to the ascent of seven narrow locks near the village of Watford. The change of level was particularly steep, involving the use of yet another type of lock. This was the staircase or 'riser', the top gate of one lock being the bottom gate of the one above, so that there was no intermediate pound between them. Grouped in sets

of two or three, they resemble a flight of gigantic steps climbing
the hillside. There were two pairs of 'risers' at Watford, and when
we had worked our way through them there lay before us twenty
miles of summit level four hundred feet above the sea. Just as we
were moving out of the summit lock we saw a horse-boat coming
in to the first of the flight, so when we came to the tree-girt mouth
of Crick tunnel a little way ahead we moored up and had tea,
thinking to offer the boatman a tow through, and so save him
the wearisome job of 'legging'. What became of him we shall never
know—perhaps he also stopped for refreshment—for he did not
appear, so, when a thunderstorm rolled up unexpectedly, we
dived into the mile-long tunnel for shelter. As we approached the
northern end we could see vivid flashes of lightning and torrential
rain lashing the water, so I put 'Cressy' astern and we sheltered
in the tunnel mouth until the storm passed as quickly as it had
come, the sun sailing clear of the towering cumulus clouds. Canal
tunnels have their uses.

We made a brief halt at the disused Crick Wharf while we
obtained a supply of milk and eggs from a nearby farm, before
continuing our journey over this lost and lonely waterway. So
far removed were we from the walks and works of man that we
might have floated out of time; it became difficult to credit the
existence of cities, and more probable that the canal would lead
us to some enchanted Avilon 'fair with orchard lawns', than to
prosaic Leicester. Tall rushes and flags of innumerable varieties
lined the margins, growing so far into the water, and leaving a
channel so narrow that on approaching some of the endless turns
it looked as though the canal would disappear altogether. Yet
the travelling was better than that on many canals of twice the
apparent width, for the water was deep and clear, and hour by
hour 'Cressy' kept her effortless gliding pace, only the laziest of
ripples fanning from her bows as she swung easily this way or that,
following a tortuous course among the folds of the hills. Though
we sighted an occasional farmhouse or an isolated labourer's
cottage, our only companions, other than the cattle or sheep
grazing by the water's edge, were the birds. Coot and moorhen
fled to the shelter of the rushes with a furious commotion of beating wings, indignant clucking and frantically paddling feet. Swans
sailed by with an air of aloof, slightly offended dignity, while
every now and again a heron would wheel away, borne up with
effortless grace on great grey pinions. As the thrush excels in song,

so, surely, does the heron in flight. The swan loses her dignity in the air—the take-off is laboured, wings flapping and feet lashing the water, while when in flight the action is ungainly, the long neck craning forward as though out of balance. The heron, on the other hand, rises into the air as lightly and swiftly as blown thistledown; the slow beat of the wings is full of rhythmic grace and the poise magnificent, the neck laid back and the legs extended to make a perfectly horizontal line, like long tail-feathers.

Our first night out of Norton was spent at a disused wharf near Yelvertoft village, and the second in a wooded cutting near the mouth of the tunnel at delightfully named Husbands Bosworth. Before reaching these moorings we had crossed the headwaters of the Avon by an aqueduct, and passed the junction of the short branch canal to Welford. Probably few people realise that there are two Welfords upon Avon, for this is not the well-known village between Bidford and Stratford, with its famous maypole and luscious raspberry canes, but an unassuming place on the Leicestershire–Northamptonshire border where the Avon is scarcely broader than a man's stride. Very occasionally a coal-boat trades to Welford, but the insignificant branch is of great importance in another respect, for it is a valuable 'feeder', supplying the Leicester Section, and through it the main line of the Grand Union, with water from two reservoirs on the ill-fated wolds of Naseby. This provision of an adequate supply of water to the summit is one of the lesser-known aspects of canal construction and maintenance, and is often a source of great difficulty during a long drought. On one such occasion the canal company were compelled to take the drastic step of draining the whole of this twenty-mile 'pound' into the main line in order to keep the latter navigable.

Midway between this junction and the tunnel is North Kilworth Wharf, where Mr. Woodhouse keeps the only inn on the canal. He is a boatman like his father before him, and the infrequent wayfarers almost invariably pause to drink a pint and pass the time of day with him even if they cannot arrange their journey so as to moor for the night beside his own boats at the wharf. Like 'The Bull and Butcher', it was a friendly, intimate place, with an atmosphere poles apart from that of the drab and impersonal urban drink-shop. It was a damp, dreary evening of low-flying cloud and driving rain-squalls when we called, and at such a time there is no more pleasant place in which to be than a hospitable country inn. The

'A Wooded Cutting near the Mouth of the Tunnel'

bar more nearly resembled a kitchen, with its stone-flagged floor, scrubbed table top, and wide fireplace a-glitter with copper and brass highly polished in real canal fashion. We were very well content to sit drinking our cellar-drawn beer, listening to Mr. Woodhouse as he talked of canals past and present, while the burnished metal about the hearth awoke in the firelight to a lambent bloom that no modern plate or stainless metal can ever equal.

Although this countryside would appear attractive enough to the townsman, there is a tragedy in its solitude which reveals itself to the more discerning eye in the deserted sheep-walks, the endless fields of ridge and furrow that have reverted to pasture, the un-trimmed hedgerows, choked ditches and gates drunkenly leaning. The husbandman has abandoned his heritage for the get-rich-quick lure of the industrial towns of the Midlands. We met some of this new generation of 'countrymen' as we walked from the wharf to the village of North Kilworth. The evening train had just brought them back from some factory or other, and they were hurrying homeward with their tin lunch-cases tucked under their arms. After this foretaste we were not surprised to find that the village epitomised the story of the deserted fields. The cottages, once thatched, had, almost without exception, been re-roofed with corrugated iron, while many stood empty and ruinous. The characteristic wattle walls, once also capped with thatch, were alike crumbling to ruin, their gaps filled with hurdles or wire. The rural arts had gone with the old rural community, and the village was dispirited and dead, the only new life a row of unsightly bungalows which had sprung up along the main road conveniently near the station. Before our journey was over we were destined to see many more of these tragic epitaphs of broken faith which are the result of 'the drift to the towns', and were able to forecast the proximity of large towns without the aid of a map by the noticeable impoverishment of the country around them.

It is true that at one point not far from North Kilworth we saw a large pasture being broken up for plough, but the way in which this task was being performed belonged to the factory, not to the fields. A most monstrous machine the height of a house was dragging itself over the ridge and furrow on caterpillar tracks larger than any tank. The simile, indeed, was fitting, man having apparently declared war on Nature and brought up his heavy artillery. In the tail of the machine two sets of revolving steel tines, each as long and thick as a man's arm, were tearing the ground like vast talons. High up under a canopy in a haze of pungent diesel exhaust fumes the modern husbandman, a mechanic in blue overalls, sat before a host of levers, as far removed from the land as a passenger on a luxury liner is from the sea. The roaring of the engine, the groaning of gears and the dull rumbling sound of the steel claws as they tore through the ground, combined to make a din that shattered the silences for half a mile around, so that I was thankful when we passed out of earshot. The advantage of these ponderous and costly machines is extremely doubtful; that no machine will ever replace the thatch on the roofs of North Kilworth, lay the hedges, rebuild the walls, or build a sound farm gate, is quite certain.

It was still raining when we cast off next morning and entered Husbands Bosworth Tunnel, but by the time we reached daylight once more the sky was clearing, and before long the sun came out. This was fortunate, because scenically these last few miles of this long summit level were the best of the twenty. The steep, bracken-covered slopes of the Laughton Hills rose sheer from the water's edge as the canal wound along their flank, and, opposite, the land shelved away more gradually into the shallow upper valley of the Welland. As we journeyed on, the hills became more gentle of contour and covered with woodland, to fall away altogether just before noon when we sighted the whitewashed cottage which I knew marked the top of Foxton Locks.

The descent at Foxton is greater and even steeper than the ascent at Watford, there being no less than five pairs of staircase locks having a combined fall of seventy-five feet. So abrupt is the change of level that when we first sighted the summit lock, the long beams with their white painted ends stood out boldly against the open sky until, on closer approach, a wide expanse of the Leicestershire plain came into view below. The paddles of these locks were extremely heavy, and we were assisted on our way down by the lock-keeper, who had a windlass with an extra long crank, made especially for the purpose. He was a most kindly and helpful old man, having only one leg, but with the aid of a single crutch he made his way about the locks with most remarkable agility and speed, balancing himself dextrously on his solitary foot when he wound up the paddles.

Such a concentration of narrow locks takes some time to negotiate, and constitutes a serious hindrance to traffic, because boats are unable to pass each other except between the groups

of 'risers'. It was with the object of obviating this delay that the
Foxton Inclined Plane Lift was constructed and opened for traffic
in the spring of 1900. Of all the many strange freaks that the
mechanical age has produced, this was one of the strangest, and
the photographs of the extraordinary contrivance which hang in
the bar of 'The Black Horse' in Foxton are well worth inspection.
It consisted of two enormous cast-iron caissons, each capable of
floating two narrow boats, these being mounted upon ten wheels
which ran on five parallel sets of rails laid down the inclined plane.
These were raised and lowered sideways by means of cables, one
counterbalancing the other, a winding engine being employed
for the extra power required. Unfortunately the rails were
constantly giving way beneath the colossal weight of the caissons,
and the infrequent traffic did not justify the expense of manning the
engine-house or keeping a boiler constantly under steam, with the
result that after a very few years had elapsed, the lift was abandoned
as a costly failure. All that we saw of it, apart from the two short
backwaters that connected the canal to it, was a steep ramp of
crumbling concrete up the face of the hill overgrown with briars,
and, on the summit, the ruins of the engine-house. Canal lifts
have never been widely employed, and the only one still in use today
is the Anderton Vertical Lift at Northwich, which lowers boats
from the Trent and Mersey Canal to the River Weaver, a fall
of fifty feet.

At the foot of the locks we joined the 'broad' canal from
Leicester to Market Harborough, once an independent waterway
called the 'Old Union', but long ago merged into what is now the
Grand Union system. Here we turned aside from the main course
of our journey, having decided to make Market Harborough our
first port of call for letters, laundry, and general stores. Occasionally a pair of Fellows Morton boats, or 'Joshers' as they are
called on the canals, in affectionate remembrance of the late Mr.
Joshua Fellows, trades to Harborough basin with a cargo of timber
from Brentford, but the trade on the branch is very small. The
swing bridge by which the village street of Foxton crosses over the
water is kept locked, and the key, so the lock-keeper informed us,
hung in the porch of the first cottage on our left turning down the
road. There seemed to be some subtle magic in this key, for when
I walked up the flower-bordered path to the cottage door the street
was deserted, yet no sooner had I lifted it from its hiding-place
than the children of Foxton appeared miraculously from nowhere.

Evidently the opening of the bridge for the passage of a boat is for them a unique and wondrous event. Some of the more sober among them helped me to swing the bridge, but this assistance was more than discounted by the majority, who jumped onto it for a ride. There were shrill shrieks of excitement and delight, and a total disregard for the admonitions of mothers who had come to their cottage doors. We breathed a sigh of relief when we had re-locked the bridge and passed out of sight, although, to do them justice, they kept a respectful distance from the boat, unlike the children of the towns whom we encountered later.

When we left Foxton we were reminded of the Oxford Canal at Wormleighton, for although it was only two and a half miles across country to Market Harborough, the canal described a wide arc of nearly six miles round Gallow Hill, overhung by trees on one side, with fine views over open country on the other. The water was deep and crystal clear, but was in places so covered with dense blanket weed as to appear a solid surface. This weed was too fine to foul our propeller, but it repeatedly choked the strainer of the engine cooling water intake, so that for a considerable part of the way Angela looked after the helm while I lay flat on the aft deck, with one arm trailing in the water clearing the weed away. Such troubles only give an added zest to the navigation of little-used canals such as this, and it was with a pleasant sense of minor triumph that we sailed into Harborough Basin at noon of our ninth day out from Banbury.

THE BOTTOM LOCK, FOXTON

Chapter XII

INTERLUDE AT MARKET HARBOROUGH

We had timed ourselves to arrive in Market Harborough on Market Day, for there is no better measure of the character of a country town than this. Yet when we walked down the hill from the canal basin, the wide main street of tall Queen Anne houses was empty of the booths and jostling crowds we had expected. The answer of a passer-by to our enquiry explained all, and accurately summarised the position of the town today. 'Go down past that cinema,' he directed, pointing, 'and you'll see the 'all. It's in there—what's left of it.' Following these instructions, we found the sorry shadow of a market which revealed that rural life in the district had fallen upon evil days. Our impression of the country around North Kilworth was confirmed, and the town might as well call itself plain Harborough, for as a market town it is dead. Its most active and prosperous institutions appeared to be a corset manufactory, a canning works and several saddleries. The inference is obvious; stays and tinned soup have become more profitable commodities than agricultural produce, while costly saddles proclaim that though 'the Shires' may be falling to wrack and ruin, they remain the playground of the fox-hunting rich.

We had a meal ashore in Market Harborough, dining one evening at a hotel which has been made famous by its host, whose unmistakable figure we had seen crossing the street when we first entered the town. The house stands in the main street, its plain but not unpleasing façade of stucco enhanced by a well-painted sign set in a frame of wrought-iron work so intricately and cunningly forged that, though probably the work of a local craftsman, it rivals the best Spanish workmanship. A wide archway beneath, giving access to a cobbled courtyard, proclaimed a coaching origin. We found the interior decoration a trifle bizarre for our taste, yet because it displayed a certain independence and originality of idea, attributes so sadly lacking today, we did not feel disposed to criticise, individual taste, however eccentric, being infinitely preferable to the pseudo or the modern super-cinema style of which the eye soon sickens to the point of nausea.

For a very modest sum we were served with a dinner which fully justified the reputation of the house, and which few London restaurants could equal at many times the price. It must be a difficult task to keep this kitchen supplied with all its manifold needs, and the meal proved that it was possible, by the use of imagination, to escape from the inevitable roast-and-two-veg, tinned soup and tinned fruit of the average country hotel dinner. Yet, for all its excellence, I was disappointed to find that the meal was cosmopolitan in origin, and not, as I had hoped, a revival of genuine English cooking. I have still to discover an inn where I could confidently take a foreign friend to dine and say to him, "This is English cooking".

The culinary craft is yet another of the useful arts which have suffered eclipse in recent years, for had not the self-sufficient rural kitchen and all that it stood for been banished by the evil genius of the can-opener, there would be no need today to introduce foreign dishes in order to produce a good dinner. The average cook knows less of the value of herbs, spices and seasonings than did her forbear in the humblest farmhouse, and, what is more, she has lost the art of taking pains. Gone are the bundles of thyme, sage, agrimony and rosemary which once hung above the hearth; and what of the others: savory, chervil, fennel, marjoram and green tarragon, whose fragrance lingers in their names? Their place has been usurped by synthetic concentrates and 'Bull-in-the-bottle'.

I would not make so bold as to presume to teach the twentieth-century innkeeper his business, because I am fully aware of the difficulties under which he labours, but this does not prevent me from creating the ideal inn of my imagination. First and foremost, I would free myself of the stranglehold of the big brewery com-

panies by which most houses are literally 'tied'. This would
enable me to make my choice of beer, or, better still, to brew myself
if I were able. Furthermore, I could then lay down a good cellar
of wine, as distinct from the vinegarish substances 'bottled at the
brewery' to promote the sale of inferior beer at the expense of the
Englishman's palate. Meanwhile in my kitchen I should aim,
not only to re-create traditional English cooking in general, but
especially to preserve from oblivion those dishes peculiar to the
immediate locality of my house, and make these my speciality.
I wager that in this way I could obtain sufficient variety to satisfy
the most critical without borrowing ideas from abroad, and last,
but not least, my bill of fare would bespeak my dishes in plain
English, not in 'menu-ese', that ludicrous jargon which is a relic
of smug Victorian gentility.

I am afraid that such an inn will never exist in actual fact, and
that if it did it would prove a costly failure, so debased has popular
taste become. Meanwhile due credit should be given to my host
of Market Harborough for creating a house of character and distinction in an unpromising neighbourhood for such a venture.

Chapter XIII

LEICESTER

BECAUSE the city of Leicester has exerted its urban influence on the countryside over a wide area, the sixteen miles of canal from Foxton to Aylestone Mill within the city boundary had little to commend them. The first few miles between the villages of Smeeton Westerby and Gumley, perched upon its hill-top, were pleasant enough, but when we emerged from Saddington Tunnel it was to behold the first portent of things to come—a livid rash of jerry-built houses surrounding Fleckney. A beautiful tree-bordered pound by Wistow Park a mile or so beyond, and the sylvan surroundings of Newton Harcourt, were the last outposts of a countryside in retreat, for the next village, South Wigston, had become industrialised, a fragment of a city slum dropped in the green fields, while Blaby was a typical urban dormitory. Railways, power-lines and roads lined by ribbon development began to converge on either hand, until as we approached the latter place we sighted, standing beside the canal, what we at first took to be an ultra-modern factory of the type which disgraces the Great West Road. On closer approach, however, the building revealed itself as a monster 'gin-palace', the ultimate apotheosis of brewers' taste manifested in the super-cinema style. There could be no doubt of its commercial success, for the place was crowded with the clerks, typists and mill-hands of Leicester, while a score of white-jacketed barmen hurried ceaselessly to and fro. Only American slang can adequately convey the atmosphere; it was 'one hundred per cent.', in place of quality an overwhelming quantity being substituted upon the same principle as the film producer's thousand extras, herd of stampeding elephants, or triple revolving stages. In one vast room there was dancing in progress, and an effete young man was crooning into a microphone, his accent a curious blend of natural Leicestershire and cultivated American. In another, equally popular, there must have been at least a dozen dart-boards. The huge expanse of car park was filled with small saloons as like as a row of beans, and there was even a playground where the future citizens of Leicester might disport themselves while daddy sank a pint or so of draught bitter, and mummy had a glass of nourishing stout, or sipped a more refined port and lemon. The friendly, intimate atmosphere of the English inn was entirely lacking, and the quality of the beer was execrable.

From our position at the bar we could see 'Cressy' at her moorings beside the tow path, and our drink was summarily interrupted when we espied several boys of fourteen or fifteen years of age clamber aboard and walk unconcernedly about the aft deck. When we were in country districts we never felt the slightest concern about leaving the boat unattended, but we soon discovered that this behaviour was typical of urban manners, a contrast that was significant. We found that grown-ups were little better, for on more than one occasion when we were passing through a lock some mother would satisfy her child's curiosity by lifting it up and thrusting its head through any window that happened to be open.

It took us little over an hour to cover the remaining distance from Blaby to the tail of King's Lock at Aylestone, where we left the canal and entered the River Soar, from whose ancient name of Leire the city derived its title. We found unexpectedly good moorings at Aylestone Mill, and later in the day journeyed into the heart of Leicester by that obsolete and ear-shattering form of transport, the tram-car.

In the seventeenth century the knitting of hosiery and other textiles became the staple employment in the cottages of a hundred rural communities in Leicestershire, but the invention of the power-driven frame in the early eighteen hundreds silenced the hand-frames of the villages for ever, and the industry soon became concentrated in a few large mills in the city. This early industrial revolution has completely changed the face of Leicester, and a few smoke-blackened fragments, scattered like ashes among the beetling warehouses, are all that remain of the mediaeval stronghold of the Red Rose. One of these remnants, an old house adjoining what little is left of de Beaumont's great castle, is reputed to have witnessed that scene immortalised by Shakespeare, the death of John of Gaunt. Surrounded by grimy mills and reeking chimneys the famous words: 'This other Eden, demi-paradise', assume a quality of bitter irony undreamed of by their author.

Two features of Leicester I shall remember: the market and the church of St. Mary de Castro. After our experience at Market Harborough, we were not very sanguine about the former, expecting to find it lurking in some gloomy hall redolent of fish. Instead we came upon a great square filled with row upon row of booths, and resounding with a babel of hucksters crying their wares. Competition was particularly keen among the numerous vendors of fruit and vegetables, each doing his best to shout down his neighbour. 'Fivepence a pound plums', one would bawl until his face grew as red as his wares and the adjoining stall cut the price to fourpence, when, not to be outdone, he would change his tune to a defiant: 'Five pound for eighteen pence—there you are now, the best value in town'. Besides these fruit-sellers there were stalls piled high with 'seconds' (blemished china from the Potteries), stalls of meat, fish and poultry, stalls of moth-ridden secondhand clothes, old limp boots and shoes, bookstalls stacked with dog-eared volumes of Victorian sermons, tattered paperbacks, and faded editions of Whyte Melville or the Waverley Novels. Cheap-jacks were offering bright baubles of every sort, and the sweet-stalls were heavy with golden brown toffee apples at a halfpenny each.

The church of St. Mary de Castro, which rears its graceful, soot-blackened spire from the top of the castle mound, was once the chapel of the House of Lancaster, but when 'Proud Bolingbroke' usurped the crown in 1399, the Earldom of Leicester was merged into the monarchy, and the chapel became a parish church which, lacking patronage or benefice, fell into a disastrous state of repair. Since that time it has suffered at the hands of many restorers, although it still presents many features of great interest. There is not only a fine north door of Norman work, but a magnificent example of a Norman triple sedillia in the south wall of the chancel, double-shafted pillars supporting the characteristic arches of dog-

tooth moulding in a fine state of preservation. From the point of
view of the archaeologist this was undoubtedly the greatest
treasure in the church, but it was the Early English triple sedillia
in the south aisle that I most admired. The years have dealt more
hardly with it, much of the carving having suffered from damp,
but the two interpretations of the same motif afford an interesting
contrast. To my eyes the stolid Norman work looked ponderous
and disproportionate beside the airy grace of the Early English
shafts, so perfectly in harmony and balance with the graceful
spring of the vaulting. One feature of the church must be quite
unique, and that is the tower. When originally built it was remote
from the body of the church, like its fellow at Evesham, but when,
at a later date, the enormous south aisle was constructed to house a
second collegiate church, the tower was enclosed, so that it now
stands upon its own foundations within the body of the church.

We emerged from the cool dimness and quiet of this most
ancient place into the full blaze of a summer's afternoon. The
sun was shining out of a clear blue sky, and in the city streets the
scorching pavements with their jostling crowds, the fumes of traffic
and the blaring horns, made 'Cressy' and the cool river seem more
than ever desirable. We caught a tram without more ado and
clanked back to the comparative peace of Aylestone, resolved to
slip our moorings and head for open country the following morning.

The River Soar is Leicester's back door, and as back doors are
apt to do, it reveals 'domestic offices' which usually remain dis-
creetly hidden from the eyes of visitors. Broad squares and
pretentious public buildings proclaim the city's commercial
prosperity to the traveller by road, but the water-borne traveller
sees a very different picture. This is no less than the ugliness and
squalor which underlie the superficial pomp and circumstance of
all great cities. We saw the reeking gas-works, mountainous refuse
dumps, the power-station with its gigantic steam-capped cooling
towers, great mills pulsating with machinery rising sheer from the
water's edge and, above all, the countless mean streets where
dwelt the servants of these monsters.

As we drifted along, passing beneath innumerable bridges,
and winding this way and that through a canyon of factory walls,
I was extremely thankful for the presence of the towing-path which
accompanies the river throughout its navigable course. For every
now and again the channel would divide, one branch passing into a
lock, while the other shot over a thundering weir, and as both

were usually invisible, only the path's unfailing guidance prevents the stranger from losing the navigable channel and heading for a weir on a swift current.

There is a great deal to be said against river navigations from the commercial point of view, as the pioneer James Brindley realised, for, writes Smiles, 'He likened water in a river flowing down a declivity to a furious giant running along and overturning everything; whereas (said he) "if you lay the giant flat upon his back, he loses all his force, and becomes completely passive, whatever his size may be".' The truth of this simple allegory is proved at least once every winter when the Soar, swollen by flood-water, becomes unnavigable, and boats are held up sometimes for weeks on end. At such times locks are liable to damage, headroom under bridges becomes very restricted, and narrow boats can scarcely make headway against the current. Travelling downstream in floodtime is extremely dangerous, because unless a boat can maintain a speed greater than that of the current it loses all steerage way, drifts out of control and is swept over the weirs. This fate has befallen over-venturesome boatmen on more than one occasion, and even when the river is at normal level the effect of the current has to be allowed for when turning broadside across the head of a weir to enter a lock channel.

Successfully negotiating these hazards, we presently entered a long, artificial cut away from the river. The water here was black and foul, the surroundings depressing in the extreme, so that we were glad when, after passing the vast Wolsey Underwear Mills, we sighted the river again and the first glimpse of open country. We had seen enough of Leicester. Urbs had one more card to play, however, for we found that Belgrave Lock, through which we had to pass to rejoin the river, was full of dead rats. The churning of our screw set their bloated, putrifying bodies bobbing up and down in horrid semblance of life. Had there been a local rat week? we wondered. Two imperturbable fishermen who sat on the lock-side gazing raptly at the water discountenanced the theory, for they appeared to accept the malodorous corpses as a part of the normal order of things. Perhaps Leicester breeds a fortuitous indifference to the more unpleasant aspects of city life.

'Moorings, Barrow-on-Soar'

Chapter XIV

COSSINGTON AND BARROW-ON-SOAR

LEICESTER has not marched so far into the country to the north; its frontiers, the suburban villages of Birstall and Thurmaston on Fosse Way, were soon passed, and we found ourselves in open fields at last, with the tall fingers of the mill chimneys fading in the smoke haze astern. Near the village of Wanlip we entered another artificial channel, the river making a wide circle to westward, and before rejoining it at Cossington we met the little River Wreak, flowing through a green tunnel of overhanging trees on its way from Melton Mowbray. From this point onwards the river scene would have delighted Cotman or Constable, and it was hard to believe that the same stream, a few miles back, had seemed little better than an open sewer. Having achieved our object of getting clear of the city, we went no farther that day, but moored up in the water-meadows below the lock by Cossington Mill.

As is the case with everything else in life, the true appreciation of travel lies in the contrasts which it constantly provides, for just as those who have not known great sorrow cannot rejoice, so ugliness must forever be the measure of beauty. With this simple truth in mind, we had decided on a route which did not seek deliberately to avoid industrial districts, and this evening at Cossington fully justified our choice. For had it not been for the city we had so lately left, the evening light in which clouds of gnats were dancing their intricate measures had never seemed so golden nor the meadows looked so richly green, nor could the eye have so delighted in the stooping willows and darker plane trees that, shadowing the water, wrought cunning tapestries of image and substance. There was new magic in the stillness, broken only by the lazy thunder of the weir, because the day before we had lurched down the Aylestone Road in a Leicester Corporation tram.

That the river had still better things in store we discovered the next day when we reached the lock at Barrow-upon-Soar. It was one of those blazing noons when everything is warm to the touch: the wooden lock beams, the crumbling brickwork of the bridge, even the grass had a sensuous warmth, as though the earth beneath were flesh. The wall of the lock cottage was covered with a climbing rose in full bloom, a wealth of white and gold flowers clustering about the windows and filling the air with their fragrance. The murmur of the bees that were busy about them mingled with the cool plashing of the thin jets of water which were leaking through chinks in the lock gates to make so drowsy a summer song that we could scarcely summon the energy to lift the paddles. We were already in two minds whether or not to continue our journey to Loughborough, as we had originally planned, but the sight of the lovely reach below the lock decided matters. We moored up, and did no more voyaging for four days. Even so, our departure was determined, not because we had grown tired of our surroundings, but for the reason that we feared a break in the perfect weather, or that some chance circumstance might conspire to spoil our recollection of such a time as falls to the lot of the average mortal all too rarely in these unhappy times.

On one side our moorings were sheltered and screened by the almost precipitous bank of Barrowcliffe, thickly clothed with trees and undergrowth, which afforded welcome shade in the heat of the day. Opposite, we looked out over level fields towards the village of Quorndon, part-screened by encircling elms, and backed by the wooded heights of Charnwood Forest. In the haze of cloudless days this farther distance grew indistinct, assuming a quality of blue that was almost indistinguishable from that of the sky itself, but by night, under a harvest moon which was near the full, the high skyline of the forest stood forth as darkly clear as a woodcut.

One day we went to the village of Woodhouse Eaves, that lovely name, and climbed up through the pungent, sun-drenched bracken to the summit of Beacon Hill, one of the highest points in the

Forest, commanding a mighty expanse of the Midland Plain.
Later, when we had returned to Barrow, hot and dusty after our
walk, we hired a rowing boat, and in the cool of the evening rowed
round the unnavigable loop of the river by Quorn Hall. Our row
ended, appropriately, at the Navigation Inn, its stone-flagged bar
overlooking the white, foaming fall of the weir. Here the mild
draught beer, a Derby brew, was the best we encountered on the
whole of our journey, a fitting climax to the day.

Determined to make the most of the perfect weather, we had
all our meals in the open, and in the evenings sat on the deck until
long after darkness had fallen, watching the last flush of colour
drain from the sky and the golden moon ride up over the shoulder
of Charnwood. As the air cooled the river smoked with rising
mist, weaving thin white veils, lambent in the moonlight, which
drifted away over the fields, a ghostly flood no higher than a man's
waist. We were constantly reminded of the wild company about
us by repeated scuffling sounds in the reeds, or by the sleepy clucking of a moorhen. Often in the daylight we would catch sight of
a small brown water-vole squatting on his hindquarters in some
green arbour of the bank not four feet away, nibbling imperturb-
ably at a juicy morsel held between his fore paws. So close did
they venture to 'Cressy's' bow that it was often the comfortable
sound of their munching that first attracted our attention.

Our most entertaining companions, however, were the little
grebe or dabchicks, in their summer plumage of black with bright
chestnut cheeks and throat. We had not encountered them before,
and to watch them was a constant amusement and delight. Their
dive was like a conjuring trick, so swiftly was it performed and
with so little trace; one moment there would be a small bird
swimming sedately across the river, and the next empty water
unbroken by the faintest ripple. Most of their time was spent
singly in the serious pursuit of food, but every now and again one
would decide to play a practical joke on his fellow and, diving,
would startle him by popping up like a cork almost directly beneath him. This was invariably the prelude to a wild game of hide-
and-seek under and over the water, accompanied by loud laughing
cries, more melodious, but not unlike that harbinger of rain, the
call of the green woodpecker. Just as the memory of some melody
can become inextricably associated in the mind with certain persons, events or places, so I shall always recall these halcyon days
at Barrow-upon-Soar when I hear the cry of the dabchick.

Chapter XV

THE BELL FOUNDERS

WHEN we reluctantly cast off from our moorings at Barrow it was not long before we once more left the river for an artificial channel, and presently found ourselves approaching the town of Loughborough. The surroundings were an unprepossessing replica of Leicester, though, fortunately, upon a smaller scale, and as the weather was still perfect, we were sorely tempted to push forward until we rejoined the river. Yet there was one feature of the town we had resolved not to miss, so we moored up and tramped through a seemingly interminable maze of mean streets, until we came upon our objective, the works of Messrs. John Taylor, a small unpretentious foundry, famous the world over as the birthplace of bells since 1366.

Loughborough is justly proud of this ancient industry, and boasts a public official whose office is unique in England. He is the Town Carilloneur, and twice a week throughout the summer months he gives recitals on what must surely be the finest War Memorial in the country, a carillon tower of forty-three bells.

There can be few countries which have not heard the sound of a Loughborough bell, nor a cathedral in England whose bells John Taylors' have not cast or re-cast. No bell is too small or too large for these craftsmen to tackle, from the sweet-toned handbells once beloved of village ringers but now alas all too rarely heard, to such brazen-voiced giants as 'Great George' of Bristol, 'Great Peter' of York Minster, and, peer of them all, 'Great Paul', the Bourdon Bell of St. Paul's Cathedral, which weighs no less than sixteen and a half tons and measures thirty feet in circumference. This enormous bell, the largest in the Empire, was cast in 1881, and conveyed to London by road—certainly no mean feat at that time. Among the most notable of more recent casts has been a peal of fourteen and a Bourdon bell 'Hosanna' for the new Abbey of Buckfast.

This foundry was full of bells of every size and for every purpose: ships' bells (one for the new Cunarder 'Princess Elizabeth'), bells for carillons, and church bells, some, destined for Catholic or monastic foundations, bearing Latin inscriptions, others inscribed as memorials of persons or events. Even in the yard outside lay numerous old and discarded bells, sadly awaiting their turn to be melted down.

The mould into which the bell-metal is poured when the cast takes place is not made to a wooden pattern or a drawing, as is the case in ordinary foundry work. Instead it is built upon a circular metal bed-plate to the measure of a sheet-metal template called a 'strickler'. This represents an exact 'slice' of the required bell, so that the moulder, using it as a gauge, can build up the mould and core to precisely the right contour. When this has been done, the outer mould, formed in a metal container not unlike a bell itself, is lowered over the core, the air space between them being the phantom bell to which the molten metal will conform when it is poured in.

When the cast has taken place the final tuning is carried out by removing a certain amount of metal from inside the mouth of the bell. Nowadays this process is carried out on a vertical lathe, but in the earlier days of bell-founding it was done by the somewhat crude means described as 'hammer and chisel tuning', which simply consisted of chipping away the metal until the bell sounded right. Many of the old bells in the scrap yard bore evidence of this haphazard method.

To anyone with a rudimentary knowledge of foundry work the foregoing procedure is perfectly straightforward, even though it is unorthodox. The secret of the bell-founder's craft is hidden in the calculations which can produce a bell to ring the desired note so accurately that only the lightest skimming on the lathe is sufficient to put it in perfect tune. We caught a momentary glimpse of this genius, a portly, bespectacled figure incongruously clad in blue pin-stripe trousers, suede shoes, shirt sleeves and gaudy braces, who emerged from some inner lair to listen attentively while overalled workmen armed with hide mallets rang several peals on a set of bells which had just arrived for re-casting. What his conclusions were and in what intricate form they would take shape at his desk we shall never know.

We saw not only the bells themselves in process of manufacture, but the massive frames in which they are hung and the slender wooden rope pulleys which lift them. Most modern frames are built of steel girders, but in the joiners' shop, where machinery was conspicuous by its absence, one of the old-type wooden frames was being constructed with great new-hewn beams of seasoned oak which were a joy to behold. The employees of Messrs. John Taylor are fortunate in their craft, for the making of bells can never fall a prey to mechanised quantity production, and the machines must forever be subordinate to the skill of hand and eye.

Loughborough may rightly be proud of her bells, and we did not begrudge the hours of sunshine which we spent in the foundry.

Chapter XVI

DOWN TO THE TRENT

INLAND navigation must be the safest form of transport ever devised, and compared to the death-dealing turmoil of the modern motor road, the canal or river is a veritable sanctuary. The nearest approach to an accident which we encountered on the whole of our long journey occurred as we were leaving Loughborough on our way back to the river. We were approaching the narrow channel under a bridge—or a 'bridge-hole', in canal parlance—when through the arch came a party of holiday-makers in a hired punt. There would have been ample time for them to have cleared the narrows and paddled to the side, but at the sudden spectacle of 'Cressy' bearing down upon them they completely lost their heads and swung broadside across our bows. From my point of vantage at the tiller it seemed that we should inevitably smash their fragile craft to pieces against the mouth of the bridge, for there was no room to alter course. All I could do was to put 'Cressy' full astern and hope for the best. The water boiled furiously under our stern and the whole boat vibrated, but the expected collision did not come. We checked with a foot or so to spare, and the occupants of the punt, righting themselves, paddled past, making such embarrassed apologies and blushing so furiously that we had not the heart to vent upon them the storm of abuse (that mythical language of the 'bargee') which they evidently anticipated.

This encounter had its sequel on the river an hour or so later, when, on drawing in to the bank to moor for the night, I engaged reverse gear without result, our propeller ceasing to revolve. When we had contrived with difficulty to get our mooring lines ashore, I made an investigation, hoping for the best, but gloomily visualising a broken propeller shaft, a sheared key, or dire happenings inside the gearbox, any of which was capable of crippling us for many days. Luckily, however, the trouble was simple. A coupling sleeve on the propeller shaft had been loosened by the rough treatment it had received, allowing the tail end of the shaft to slide out through the stern tube until the propeller had fouled the rudder stock. It was simply necessary to push the shaft home and re-tighten the coupling, a job that was soon done, although it involved an impromptu bathe in the river. Because the evening was warm, this was no hardship—in fact the tonic of cold water gave me a wonderful appetite for the dinner which was awaiting me when I had finished.

The numerous slender spires of the village churches are a feature of the soft river scenery between Loughborough and the Trent. First comes Normanton, so close upon the bank that it ponders its image in the water, then Kegworth, rising from a screen of sheltering trees, and lastly Radcliffe, a church of more humble proportions crowning a knoll in the open fields.

Was it chance or an innate sense of fitness that inspired the masons of old time to build their spires so often in the flat lands? Dwarfed in a hill country, where the bolder tower is better suited, there can be no doubt that the soaring grace of the spire appears to the best advantage in a setting of willow-fringed pastures and winding streams.

When we landed at Normanton in quest of milk we were gladdened by the sight of old buildings in good repair, some newly thatched, the first examples of living country craftsmanship we had seen since we had left Oxfordshire. A similar excursion into Radcliffe-on-Soar the next day was even better rewarded, although we could obtain no milk. In order to get to the village we had to repeat our adventure on the Avon at Harvington by wading the weir channel of the river at a ford. A bed of sharp stones made the crossing extremely uncomfortable, but Radcliffe church was worth a tender foot-sole and an empty milk-can.

It appeared to have escaped alike the unwelcome attentions of the Cromwellians and of nineteenth-century restorers, so secluded is this hamlet by the river. The magnificent alabaster tombs of the Satcheverell family in the chancel were intact, the calm features of the knights and their ladies undefaced, while the whole church, innocent of Victorian make-up, glowed in its original simplicity. Nor was this all; more remarkable still, it had been furnished in rare and perfect taste. All too often the austere beauty of naked stone or mellow woodwork is marred by garish scarlet hassocks and carpets, while altars of effective simplicity are covered by hideous cloths of green, magenta or royal blue. Here the carved altar table of natural oak, scorning all such tawdry pretensions, was quite bare and, by a stroke of genius, the narrow strip of carpet up the centre of the aisle was of a certain shade of azure blue that harmonised to perfection with the greys and browns of stone and wood. The beauty of the average country church would be enhanced tenfold if the clergy could have a few lessons in the art of church furnishing from this incumbent. Yet all was not well with this lovely church, for the fabric was in a sorry state of repair, the fine oak roof showing signs of rot, and the walls so stained with damp at floor level as to suggest that it had been invaded more than once by winter floods.

In the surrounding churchyard were some outstanding examples of the slate tombstones which are peculiar to this district. They hail from the famous quarries of Swithland in Charnwood, their lettering and ornamentation, which are of remarkable grace and delicacy, being the work of a group of village craftsmen founded in the seventeenth century.

Half an hour after leaving Radcliffe we passed through Red Hill, the last of the Soar locks, where we gave up the pass which had carried us from Norton Junction, and presently entered the broad Trent at a meeting-place of many waters. Immediately on our right the river flowed over Thrumpston weir, while the mouth of the navigable channel, or Cranfleet Cut as it is called, for craft proceeding downstream to Nottingham, Newark and the Humber, lay two hundred yards upstream. Directly opposite was the entrance lock of the Erewash Canal, leading north to Derby and Langley Mill. Save for an occasional pair of 'Joshers' or Erewash Canal boats, we had met little traffic on the Soar, but now we found ourselves in the midst of a *mêlée* of boats of every sort and size. A pair of narrow boats were coming out of the lock opposite,

numerous holiday-makers in minute pedal-driven craft were darting hither and thither like so many water-fleas, with a joyous
abandon that cared nothing for the rules of navigation, while, to
complete the congestion, a race was in progress for small sailing-
boats and, since there was a head wind, these last were tacking
from bank to bank across the stream. Turning left-handed, we
forged steadily up-river, keeping a wary eye on the pedal boats,
which were reminiscent both in appearance and behaviour of the
'Dodgem Cars' at a fair, and at the same time taking care to pass
the amateur sailors on the right tack. In this fashion we came to
Sawley Lock, the only one of the big Trent Locks which we had
to pass.

As this was the height of the holiday season, we had been surprised at the absence of pleasure craft on the quiet reaches of the
Soar, but the next few hundred yards of the river above Sawley
amply accounted for the deficiency. A dozen or more cabin
cruisers were moored head to stern along the banks, whose grass,
bruised and flattened, was bestrewn with an untidy litter of paper
bags, empty tins, orange peel and the embers of picnic fires.
Nearly all the boats had crews aboard, of whom some were bath-
ing, while others lolled on the decks to the accompaniment of the
inevitable gramophone or radio. Evidently the townsman afloat
is as gregarious as his *confrère* of the roads, whose habits I have
frequently pondered with amazement. Often on a bank holiday I
have walked or driven through fields and lanes for hours on end
without meeting a soul, but, on coming upon a main road, found
its verges crowded with cars and picnic parties within a bun's
throw of each other. It would seem that the close confinement of
great cities has re-awakened the herd instinct of the primitive. The
countryman knows no unease in the elemental silence of lonely
places; but when the people of the towns return to the land they
have forsaken, impelled by a craving they do not understand, it is
to find its solitude intolerable, so complete is their estrangement.
This is one of the tragic results of the drift to the towns.

We had thought of spending a night on the Trent, but the
spectacle of this throng at Sawley induced us to change our plans,
and so we continued upstream, passing under the great girder
which carries the Leicester pipe of the Derwent Valley water supply
over the river in a single span. The river hereabouts must have
been fully a hundred yards wide, and since the westering sun was
dead ahead, it was over a dazzling golden pathway that we came

to the end of our river journey at Derwent Mouth. On our right was the mouth of the tributary Derwent, and between the converging rivers lay the entrance of the Trent and Mersey Canal, England's first coast-to-coast waterway, and James Brindley's masterpiece.

By this time we had become so accustomed to travelling on broad rivers that it seemed strange to find ourselves once more confined to such a narrow channel of dead water. The banks, overgrown with tall reeds, appeared to crowd in upon us, an effect that was heightened by the great clumps of reed which had broken away from the banks and floated into deep water, often forming what appeared to be an impassable barrier until they were swung aside by 'Cressy's' bows. By the time we had worked our way through the first two canal locks and had come to Shardlow, darkness was falling fast, so we moored for the night in the meadows just beyond the village.

Chapter XVII

SINGING SHARDLOW AND STORM AT FINDERN

THE wharves and warehouses of Shardlow constitute the eastern terminus of Brindley's great canal, and the village has sprung up around them in the same way that Crewe has grown up beside its railway yards. Here the parallel ends, however, for, when Crewe was built, the new industrial order was already firmly established, and the short-sighted aim of immediate commercial gain had finally swept away the last remnants of permanence and grace from architecture. Shardlow dates from the dawn of the new era, and the canal buildings bear witness to the fact that these qualities had not then been lost. The masons of a century and a half ago built them to endure, and endowed them also with the dying spark of that fire which once made the humblest barn a thing of beauty.

One large, three-storeyed warehouse, which in modern hands would have been a featureless barrack, was miraculously transformed by a combination of detail so subtle that it was difficult to discover why it should be so satisfying to the eye. Doubtless the secret lay in the pitch of the roof, in the shape and spacing of the windows, and in the colour of the wide-morticed bricks, while a low, wide arch under the foundations, beneath which the boats could run to unload, gave the whole ponderous mass an unsubstantial air which called to mind the fairy-like, painted castles of the boat cabins. In the same manner, round-headed doorways and a curious projecting gable end lent character and charm to an old Malthouse adjoining 'The Malt Shovel' inn.

We found no less than three canal-side inns at Shardlow, each with its staunch little clientele of 'regulars' playing each other at darts, or setting the affairs of villages and nations to rights over a pint of Burton ale. No club is more exclusive than the bar of a village inn, and perhaps it was because we respected this fact that we were greeted with kindliness and natural courtesy, two qualities which the townsman of today has lost.

Least prepossessing externally, but most entertaining of the trio, was 'The Canal Tavern', beside Shardlow Lock. By day the jovial landlord of this inn plies his trade as a blacksmith, but in the evenings he turns musician, settling his burly figure onto the stool before the old bar piano and rattling off all the old familiar songs, simple, sentimental or bawdy, while his patrons sing themselves hoarse. We heard the strains of 'Daisy Bell' drifting over the water long before we reached the house, and when we entered we were at once invited to swell the chorus of singers who lined the benches round the walls, with their pint glasses set before them. The company was representative of both sexes and every age, from a party of village youths who evidently preferred an evening's full-blooded entertainment at the 'Tavern' to two hours synthetic sentiment in the cinema, to an old lady who, we were informed in a stage whisper, was over eighty years of age and would, when the mood was upon her, dance in the clear space between the tables, footing it as lightly and nimbly as a girl. Unfortunately this spectacle was denied us, but it was enough to watch her as she entered heart and soul into the singing, with a harsh but surprisingly tuneful voice, like a male falsetto, nodding her head and swinging her glass in time to the music. Despite innumerable wrinkles and an almost total lack of teeth, her features were wonderfully firm and youthful, while her hair was as dark and lustrous as her eyes.

After several songs in chorus, notably a long and bawdy version of 'Old King Cole', with a rousing refrain which echoed to the rafters, we were treated to a solo by the local lock-keeper, a swarthy, handsome fellow in his early thirties, who gave a most able rendering of 'Old Macdonald' with great fluency and spirit. Then, acquiescing coyly to insistent requests, the landlady obliged with a very sentimental ditty, sung in a quavering contralto, which drew silent tears from the old lady.

Meanwhile the drawing and carrying of beer were entrusted, with delightful informality, to voluntary helpers, most notable among these being an elderly engine-driver. 'Uncle Jack', as he was affectionately called, bustled untiringly to and fro in his shirt sleeves, singing lustily, a cloth cap perched on the back of his silvery head. His rosy countenance radiated benevolent good humour in a perpetual grin, and his blue eye was as sharp and quizzical as a robin's.

For all its mediocre appearance, the landlord and patrons have brought 'The Canal Tavern' nearer to the spirit of an older and happier rural past than all the 'olde innes' with their sham timbering and bogus brasses. The scene in the bar would have delighted Hogarth or Rabelais; it swept the imagination into that past when the countrymen of England were still merry, to the days before the repressive effects of Puritanism and the Enclosure Acts had, between them, contrived to kill the spontaneity and break the ties of the rural communities. It was with genuine regret that we took our leave of this jovial company, and on the morrow looked back until a bend in the canal hid the wharves and inns of Shardlow from our sight.

The weather was overcast and threatening, for a thunderstorm in the night had not cleared the air, and when we met our friend the lock-keeper at Aston Lock it began to rain heavily. Nothing daunted, we continued on our way up the valley towards Weston-upon-Trent, and were rewarded not only by an improvement in the weather, but by a more than usually attractive canal scene. For a mile or more the waterway hugged the wooded slope of the river bank, and between the boles of the trees which leant gracefully over the water we caught glimpses of the winding river, with the green slopes of Donnington Park beyond.

The locks hereabouts were wide, and so deep that it was sometimes impossible to clamber from 'Cressy's' deck onto the lock parapet. Several of the cottages beside them were small shops, selling twist tobacco, highly coloured sweets or mineral waters, and one at Weston Lock served as a Toll Office for west-bound boats. By the time we reached the lock at Swarkestone, the junction of the Derby Canal, the sun, which had at last struggled clear of a sultry, steaming haze, was blazing down from a cloudless sky with such intensity that every solid outline appeared to waver in the shimmering air, and the tar blistered on our deck.

A canal lock, with its outspread beams, graceful bridge and attendant cottage ringed about with flowers, is an addition to any landscape and the dominant feature of the canal scene. The lock at Swarkestone was still further enhanced by the garden of a second cottage, which occupied the narrow triangular plot of ground between the two converging waterways. With its massed borders of sweet-scented country flowers, smooth lawn and heavy-laden apple trees, it resembled an enchanted island in the still water, and so beguiled us that it was not until we had journeyed some two miles on our way that we realised that we had left both our lock windlasses behind.

It seemed that there was nothing for it but to trudge back along the tow-path, for one of the minor drawbacks of canal travel is the impossibility of turning the boat round at will. In the heyday of the canals, when boats traded to every village wharf, turning-places or 'winding holes' were common enough, but as the wharves fell into disuse they became filled up with mud or overgrown with reeds, with the result that junctions or the basins of the larger towns are often the only turning places. We had therefore resigned ourselves to a weary tramp, and were arguing whether one or both of us should go, when we sighted a large farm on the right bank, called, according to my map, Arleston House. Thither we went on our usual quest for milk and with the idea that I might perhaps be able to borrow a bicycle. We found substantial outbuildings in good repair, and received a general impression of prevailing order and efficiency, a welcome change from that dispirited air of neglect and decay which pervades the majority of English farms today. Owing to the abnormally wet season, the hay harvest had evidently only just been completed, although August was almost at an end, for several Hermaphrodite wagons were standing in the yard beside new-made ricks as yet unthatched. I had never actually seen a wagon of this type before, although I recognised it at once from the drawing and description in Mr. Hennell's fascinating but tragic book 'Change in the Farm'. It consists of an orthodox two-wheeled tumbril which can be speedily converted into a light harvest wain by the addition of a fore-carriage, the whole making a combination so serviceable that it is surprising it is not more widely used. A measure of the charm of these old agricultural implements built by local craftsmen, however, is their regional character, and according to Mr. Hennell the home of the 'Mophrodite' or 'Mufferer', as countrymen call it, is in North Lincolnshire and part of Norfolk.

Whether or not the farmer of Arleston was a Lincolnshire man we did not discover, but he was certainly extremely obliging, not only filling our can with new milk, but prevailing upon his cowman to lend me his bicycle. So, while Angela laid tea on the fore-deck, I pedalled furiously back to Swarkestone, found one windlass after some search, and returned, all in less time than it had taken

'Cressy' to make the single journey and no longer than the tea kettle took to boil.

We had not gone much farther upon our way that evening before the sky began to darken ominously, towering thunder-clouds sweeping up astern. We heard the first distant roll of thunder as we left Stenson Lock, and though we ran before the storm for a mile or so, it became obvious that we could not hope to evade its swift advance, so we moored hurriedly by the village of Findern just as the first heavy drops of rain were plopping sullenly in the water.

It was the worst storm either of us had ever experienced, raging without pause for over three hours. Many-branched forked lightning flickered incessantly on three sides, illuminating the cabin with its vivid glare as the great storm-belt travelled slowly northwest from the direction of Ashby-de-la-Zouch, across the Trent valley and over Needwood Forest. We had to shout to make ourselves heard above the roar of the tropical deluge on the roof and the repeated crashes of thunder.

At half-past ten that night, when the fury of the storm had at last abated, we were surprised to hear the familiar exhaust beat of an approaching motor-boat. Looking out, we were in time to watch her, a loaded Fellows Morton, glide by and to exchange greetings with her steerer. His legs were distinguishable in the light from the cabin, but his head and shoulders were invisible, for the boat carried no external lights and the night was black as pitch, save when an occasional flicker of lightning afforded a momentary glimpse of a dark skyline of trees. Only once have I tried navigating a narrow boat by night, and then decided to give the boatman best. He rivals the owl or the cat in his ability to find his way over the most tortuous waterway in almost total darkness.

Chapter XVIII

THE BREWERS

ON the afternoon of the day following, which was fresh and clear after the great storm, we reached Horninglow Wharf, in the home of beer, Burton-on-Trent. As usual, the proximity of the town had been marked by suburban villages and impoverished country, the only point of interest being the aqueduct of twenty-three arches by which we crossed the River Dove. Although dwarfed by the modern concrete road bridge beside it, this is a monumental work, considering the age in which it was built and taking into account the enormous weight of the canal in its puddled clay bed. No other work of the day compared in magnitude with these aqueducts of Brindley's making. Crowds flocked to see them, while they were described by contemporary writers as 'the greatest artificial curiosities in the world' or 'rivers hung in the air'. They are a distinguishing feature of Brindley's canals, for Rennie and Telford, who followed after him, dispensed with the great weight of the puddled bed by carrying the water in a trough of cast-iron sections bolted together and enclosed in masonry.

Walking through Burton's dirty streets, it is impossible for a moment to forget the town's major industry. Brewers' drays or lorries rattle past over the uneven setts, and the air is filled with the pungent aroma of the tall brewhouses and maltings which meet the eye on every hand. These streets are intersected by innumerable level crossings. Every now and again, at the strident clang of a bell, the gates swing to, compelling the traffic of Burton to wait with patient deference while a squat, shunting locomotive, glittering with polished brasswork and bright paint, puffs fussily across with a lumbering trainload of great pot-bellied casks bearing the familiar names of Bass, Worthington, Allsopp, or Ind Coope.

Obviously we could not leave without visiting a brewery, and we singled out Allsopps for no better reason than that their products appealed most to our taste. We found a resplendent commissionaire in a lofty entrance hall as grandiose as the Bank of England, and a striking testimony to the profits derived from slaking the national thirst. When we had made our wishes known we were conducted from one reception-room to another, questioned by another and even more resplendent commissionaire, then by a girl secretary, given a final inspection by a still more authoritative personage, who, having apparently satisfied himself that we were neither anarchists nor unscrupulous competitors, deigned to unbend and grant our request. Actually we were doubly fortunate, not only in being allowed round at such short notice, but in the fact that for this very reason we escaped the more usual fate of being members of a large party with a uniformed guide. Instead our philosopher and friend was a 'spare man', one capable of taking the place of any absentee workman, and who therefore was familiar with the whole process. His natural, diffident explanations, made in a broad Staffordshire dialect, were infinitely preferable to the glib, parrot-like monologue of a professional guide.

The beer barrel is ubiquitous in Burton; it is the town's one inescapable feature, so that when I recall it to my mind it is to picture not streets, buildings or faces, but the mountainous piles of barrels which we saw as we crossed the cobbled yard to Allsopps' brewery. There were barrels, too, in railway wagons and lorries; even the air above was not free of them, for they rumbled high overhead on a roller conveyor, lurching along like a row of drunken men.

Climbing many flights of steps, we saw how the malt was forced up through pipe-lines from the maltings into yawning hoppers the height of a house, and we followed the 'liquor' on its complicated course from the great hooded copper vats, where the delicate process of brewing takes place, up to the cooling-room at the very top of the tall building, down again through the foaming open vats, where the yeast does its work, and finally to the cold bottling-rooms and cellars, where bottles and barrels are filled with the finished product, which only then goes by the name of beer.

Brewers are slaves of time and temperature, for an error of a few degrees Fahrenheit or five minutes on the clock may spell ruin to a thousand gallons. Clocks and thermometers were everywhere, and beside each open vat hung little blackboards covered with cryptic symbols and times which revealed to the initiated at a glance the stage each had reached in the process of fermentation.

No mistake had been made over the brew we sampled in the cellar, of that there could be no question. It was a dark mild beer which glowed the colour of deepest amber in the tall sampling glasses, and it tasted as good as it looked. There could be no question, either, of work in a brewery destroying the taste for beer, for our companion obviously relished this conclusion of our conducted tour, and we toasted each other several times, still surrounded by the inevitable barrels, until we finally bade him farewell and, blinking, climbed the cellar stairs into the bright sunlight of the yard.

We carried away an impression of cleanliness and efficiency calculated to heighten rather than detract from the pleasure of drinking a glass at the sign of the red hand; moreover, it was obvious that brewing was a trade which still demanded individual initiative from the operative. Nevertheless, I still feel the old regret that such an essentially rural and individual process should have become industrialised upon so vast a scale. As we walked back to the boat I recalled somewhat wistfully the little brewhouse of Cotswold stone behind the 'Noel Arms' at Chipping Camden, one of the last licensed houses in England to evade the clutches of big business and preserve its ancient rights.

ESSEX BRIDGE, GREAT HAYWOOD

Chapter XIX

HORNINGLOW TO HAYWOOD

WE found that the seven miles of canal from Horninglow Wharf to Wichnor Bridges were the most uninteresting we had so far encountered. The canal crossed a flat plain of semi-derelict pasture whose boundaries were the chimneys of Marston's Brewery, the low hills of Needwood, and the Burton–Lichfield main road. We soon approached to within a few yards of the latter, following it for several straight and seemingly interminable miles. The knowledge that this busy highway was once the Roman Rykneld Street was small compensation for the din of hurrying traffic, the glaring road-signs, ribbon-built bungalows and all the tawdry ugliness which the motor-car has brought to the English road.

Watching the speeding cars from 'Cressy's' deck as she drifted along at her placid three-miles-an-hour gait, I found myself marvelling at the mania of hurry which has infected our unhappy civilisation. It would seem that I was beginning to acquire something of the boatman's philosophy, for when I was a motorist myself I was never so struck by the absurdity of expending such prodigality of power and effort, risk and nervous strain, for the sole sake of saving an hour or so of time which was seldom or never utilised to any creative purpose. Cumbersome lorries were thrashing down the long, straight road with their engines running at peak revolutions, little, mass-produced saloon cars clinging like terriers to their swinging trailers, dodging in and out in their attempts to pass, being evidently determined to maintain their fifty miles per hour, regardless of risk. No doubt when they reached their destination their drivers would spend the precious time they had risked lives to save by going to the talkies to relieve their boredom. At one point traffic was held up by a herd of cows which were wending their slow, imperturbable way across the road to the milking-shed, and the expressions of impatience on the drivers' faces were wondrous to behold. We were thankful when, just as dusk was beginning to fall, we reached Wichnor Bridges, where canal and road diverged.

The lock-keeper at Wichnor by whose cottage we moored was even more agreeable than most, which is saying a great deal. Not only did he provide us with a windlass to replace the one we had lost at Swarkestone, but he insisted on making us a present of a fine basket of blackberries. Lock-keepers lead solitary lives, for their cottages are often remote from villages or even roads, so that they welcome a gossip with the crew of a passing boat. Their job is not as easy as it would appear, for their responsibility is not confined to the lock by their cottage, but extends over some miles of canal, which may include several more locks. As the prosperity of the canals sinks into eclipse, so each man's length grows longer and longer, intermediate lock cottages being either let to agricultural labourers or left to fall to ruin. In addition to maintaining the locks in working order, there are the hedges to be trimmed and banks to be mown, while the towing path must be kept in a reasonable state of repair. It is also the lock-keeper's task to maintain a more or less constant level of water in the pounds under his charge through winter floods or summer droughts, by adjusting the sluices which govern the flow of water from feeders or outfalls. Any minor leaks which may develop in the banks must be stopped with clay puddle before they assume serious proportions, and it is his duty to notify the maintenance department of any major repairs which may become necessary, or of sections which may require dredging.

The lock-keeper of Wichnor had been born in his cottage, for his father had spent his lifetime on the same job. He was a mine of local information, as well he might be, and it was he who told us the history of the great farm which stood by Rykneld Street at Wichnor Bridge. The generous size of many farmhouses recalls the vanished prosperity of the countryside, but this house was bigger than any I had ever seen. Built of typical Midland brick, it presented a long and towering three-storeyed façade to the road, the doorway flanked by pillars which supported a bow-fronted bay extending through both upper storeys. Of no less impressive magnitude were the buildings set about the spacious cobbled courtyard, to which a lofty archway gave access. Yet the whole made a sorry contrast to the last farm we had visited at Arleston, for to walk through this arch was to see desolation, poverty and its attendant ruin stalking like a malignant disease. The cobbles of the courtyard were covered with weeds, slates had slipped from the roofs to reveal skeletal rafters beneath, broken window-panes stuffed with sacking had an air of shabby villainy, like the patch over a pirate's blind eye, while only a few rooms in the enormous house appeared still to be inhabited. This, we learned, was 'The Flitch of Bacon', once one of the latest and greatest of posting-houses, its name now bestowed upon an insignificant modern inn a mile down the road. In the light of this knowledge the place appeared even more forlorn. The serried rows of blank windows gazed down with an air of witless bewilderment on the hurrying cars they knew not and over the ruined courtyard, which never more would echo to the ring of hooves or the urgent cries of postboys and ostlers.

Midway between Wichnor and Alrewas the River Trent flows through the canal. It enters at the tail of Alrewas lock, to flow out over a weir some two hundred yards below. It seemed a strange negation of Brindley's declared policy of avoiding rivers, being a source of danger and delay in time of flood, when empty boats are easily drawn towards the weir by the swift current. Our friend the lock-keeper, who insisted on accompanying us as far as Alrewas lock, complained bitterly of the trouble caused to him by the masses of floating weed which the river was continually piling against the gates of the lower lock.

Alrewas scarcely lived up to the beauty of its name, for the old village of timbered brick and thatch was beleaguered by that all-too-common fringe of alien Council houses. We therefore passed by to moor in open country midway between it and the junction of the Coventry Canal at Fradley Locks.

The ancient village of Fradley lies some distance to the east, but a second village has grown up about the canal junction, centring around the yards of the district maintenance department and 'The Swan', a typical canal inn, with stabling attached which overlooks the wide basin formed by the meeting of the two waterways. As is only fitting, the main street of this little hamlet is the canal climbing easily up a gentle slope by a flight of four locks, and access to it by road is provided only by the towing-path, which has been broadened to admit wheeled traffic as far as the 'Swan'. Here we had reached the southernmost point on the canal, Fradley being situated at the apex of the broad Vee which its course from coast to coast roughly resembles. When the waterway was originally proposed it was referred to as 'the canal from the Trent to the Mersey', but although this is the name which has survived in current usage among boatmen, Brindley urged that it should be called 'The Grand Trunk', and it was in this name that the Act was passed through Parliament which enabled Josiah Wedgewood to cut the first sod of the great undertaking at Bramhills on July 26th, 1766. Brindley's choice of title was made because he foresaw that the projected canal was destined to become the central connecting artery of the whole system of inland waterways, the truth of his contention being proved some years later, when, by the construction of the Staffordshire and Worcestershire Canal to Great Haywood, and the Coventry Canal to Fradley, his 'Grand Trunk' was linked to the Severn at Stourport and to the Thames at Oxford. Perhaps when these canals were at the height of their prosperity—and in their day they were more successful than the railways have ever been—Fradley Junction was aware of its significance. No doubt the stables of the 'Swan' were nightly filled with horses and the bar with boatmen, while by day the water in the locks was seldom still. Now, however, Fradley has fallen asleep. It has ripened to a mellow old age, like any other country village, and, less disturbed by the present age than they, it slumbers in the sun, the dreams of a busier past unbroken by the rare passage of a boat through the locks.

We moored 'Cressy' to the rings conveniently placed before the door of 'The Swan' while we drank a glass of mild beer in the cool but sunlit bar. The window of the little-used toll office opposite was set out with bowls of fruit for sale, and when Angela crossed over the lock to buy some it did not seem in any way remarkable, so naturally was it in keeping with the character of the place, that her purchase should be weighed upon a steelyard, that early form of hanging balance once common in the English farmhouse, but now one with the bread peel, the skimmer and the spit in the ranks of rural 'by-gones'.

It was after we had left the inn at Fradley and had come to rest in Shade House Lock that we first noticed the *smell*. At Wood End Lock it was worse, while at Bramley Common, the last of the flight, it was positively nauseating, the water black and foul, the banks and lock-sides covered with a noxious slime. We were at a loss to understand the reason for this, for we were passing through a remote tract of heath and woodland on the fringe of Cannock Chase. The captain of a passing 'Josher' gave us the answer: 'It's the Milk Factory,' he explained, with a jerk of his head in the direction in which we were travelling. Sure enough we presently came upon it—an unsightly blot in the fair green fields. A steel chimney was belching black smoke, and a reeking, milky affluent was pouring into the canal through several pipes. Evidently the canal authorities take no exception to this proceeding, but it seemed well-nigh incredible that the angling society owning the fishing rights on this section had apparently taken no action, for we noticed many dead fish. In view of the elaborate apparatus introduced in modern times to dispose of domestic sewage at the expense of soil fertility, it seems criminally illogical that industrialists should be allowed to pollute miles of water in this indiscriminate and wanton fashion. Factory effluents such as this and the bitumen-laden surface water from modern motor roads are between them slowly but surely driving the wild life from the canals, rivers and streams, a lamentable fact which any fisherman will corroborate.

It was a welcome relief to be in clear water again, heading for the villages of Handsacre and Armitage, and once more in sight of the Trent, which we had left to the north at Alrewas. There was evidence that Armitage had once been an exclusively rural community attractively placed on the edge of the Chase overlooking the river, but, thanks to the establishment of a large sanitary pottery in the vicinity, the village now bears a sadly blackened and semi-industrialised appearance. The most interesting feature we encountered there was the canal tunnel. Though only a hundred and thirty yards long, it more nearly resembled a natural cavern, Brindley's 'navigators' having roughly hewn their way through an

'ARMITAGE TUNNEL . . . MORE NEARLY RESEMBLED A NATURAL CAVERN'

outcrop of solid sandstone, the marks of their crude implements appearing so fresh that it was difficult to believe that they had been made a century and a half ago.

Armitage was scarcely a beauty spot, but there was worse to come in the shape of Rugeley, which we decided was one of the drabbest and dreariest small towns we had ever seen. Fortunately, however, its squalid cottages, neglected allotments, and odorous tannery were soon left behind, our surroundings changing with almost magical suddenness, so that we presently found ourselves traversing one of the most beautiful pounds we had so far encountered. On the right bank the fields sloped gently upwards to that thinly populated and little-known tract of country which stretches northward to the great park of Chartley, last sanctuary in England of the wild boar and of the ancient breed of wild white cattle. Until recent times, when the herd became interbred and died out, the birth of a black calf among them was said to be an infallible portent of death in the family of Shirley, Earls Ferrers, Lords of Chartley since the time of Henry the Third.

On our left the river wound through sunlit levels of pasture which glowed most richly green against the steep slopes of the Chase beyond, which were in deep shadow. These included Oakedge Park, Haywood Warren and the Satnall Hills, heights of bracken and ancient trees that have seen little change since Plantagenet and Tudor hunted the boar along their flanks. Below Colwich Lock an ancient labourer, with long white side-whiskers, clad in a sky-blue overall jacket and trousers of buff corduroy buckled below the knee, was sitting at his cottage door enjoying the last of the evening sun, and waved cheerily as we passed by. In Shuckburgh Park at Great Haywood they were loading the last wain of a belated hay harvest, although by this time the sun had set and already a thin mist was gathering in the meadows, a portent of September and of summer's end. On the opposite bank trees leaned so far and low over the water that their branches scraped along our deck, bestrewing it with leaves and twigs, while the stove chimney fell with a clatter, to dangle by its safety chain. At Haywood Lock they grew on both sides of the canal, but were taller, their branches interlacing overhead to make a tunnel of cool green shade whose intricate pattern the water reflected with unruffled perfection of detail. It was in this quiet, dim place that we moored for the night, awaking to see moted beams of sunlight glancing on the water through gaps in the network of branches, as through the clerestory windows of some cathedral nave. Between the boles of the trees we could see the river spanned by Essex Bridge, surely one of the most beautiful and least cele- brated in England. It is a pack-horse bridge reminiscent of Hugh Clopton's bridge at Stratford, but executed in stone. To my mind it surpasses Clopton, even if due allowance be made for its more favoured and secluded setting. The impression of permanence and power conveyed by the massive cut-waters of the buttresses is perfectly counterbalanced by the graceful pitch of the arches, a curve which is subtly emphasised by the concentric string courses above them. Essex Bridge is an enduring memorial to the ability of the early masons to combine simplicity and utility of con- struction with beauty, a gift that was once as instinctive and unselfconscious as the poetry of country speech.

Great Haywood is not only a junction of canals, for the Rivers Trent and Sow unite just above Essex Bridge. The waters of the Sow run clear and unpolluted from their source in the high ground of Staffordshire's western border, but the Trent is so black and foul after its journey through the Pottery towns that even the grass shrinks from its banks. For several hundred yards below their confluence the smoky line of demarcation between the two streams is clearly visible, and constitutes a striking natural commentary upon the old age and the new.

There is a second bridge worthy of note at Great Haywood. It carries the towing path of the Trent and Mersey over the mouth of the canal to the Severn, the breadth of its single span being remarkable in a bridge of this type. The reason for this is not readily apparent, for it exceeds the combined width of the water- way and tow-path beneath by several feet. The line of the low balustrade is also unusual, for instead of following the curve of the arch in the customary manner, it consists of two slight reverse curves culminating in a pointed apex over the keystone. Whatever may have prompted the canal engineers so to depart from the ortho- dox will never be known, but the result is an arch so light in its flight from bank to bank, so airy and insubstantial that it might have been inspired by a Dulac fantasy. Beside this bridge, an ivy- covered warehouse crumbling to ruin, a dock filled with tall reeds, and a shuttered toll office no bigger than a garden tool-shed are all that make up this meeting-place of coast-to-coast waterways. It seemed typical of the remote and unassuming manner in which the canals make their way through the countryside that the village of Haywood, although only a quarter of a mile distant, had remained aloof from this important junction, as though unaware of its existence. It would have presented a very different aspect had it been chosen as the meeting-place of railways or of trunk roads. Green fields and tall trees whose beauty the canal enhances would have given place to blackened railway yards or petrol pumps and road-houses. But because the canal is a forgotten relic of a more leisured past, its banks are not considered 'desirable building plots', and so remain the haunt of coot and heron.

MOORINGS, GREAT HAYWOOD

Chapter XX

YOCKERTON HALL

THE Trent valley once more becomes broad and shallow above Haywood, and our journey thence to Stone, though pleasant enough, lacked any special feature worthy of mention. It included four locks, at Hoo Mill, Weston, Sandon and Aston, but with the exception of these villages the canal wound through open pastures close to the river bank and overlooked by the tree-girt slopes of Ingestre Park, seat of the Earls of Shrewsbury. It may be recalled that we passed two villages named Weston and Aston soon after we left Shardlow, so it should be explained that there are two pairs of villages so called upon Trent, a state of affairs that must cause no little confusion in postal sorting offices.

When we landed at Stone it was to find that the well-worn phrase 'we lost account of time' had in our case literally come true. We had believed the day to be a Friday, but the crowds of late shoppers aroused our suspicions, and we bought a '*Staffordshire Evening Sentinel*' to discover that we had mislaid a day on our week's journey from Shardlow. There are two breweries and a pottery works at Stone, while the city of Stoke is dangerously near, but in spite of this it seems to have escaped the desolation of Rugeley, for to walk down the single main street from the church past 'The Crown Hotel', with its graceful bowed front, is to feel that the place is still at heart a small country market town.

One of the many respects in which the industrial district of the Potteries differs from any other is in the sharp definition of its boundaries. From any one of the Five Towns a sixpenny bus ride will carry you into practically unspoilt country. No doubt the reason for this lies in the fact that they reached the limit of their growth at a very early stage in the Industrial Revolution, so that, unlike manufacturing areas of more recent date, their dormitories have never marched far into the surrounding country. Furthermore, the exclusive and highly specialised craft of the potter has not attracted the usual drift of labour from the surrounding rural areas. Thus it was hard to believe that at Meaford Locks, a mile north of Stone, we were only six miles from the heart of Stoke-on-Trent. From the rose-covered cottage at the foot, the flight of four locks climbed in leisurely fashion up a gentle grassy slope set about with trees in a manner reminiscent of Great Haywood. There is something incomparably restful and unfailingly satisfying to the eye in this combination of woodland and still water, so we paused by the top lock to eat a simple lunch of bread and cheese in the sunshine on the foredeck. It was here that we met the first horse-boat we had seen since we left the Oxford Canal—a boat of the Mersey Weaver Company, travelling empty towards the Potteries. Whenever there was any likelihood of our encountering horse-drawn craft we always took good care to moor away from the towing-path, so that we should be clear of tow-lines, but on this particular occasion we were caught unawares, so that I had to clamber on deck to pass the line over tanks, stove chimney and shafts as the boat came by.

Soon after we drew clear of the trees of Meaford we sighted the village of Barlaston, backed by the chimneys of the Potteries, and half an hour later we found moorings immediately above Trentham Park Lock, a point within easy reach of the city, but just outside the suburbs. Here, ten years before, 'Cressy' had been moored for a period of months when her former owner lived nearby, and the old lock-keeper, recognising her as soon as she hove in sight, welcomed her like an old friend. Later that evening he presented us with a basket of the finest runner beans we had ever seen, and when we thanked him, expressing due admiration for their size, he explained proudly that they were a special strain of his own nursing, which he called 'Yockerton Wonders'. Now, the Pottery folk have a great sense of humour, which finds a favourite and time-honoured expression in the mischievous art of gulling the unsuspecting or inquisitive stranger, and in this direction the name of Yockerton Hall has a prominent place. A guileless enquiry as to the whereabouts of an individual or the destination of some parcel or product is sufficient to set the old joke in motion. 'Yockerton Hall', replies the citizen of Stoke, with a sly wink at his fellows. The victim invariably falls heavily into the trap by asking, to the general delight, the whereabouts of this unheard-of place, receiving the surprised and surprising answer: 'What, dunna tha know? It's where there's neither land nor water an' they walk about on plonks.' Convinced that this curiously insubstantial place was a figment of local fantasy, I was determined not to be caught, and so replied warily that I thought the curious conditions prevailing there were hardly likely to produce such a fine-quality bean. To my surprise, however, he insisted—apparently in all seriousness—that this narrow strip of country between Barlaston and Trentham was in actual fact Yockerton. I allowed myself to be half convinced, but knowing the local ability to sustain such a joke with a poker face, and finding that my inch-to-the-mile survey map was suspiciously uninformative, I still have my doubts about Yockerton Hall.

Chapter XXI

TRENTHAM AND THE POTTERIES

TRENTHAM HALL, once the seat of the Leveson-Gower family, Earls Gower and Dukes of Sutherland, is beautifully placed at the head of a large artificial lake situated between the river and the wooded slopes of the park, which in places rise steeply to a height of over six hundred feet. As early as 1758, before canals were heard of in this country, it was the Earl Gower of that time who first commissioned Brindley to survey a line of water-way that would connect Liverpool, Hull and Bristol, and in the following year the engineer, as his diary records, frequently visited the Earl at Trentham 'a bout the novogation'.

It is now many years since the family left Trentham, however, and of the great Palladian mansion only the stabling and an arbour of the type beloved by Victorian romantics remain. Local legend has it that the smell of the polluted river flowing through the grounds was responsible for this exodus, and if this be true, the inhabitants of the Potteries have to thank the reeking effluent of their factories for providing them with one of the finest public parks in England. They were taking full advantage of their splendid playground when we walked through the park on a warm and sunny Sunday evening. The wide, gravelled walks of the terraced gardens sloping to a stone balustrade above the water were thronged with promenaders, and the lake was dotted with small boats. On one lawn the potter was trying his hand at archery, on another at clock-golf, while he seemed to be deriving as much amusement as his clamorous offspring from the see-saws, whirligigs and swings of the children's playground. There was a finely built bathing-pool so set in the woods by the margin of the lake that it did not interrupt the skilfully achieved vista of the original landscape gardeners, also a ballroom and restaurant that were similarly unobtrusive, and glasshouses where those who possessed no gardens of their own could buy cut flowers to brighten the blackness of their homes. The flowers and trees, even the grass of the average urban park, bear the drab, dispirited look of the caged animals in a zoo, but there was little of this air of artificiality about Trentham. The bright green lawns could not have been more smoothly shorn, hedges of yew or box more trimly clipped, nor could flower borders have blazed more bravely with intelligently balanced masses of colour had they still been preserved for a Duke's pleasure, instead of being free for the enjoyment of all who could afford a threepenny bus ride and sixpence at the turnstile. To a people who spend six days of every week in the heart of a smoky industrial city the value of such an outlet is inestimable, and the general orderliness and lack of litter made it evident that the people of the Five Towns appreciate their good fortune.

The young pottery worker and his girl who may be seen strolling in these gardens on any fine Sunday, or dancing in the ballroom if it is wet, are not only infinitely better dressed than their cousins in the south, but although often still in their teens, they are remarkably independent and self-assured. It is more than likely that they both work 'on the Pot Bank', he as an oven 'placer' and she in the decorating room. Bound together by the ties of their skilled and exclusive craft, the potters have always been a highly individual community, in which there is no social distinction but that of capability. It frequently transpires that Jack and his master were born and bred in the same humble row of cottages, and the southerner of the so-called middle or upper classes must drop his social pretensions if he wishes to be accepted by either. The thin veneer of Eton and Oxford culture, often only a generation thick, is no match for the shrewd realism of the potter, whose life is founded upon an inherited tradition of craft. For no matter how the more class-conscious southerner may try to conceal the fact, he is aware that since England became a nation of industrialists and shopkeepers the common denominator of class is no longer one of ability and wisdom, but of irresponsible wealth.

The potter's craft does not lend itself to organisation on modern mass-production lines, and for this reason it is still carried on by a prodigious number of small and comparatively intimate family businesses. Thus it comes about that the pottery owner not only has a thorough working knowledge of his trade which rightly earns for him the respect of his employees, but he is on terms of easy familiarity with them, knowing most of the older hands by their Christian names. Master and man will drink tea together in the works canteen and discuss the merits of the latest cup shape. In this way there is preserved among them that spirit of community in craft which is yet another tradition of the past that the modern industrial organisation has broken to its own despite.

Though the immemorial art of 'throwing' on the potter's wheel has suffered eclipse in the modern pottery, the process of casting by pouring liquid 'slip' into plaster-of-Paris moulds being more widely used, the craft still demands a considerable degree of skill and delicacy of touch. The unfired ware or 'bisque' is naturally extremely fragile, and the operations of 'bisque placing' and 'setting in' are both highly skilled. The first consists of packing the ware into the earthenware 'setters' and 'saggars' in which it is fired, and the second of stacking the saggars in the bisque oven for firing. Every craft has a language all its own, and that of the potter is no exception. Thus the head placer is known as a 'cod placer', and the ladder on which he stands as a 'horse'.

Time and temperature are as critical in the firing of a pottery oven as they are in the brewing of beer, and the fireman is no mere coal-heaver. An attempt has been made on the Continent to mechanise this process by the introduction of an electrically heated oven with automatic temperature control, through which the ware travels on a slow-moving conveyor, but the conservative potters of Staffordshire are not easily wooed by the tempting bait of mechanisation, preferring to trust their valuable ware to human skill rather than to a fallible electricity supply emanating from some remote source. The firing of the bisque oven takes fifty-five hours, in which time fifteen tons of coal are consumed. The skill lies in maintaining a slow and steady rise in temperature to the maximum of 1,300 degrees Centigrade and an equally steady cooling. Test-pieces of clay placed in small peep-holes in the walls of the oven are a guide to the progress of the firing. When the oven has been allowed to cool for a further forty-eight hours it is emptied, and when it has been scoured, the fired bisque ware is passed to the 'dipper', who applies the glaze by dipping each piece in a tub of powdered borax-flint-lead glass mixed with water to the consistency of cream. This looks a simple operation, but generations of skill inform the dextrous, almost careless flick of the wrist which causes the glaze to spread evenly over the surface of the ware. The ware is then once more packed into saggars and fired in the 'glost oven'. A firing of twenty-six hours is then required to set the glaze, but the same interval as before is allowed for cooling. After it has passed this stage the ware is stored in the 'white warehouse'

until it is required for decoration, after which it receives the third
and last firing in the enamel kiln. This occupies only fourteen
hours, and the temperature is considerably lower.

The pottery designer paints his pattern upon the china, but
when it is decided to put a design into production a copper-plate
engraving is made, from which transfer papers are taken to apply
the outline of the design to the pottery. Colours and banding are
then filled in by hand by the decorators. The design department
of a famous pottery is as bombarded with the efforts of aspiring
designers as a publisher with manuscripts or the Patent Office with
specifications of perpetual-motion machines. Needless to say, a
minute proportion are purchased. The modern pottery designs do
not, in my opinion, compare with the unaffected grace of the old
Staffordshire forms of fifty or more years ago, and we saw nothing
to equal our own Gloucestershire slip-ware, for all its technical
crudity. There appears to be too much striving for effect, which
results in over-pretentiousness, and an insistence upon novelty to
the exclusion of traditional form or artistic quality. The designer
at the pottery we visited admitted this, but maintained that his job
was to give the public what it wanted, and that the modern designs
were the answer to that demand. I would like to believe that this
is the truth, though it is difficult to determine, in this case, which is
the cart and which the horse, the producer or the consumer.
There can be no doubt that the modern manufacturer has been
responsible for the lamentable decline in popular taste by blud-
geoning the public into accepting his shoddy mass-produced goods
by means of mass advertising and the elimination of competition.
Yet, because it is a skilled craft, and since good or bad designs are
equally costly to produce, I believe that the pottery trade has not
been a party to this debasement, but has been forced to pander to
it in order that it may survive.

The slip from which fine bone china is made is a composite substance consisting of one part Cornish china clay or kaolin, one
part china stone of the same origin, and two parts of calcined beef
bones, which give the china its distinguishing toughness and trans-
lucency. A considerable quantity of the china clay and stone used
is still carried by coasting steamers from the ports of Fowey and
St. Austell to the Mersey, where it is transferred to narrow boats
and conveyed to the Potteries via the River Weaver, the Anderton
Vertical Lift and the Trent and Mersey Canal. It was this vital
water communication which was responsible for the growth of the

Pottery towns from a row of straggling villages housing no more than 7,000 inhabitants, to a densely populated district of 120,000 persons a hundred years later. The growth of Manchester following the construction of the Duke of Bridgewater's canal, still referred to by boatmen as the 'Duke's Cut', was equally meteoric. Few people realise in how great a measure the forgotten canals contributed to the vast upheaval of the Industrial Revolution, which changed not only the face of England, but the whole course of our lives in a period incredibly brief—so brief, indeed, that we are still frantically endeavouring to induce our toddling social order to keep pace with the giant stride of the machine, and bitterly regretting, like Goethe's sorcerer's apprentice, that we should have gaily pronounced the spell which set the genie to work before learning how to control it. Meanwhile, by one of those strange anomalies with which the pages of history are filled, the canal—the spell which loosed the machine—has not merely fallen into obscurity, but has become the last remaining stronghold of a people whose way of life has survived the whole course of the revolution substantially unchanged, and who therefore retain to this day many of the characteristics of the pre-machine age peasant. The canal has also become so much a natural part of the rural scene that it is almost impossible to associate it with the great towns it has brought into being. Yet to realise the conditions existing in England when James Brindley set about the building of his canals is to appreciate the vast changes which have occurred in the last hundred and fifty years.

Young in his 'Six Months' Tour' of 1770 relates, with the typical self-righteous *naïveté* of the period, that the inhabitants of North Staffordshire were devoted to 'laziness, drunkenness, tea-drinking and debauchery', while John Wesley, who visited the district on a preaching tour, was pelted with clods of earth for his pains, concluding, somewhat understandably, that 'their manners were coarse', and adding that he found them given to brutal amusements such as bull-baiting, cock-throwing and goose-riding. From these comments it is easy to picture the conflict still waging with mutual intolerance between the old full-blooded rural order, which, though already impoverished and debased, was not yet dead, and the new spirit of repressive puritanism which was the first child of the commercial age. Of the prevailing conditions in the country at that time Samuel Smiles gives an excellent impression in his 'Life of James Brindley'. Although referring to this particular district of the Midlands, it applies equally to the rest of the country.

'The earthenware manufacture,' he writes, 'though in its infancy, had already made considerable progress, but, like every other branch of industry at that time, its further development was greatly hampered by the wretched state of the roads. Throughout Staffordshire they were as yet, for the most part, narrow, deep, circuitous, miry and inconvenient; barely passable with rude waggons in summer, and almost impassable even with pack-horses in winter. Yet the principal materials used in the manufacture of pottery, especially of the best kinds, were necessarily brought from a great distance—flint stones from the south-eastern ports of England and clay from Devonshire and Cornwall. The flints were brought by sea to Hull and the clay to Liverpool. From Hull the materials were brought up the Trent to Willington; and the clay was in like manner brought from Liverpool up the Weaver to Winsford in Cheshire. Considerable quantities of clay were also conveyed in boats from Bristol, up the Severn to Bridgnorth and Bewdley. From these various points the materials were conveyed by land carriage, mostly on the backs of horses, to the towns in the potteries where they were worked up into earthenware and china. The manufactured articles were returned for export in the same rude way. Large crates of pot-ware were slung across horses' backs, and thus conveyed to their respective ports, not only at great risk of breakage and pilferage, but also at heavy cost.

'The indispensable article of salt, manufactured at the Cheshire Wiches, was in like manner carried on horses' backs all over the country and reached almost a fabulous price by the time it was sold two or three counties off. About a hundred and fifty packhorses in gangs were also occupied in going weekly from Manchester, through Stafford, to Bewdley and Bridgnorth loaded with woollen and cotton cloth for exportation. Even corn, coal, lime and ironstone were conveyed in the same way, and the operations of agriculture, as of manufacture, were alike injuriously impeded. There were no shops in the Potteries, the people being supplied with wares and drapery by packmen and hucksters, or from Newcastle-under-Lyme, which was the only town in the neighbourhood worthy of the name.'

This is Smiles' picture of England on the eve of the Industrial Revolution, the England from which we have travelled so fast and far. Can it be wondered that we stand bewildered?

Chapter XXII

INDUSTRIAL LANDSCAPE

BECAUSE the canal was the nucleus around which the Potteries developed, we formed a better general impression of the district from the water than was possible in the confining maze of narrow, cobbled streets. Planning to cross the border of Cheshire before nightfall, we made an early start from Trentham Park Lock, and were soon passing the collieries of the Stafford Coal and Iron Company—monstrous black slag-heaps, droning fans and gaunt pithead gears whose spinning wheels whirled in shrouds of drifting steam from the winding houses.

The approach to Stoke presented a scene of utter desolation and ruin, on the one hand a dismal water-logged waste caused by the subsidence of old worked-out coal seams, on the other derelict blast furnaces, cold and rust-reddened. Beyond these we passed two ruined locomotive works, whose silent shops, with their shattered windows, constituted a mute but eloquent warning to those who entrust their livelihood to the shifting and fickle fortunes of mechanised industry. After this sombre scene the low comic relief provided by a warehouse full of chamber-pots was very welcome. I had supposed that this homely utensil, like the hip-bath and the mahogany commode, was a Victorian relic fast becoming obsolete, but if the smoking ovens of this pottery were any criterion, their manufacture still constitutes a profitable branch of the industry.

Mooring by Stoke wharf, we walked into the city to buy supplies. This was not easy, for in a district where so many housewives work the day through in the decorating-rooms, the modern
method of cooking with a can-opener is so popular that butchers
and greengrocers were few and far between, the streets being lined
by the shop fronts of cheap chain grocers stacked with canned
foods. One shop, however, was strange to our eyes—that of the
bird fancier, his window filled with packets of bird seeds and
medicines of every sort, while through a doorway festooned with
gaily coloured cages floated the rich fluting of roller canaries and
the thin, gossiping chatter of budgerigars. Just as the potter's
favourite hobbies of pigeon and whippet racing are a legacy from
his bull-baiting and cock-fighting ancestors, so perhaps his love of
birds may be derived from forgotten associations of ever earlier
origin.

Situated among the broken southern foothills of the Peak district of Derbyshire, the Potteries present some unique industrial
landscapes. As we climbed the four locks out of Stoke, the grimy
slate roofs of cottages and factories rose tier upon tier towards the
black tower of Shelton church, while mean streets covered with a
geometrical pattern the opposite heights of Hartshill and Basford.
These were indistinct in the haze of steam and smoke which rose
from the valley bottom, like steam from a cauldron. But the dominant, inescapable feature of the scene were the pottery ovens.
Rows of them met the eye on every side. Shaped like gigantic
bottles, blackened and squat, those that were belching dense coils
of smoke from their necks looked as actively satanic as a volcano,
but those that stood cold and dead had an appearance that was
strangely ancient and oriental. They might well have been the
pagodas of some temple to strange gods, or monuments that
marked the burial-places of kings who held court when the sabre-
toothed tiger ranged the forests of Europe.

At dusk, when the waning light softens its stark outlines and the
sunset sky flaunts sable banners of drifting smoke, or at night,
when street lamps star the hills with points of light and the flare
from open furnace doors flickers skyward, it is impossible to deny
this rolling forest of bricks and mortar a certain sombre grandeur.
The men of North Staffordshire are proud of their smoky sky, for
to them it is the symbol of prosperity, and local stationers display
picture postcards of typical 'smokescapes' for the benefit of rare
visitors. Though trade was said to be slack, there appeared to our

'POTTERY OVENS . . . SHAPED LIKE GIGANTIC BOTTLES'

eyes, fresh from the country, to be enough smoke in the air to please the most pessimistic potter, as we approached Etruria summit lock and the junction of the canal to Leek and Froghall, yet another branch of the 'Grand Trunk'. Just beyond the lock head we passed Josiah Wedgewood's famous pottery, and presently found ourselves in the heart of the Shelton Steel Works, scene of H. G. Wells' macabre short story 'The Cone'. 'Cressy's' white windows, that for so long had seen unfold before them a slowly moving pattern of field, hedgerow and tree, now looked directly into a clangorous rolling mill, lofty as the nave of a cathedral, where white-hot billets of steel were being flattened as easily as pastry under a rolling-pin, or grappled by the electric cranes which rumbled high overhead. Workmen, their faces streaked with sweat and grime, looked up from their task of feeding the rolls to grin and nod, while at one point where the crane track projected over the canal a crane driver leaned from his cabin directly above our deck to call after us, 'What about a trip?' A damp white mist shot through by the sunlight with miniature rainbows momentarily enveloped us as we passed the cooling towers, and beyond these the coke-ovens were belching steam and flame alternately. Opposite them, towering above us, reared the fiery heart of this monstrous organisation—the blast furnaces. Lifts were creeping up and down their pitiless steel sides, feeding them with fuel, and, as we passed, one of the cones that close their throats was lowered to admit a charge, the air above shimmering in the sudden blast of intense heat which shot skywards.

A sharp turn under a bridge, and a canyon of slag as barren and desolate as the mountains of the moon hid this modern Gehenna from our sight. Not a blade of grass finds foothold on these wastes, and the smoke of internal fires filters through fissures in their lava-like crust. Occasionally, owing to this internal burning, a large area will cave in, subjecting the unfortunate inhabitants of nearby streets to a shower of fine ashes and grit. These mountainous tips are also the scene of the steelworks' most spectacular display. Just as we emerged from their shadow on to a long embankment, we saw a locomotive panting up to the summit, pushing before it a ladle of slag, and appearing from our vantage below to be no bigger than a fly. Minute figures appeared, coupling the chain which operated the tipping mechanism to the front drawhook of the engine. Then the latter ran backwards, and the ladle discharged its contents down the precipitous slope. On its journey

from the furnaces the slag had cooled enough to form a hard
outer crust, so that for some yards it bounded along like a great
boulder, until, striking an obstacle, it burst with a flash of light
that was blinding even in the bright sunlight, and its molten heart
coursed downwards like some infernal mountain torrent, a livid
vein set with flickering tongues of flame.

As we approached the forest of pottery ovens that was Burslem
it was difficult to believe that we were still travelling over the same
canal which had slumbered beneath the trees at Great Haywood,
for it had become a busy highway thronged with boats. There
were chocolate-brown Cowburn and Cowpar motor-boats from
Manchester, all named after wild birds, and carrying cargoes of
chemicals in tanks or carboys, horse-boats of the Mersey–Weaver
and Anderton Companies, laden with coal, clay or stone, and even
an occasional 'number one'. Their external finish did not compare
with that of the Oxford canal boats, but through open cabin doorways we caught the gleam of polished brass knobs and rails, while
many of their crews were dressed in the true tradition, captains in
corduroys, broad-belted, their wives wearing the graceful full-
skirted dresses, tight-waisted and most elaborately pleated.

Beyond Burslem we passed by a busy boatyard where we heard
the familiar sound of caulking mallets, while at Longport wharf
many boats were unloading their dazzling white cargoes of china
clay. At Chatterley by Tunstall the seemingly interminable vista
of ovens and chimneys began to thin out, the valley to close in
upon us, and soon we sighted the portals of the two tunnels under
Harecastle hill. We had reached the head-waters of the Trent, and
the northern boundary of the Potteries.

Chapter XXIII

HARECASTLE TUNNELS

THE greatest obstacle in the path of James Brindley's canal was the ridge of high ground, a continuation of the Pennine Chain, which divides the valley of the upper Trent from the great plain of Cheshire and extends as far south as the Wrekin in Shropshire. Harecastle Hill being the narrowest point of this ridge, it was here that the engineer decided to drive a tunnel 2,880 yards long. No work of such magnitude had ever been contemplated in eighteenth-century England, and the project appeared so fantastic that it was referred to by local sceptics as 'Brindley's air castle'. Nevertheless, as soon as the Act authorising the construction of the canal had been passed, Brindley set to work upon his 'impossible' task. He first sank vertical shafts at various points along the hill-top down to canal level, the spoil being drawn up by horse-gins, while the workings were kept free from water by windmills. As the work progressed, however, water was encountered in such quantities that the wind pumps were no longer adequate, but Brindley was nothing daunted, having actually counted on the presence of such springs for the necessary supply of water to the summit level. He therefore erected a beam pumping engine, or 'fire-engine' as it was then called, which, working night and day, effectually kept the waters under control. Meanwhile the attitude of the local inhabitants changed swiftly from ridicule to awe, for in 1767 a resident of Burslem wrote to a distant friend: 'Gentlemen come to view our eighth wonder of the world, the subterraneous navigation which is cutting by the great Mr. Brindley, who handles rocks as easily as plum-pies, and makes the four elements subservient to his will'.

The great engineer never lived to see the work completed, for he died in September 1772 as a result of a chill contracted during his survey of the Caldon Branch, and although the rest of the canal works from Mersey to Trent had long since been finished, it was not until 1777 that the tunnel was at last opened, after eleven years of unremitting toil by six hundred men. Even so it proved a serious handicap to traffic, for the shaft was extremely small, being only nine feet wide and twelve feet high, so that boats could not pass each other. Since it took two hours to 'leg' through, there being no towing path, the delay and congestion can readily be realised, and it is not surprising to read that fierce arguments, frequently leading to blows, occurred among the boat crews waiting at the tunnel mouths for the privilege of the next turn through.

In 1824 the canal company decided to remedy this state of affairs, and sought the advice of Brindley's successor, Thomas Telford. His solution was to construct a new tunnel parallel with the old, so great being the advance of civil engineering in the intervening years that although of far larger section, it was completed in less than three years. For ninety years thereafter both tunnels continued in use, the old tunnel carrying the southbound traffic, and vice versa, but in 1914 an electric tug was installed in the new tunnel, and the old, though it remained theoretically navigable for a few more years, soon fell into disuse. The subsidence of old workings has since still further reduced the restricted headroom, so that it is now quite impassable, the weed-grown entrance, little larger than that of a city sewer, being all that the canal traveller can now see of Brindley's 'eighth wonder'.

The Harecastle tunnel tug must be one of the most curious craft ever constructed. Drawing its current from an overhead cable, it has no propeller, but hauls itself along on a second cable laid in the bed of the canal, picking it up on a winch and paying it out astern. Owing to the possibility of their screws fouling this sub-

merged cable, motor as well as horse-drawn craft are compelled
to make use of this weird contraption, so, as it was not in sight
when we arrived at the tunnel mouth, we moored up and had tea.
Before long a string of horses appeared over the hill, while from
the dark depths ahead a distant muttering slowly grew to a prodigious groaning and grinding sound, like that of a decrepit tram-
car climbing a steep hill. At long last the tug crawled out into the
sunshine, and for a few minutes the tunnel mouth was a scene of
great activity, as the string of boats were detached, engines started,
and horses re-attached to their respective boats. It was then our
turn to be taken in tow, so we moved ahead till we were beneath
the overhead wire.

One narrow boat always accompanies the tug, its cabin doing
duty as a 'guard's van' for the old man who issues the boatmen
with 'tug tickets' on receipt of their fares. It was therefore to the
stern of this boat that we made fast. Driver and 'guard' then went
into deep conference over the height of 'Cressy's' cabin, shaking
their heads so dubiously that we began gloomily to visualise the
prospect of having to beat an ignominious retreat. Subsidences
have affected the headroom in the new tunnel also, and the presence of a towing-path, which forces boats to hug the side wall,
does not help matters. Anticipating difficulty, we had already
removed the water-tank from the roof, placing it, filled, on the
fore-deck to ballast her, but this, in the opinion of these experts,
was not enough. A pile of sand-bags round the electricity sub-
station saved the situation. When these had been stacked for'ard
and a baulk of timber lashed slantwise from the gunwale to the fore-
corner of the cabin top to act as a fender, the tug crew declared
themselves satisfied, so, as there was still time in hand before we
were due to start, we sat talking in the sunshine on the fore-deck.

Even on the canals they have built, the names of Brindley and
Telford have been forgotten, so that it was a surprise to find that
the tug driver was as well-informed as any historian regarding the
building of the two tunnels. More interesting still, he recalled
Turnhurst, where Brindley spent the last years of his life. He had
actually attended the demolition sale, where he had purchased
some iron-hard oak timbers from this old mansion, once the seat
of the Bellot family, said to have been the last in England to em-
ploy that admirable figure the family fool, but of late years surrounded and undermined by collieries. He had also traversed the
old tunnel in a small boat before it became impassable even to the
lightest craft.

The 'guard' was eyeing his watch and we were preparing to set forth when we heard the unmistakable beat of an approaching motor punctuated by prolonged blasts of a siren imploring us to wait. 'Come along, then,' the tug driver admonished, and presently a pair of Fellows Morton boats swung round the turn and made fast to our stern. Then with a jerk we were off at last.

For all its prodigious noise, the tug travelled even more slowly than a fully laden horse-boat, so that the dark journey seemed interminable. Lashed as she was bow and stern, there was no need to steer 'Cressy', so we sat among the sandbags on the fore-deck looking into the darkness ahead. Vivid blue sparks spluttered from the overhead conductor of the tug, and in the bar of light which streamed through the aft doors of the guard's cabin we could watch the uneven roof of dripping brickwork skimming perilously close to our cabin top. At one point the tunnel was intersected by another at right angles, a relic this of a system of subterranean canals which Brindley drove direct to the coal-faces of his collieries at Golden Hill, thus not only draining the pits, but enabling the coal to be hauled away without having first to be drawn to the surface. These ingenious underground waterways have not been explored within living memory, for the coal-seams at canal level have long been exhausted, but the guard could remember in his early youth an old boatman who had worked through them. The boats, which were drawn along by means of staples fixed in the walls, were necessarily very small and finely built, of only ten tons capacity, in order that they could negotiate the sharp right-angle turns between one tunnel and another.

We were nearly three-quarters of an hour below ground before we crept out into the evening sunlight at Hardings Wood, transhipped our ballast, re-started the engine and bade farewell to the tug crew. We had scarcely lost sight of the tunnel mouth before we passed the junction of the Macclesfield canal. This waterway branches off to the south, but shortly afterwards crosses over the Trent and Mersey by an aqueduct and heads due north, along the edge of the Derbyshire uplands, to its junction with the Peak Forest Canal at Marple. A further half-hour's travelling brought us to our day's objective, 'The Red Bull Inn' at Lawton, on the Cheshire border, once a well-known stage on the pack-horse route between the Potteries and the Mersey. It was almost dark by the time we had moored at Red Bull Wharf, and astern the lights of the Five Towns made a glare in the sky over Harecastle Hill.

Chapter XXIV

THE VALE ROYAL

Of our day's journey from Red Bull to Middlewich there is little to be told, except that it involved a deal of hard labour, the canal descending into the great plain of Cheshire by a seemingly endless succession of thirty-two locks. Owing to the heavier traffic on this section, these 'Cheshire locks', as the boatmen call them, are arranged in duplicate, an interconnecting paddle allowing a full lock to discharge into its empty fellow, so that one acts as a side pond to the other. All day long we slowly worked our way downwards while the solitary bastion of Mow Cop and the long scarp line of 'the backbone of England' receded into the distance astern. Not only were the locks very heavy to work, but the surroundings depressing in the extreme—a dreary industrial hinterland that was neither town nor country. The poverty-stricken farms and ruined factories of Rode Heath, Hassall Green and Wheelock spoke only too plainly of a rural life transformed by a brief period of industrial expansion, which, having laid waste the land and claimed its husbandmen, had passed on to factories new. The only redeeming feature of the day was the number of horse-boats that we met—more than we had ever before encountered on the whole of our journey. Among their crews were some fine types of the old race of canal folk, one boat captain attracting our attention particularly. With his clear skin, proud aquiline features and dark eyes, he was a perfect specimen of true Romany stock. His face was fittingly framed by the dark ringlets which curled from beneath his cap, and as he moved about the locks, every movement graceful, his gold earrings flashed in the sunlight.

At dusk the tall chimneys of the Middlewich salt works were a welcome sight ahead, for we knew that they marked the end of the locks and the gateway to open country. We had had our fill of the industrial Midlands by this time, and could think only of quiet waters and green fields.

Our seventy-six-mile journey on the Trent and Mersey Canal came to an end the next morning, when we entered the Shropshire Union Canal at Wardle Lock Junction. Like most of the Shropshire canal system, the Middlewich branch is one of the more recent waterways constructed by Thomas Telford, and although it is now well over a century old, it is habitually referred to by Trent and Mersey boatmen as 'the New Cut'. Following the edge of a shelf of high ground on the right bank of the River Weaver, its more recent origin was at once manifested in the bold embankments and cuttings by which it crossed the narrow, wooded valleys of tributary streams or the intervening ridges, obstructions which Brindley would have carried his canal many tortuous miles to avoid. Though we were actually travelling at no great height, the level of the Cheshire Plain was such that our view from the deck commanded a fine sweep of country stretching northwards over the Winsford Flashes to Delamere Forest, and southwest to the Peckforton Hills and that dominating feature of the Cheshire scene, Beeston Crag. Perched secure upon the eyrie of its precipitous slope, the ruined keep of Beeston still holds a brooding watch upon the plains from the Wrekin to the Breiddens and from Mow Cop to the Marches of Wales. Built by Ranulph de Blundeville, Earl of Chester, when he returned from the Holy Land in 1220 with the memories of the great fortresses of the first crusaders still fresh in his mind, the castle's eventful history did not come to an end until after the Civil Wars, during which it was occupied successively by Cavalier and Roundhead. It was at Beeston that that unhappy king, Richard II, left his treasure, only to lose it when the garrison surrendered at the approach of Henry Bolingbroke, and for centuries from the castle's upper ward beacons have flared their message to the yeomen of the Vale Royal, spreading the tidings of the death of kings or of the approach of Spain's Armada.

As the sun sank towards the shoulder of Peckforton, the subtle alchemy of twilight transformed this broad vale of woodland and pasture into a dim sea that lapped the knees of the far hills. We had reached a point where the bank between the canal and the Weaver was particularly steep, the river meandering in great loops through the levels directly below, its slow-moving surface reflecting the evening sky like a burnished shield. In the middle distance the stream was spanned by a bridge of several arches, and on the farther bank a church tower rose above encircling trees to catch the last rays of the sun, which had already left the roofs of the village which clustered about it. This, we learned from our map, was the village of Church Minshull, and here we made our first prolonged stay since we had left Barrow-upon-Soar.

We could scarcely have chanced upon a better surviving example of the traditional English village had we purposefully scoured the countryside. Here was no show village of stock-broker-Tudor as false as a harlot's smile, and, more surprising still, it had escaped the fate of becoming an industrial dormitory, Crewe, aptly described by one of the villagers as 'no more than a ruck o' houses', being perilously near. Happily immune from these evils, and too unassuming to attract the sightseer, Church Minshull shelters securely under Weaver bank, a self-sufficient rural community that in numbers and activity has changed but little through the centuries. The reason for this survival undoubtedly lies in the comparative prosperity of local agriculture. Never before on our journey had we seen such well-drained pastures, trim hedgerows or prosperous farmsteads. They were a sight to gladden eyes grown accustomed to leagues of derelict land fast reverting to wilderness. Yet there was the same conspicuous lack of arable land as elsewhere, the Cheshire farmer's great cow-byres representing the mainstay of his livelihood. Possessing the finest dairy pasture in England, he is a milk manufacturer, and, as such, he has the better been able to withstand conditions which have brought the orthodox mixed farmer, who is the backbone of a healthy agricultural community, to the brink of ruin. Thus it is that conditions in the Vale Royal are not as rosy as they at first appear, although prosperity of any sort is preferable to neglect and decay, if the lease of rural life in villages such as Church Minshull is thereby prolonged.

BARBRIDGE

Chapter XXV

CHURCH MINSHULL

CHURCH MINSHULL contained many excellent examples of the timber-framed house built in the genuine regional style, interspersed with a few substantial farms of brick, a medium which superseded timber as the local building material from the eighteenth century onwards. Only one cottage represented our enlightened age—a featureless block of raw brick and slate which replaced an older building demolished under the Slum Clearance Act, whose misapplication is the latest menace to the English village. This incongruous newcomer might have been transplanted from the suburbs of Crewe, a tawdry paper rose dropped in a bed of wild flowers.

In a vale country such as this, where timber was once the most plentiful material, the tasks of the quarrymen and masons of the hills fell to woodmen and master carpenters. These characteristic walls of timber framing filled with lath and plaster work were the result, and their survival is an enduring tribute not only to the surpassing skill with which these local craftsmen wrought, but to the excellence of their materials. Because we have squandered the resources of forest and coppice with no thought of the future, such timber is no longer known, and our impoverished erections of brick and stucco compare to our discredit with these old buildings, whose every ageless beam cries eloquent reproof. It seemed most fitting that the church and the inn should stand side by side in easy intimacy at the centre of the village, for these immemorial institutions are the core of rural life. Side by side the living and the dead rested after their labours, for the gleaming and spotless tap-room of 'The Old Badger' was not a stone's throw from the quiet churchyard. The two buildings seemed to regard each other with the benign tolerance of old age, the church tower overpeering the wall of the inn yard, and the inn windows gazing undismayed at the tombs of patrons long dead and gone, as one who would with calm acceptance say: 'In the midst of life we are in death'.

In the church the ancient parish register brought home as nothing else could the strength and permanence of those ties which once held the countrymen to their land and to each other. This record, wonderfully preserved and legible, dated back to the sixteenth century, the same names recurring in birth, marriage and death generation after generation. To turn these pages of heavy vellum was to realise how, in the span of a lifetime, the bloodless revolution of the machine has loosed a bond which has survived plague, persecution and war for at least six hundred turbulent years.

Most remarkable of all the long-dead yeomen of Cheshire recorded here was one Thomas Damme of Leighton, who, it is written, 'was buried on the twentieth of Februarie 1649, being of the age of seven score and fourteen'. Assuming this entry to be correct—and there seems no good reason to doubt its authenticity—old Thomas Damme beats the better-known Shropshire patriarch, Thomas Parr of Glyn, by two years. Both these stalwart countrymen attained their great age under conditions which we now regard as barbaric, and without the aid of our much-advertised patent medicines, whose names are legion, and whose popularity does not flatter our much-vaunted standard of living. We shall not see such years again until we have recovered sufficient sanity to simplify the pattern of our lives.

From the churchyard gate it was possible to look right and left along the village street, from the Post Office at one end to the smithy and wheelwright's shop at the other. The post-mistress, white-haired and benevolent, as such a personage should be, supplied the children with the same sticky, vivid sweets as their mothers and grandmothers sucked when they, too, were young. Of an evening, when the menfolk repair to 'The Badger' for a glass of mild, the housewives foregather in the post office for a gossip, on the pretext of a stamp or half a pound of tea.

The music of the street was the clink of the blacksmith's hammer, and there was seldom a day when a pair of cart-horses patiently awaiting their turn to be shod, or a new-painted cart with scarlet shafts up-reared, were not to be seen standing outside his forge, for Mr. Eggerton was wheelwright as well as smith. The wind of increased motor taxation had swept much well-merited business into a shop redolent of paint and new-hewn timber. Gigs and traps which local farmers had dragged from long years of retirement in dim and dusty cartsheds shone bravely with new paint and varnish, their frames and shafts, wheel-spokes and felloes all delicately lined out to contribute to that rich and graceful finish which the invention of the cellulose spray gun has blown into the past. One gig bore proudly a hand-painted crest, proof positive that the hand of this craftsman had lost nothing of its cunning.

Of the several institutions that contributed to that self-sufficient and corporate whole of village life, the mill was among the most important, but because the farmer no longer brings his corn to be ground, nor the cottager his humble gleanings, it has generally suffered eclipse of recent years. Yet we discovered that the waters of the Weaver still turned the wheels of Minshull Mill, the enterprising miller not only grinding cattle-meal for the local farmers, but supplying the whole village with electric current at a paltry rate, in defiance of the local supply companies. Born of a family of millers, he had taken over the concern in a derelict condition, and the fact that he was now deriving a comfortable livelihood from it refutes the popular conception of the water-mill as a picturesque 'by-gone' of no practical value.

For all its wheels and shafts, anything less like a factory than Minshull Mill would be difficult to imagine. The dim interior was heavy with the inimitable smell of musty sacks and dust of fresh-ground meal, a compound that is incense to the imagination. Like the rime of an autumn frost, the flour had whitened the cobwebs which hung from the rafters, and the hands of generations of millers had polished the woodwork of bins and traps to a smooth, honey-coloured bloom. From beneath the floor the water boiling under the mill wheels made distant thunder, a deep undercurrent of sound to which were added the rumble of the stones and the subdued chatter of the gearing. This was the ancient voice of the mill—no high-pitched, distracting clamour, but a soothing rhythm, as measured and purposeful, as tireless and enduring, as the cycle of the seasons. The miller remains as close to the heart of essential things as the ploughman with his team or the shepherd at watch over his flocks.

A breakdown of this machinery was practically unknown, although it had been running for centuries. The two undershot water wheels had not needed repair within living memory; they were fifteen feet in diameter, their naves formed of the trunks of well-grown oak trees with the bark still upon them. The gearing was paired, wood meshing into iron, the best combination for silence and durability, but in the rare event of a tooth breaking the miller sent for a millwright from the Potteries who had not forgotten the art of shaping a new tooth, morticing and pegging it into place. Crab-apple—that magic wood of the Druids—has been found the most suitable for this purpose, and the miller of Minshull kept some by him in case of need.

In mediaeval times, and before the enclosures destroyed the truly socialistic character of the village community, the miller was paid in kind, claiming his portion or 'knaveship' with a measure called a 'toll-dish'. In this connection Messrs. Hopkins and Freese, in their book on the English Windmill, quote the following extract from the Red Paper Book of Colchester:

'Furst, the sise of a Myller is that he have no mesure at his myll but it be sised and sealed accordyng un to the Kyng's standard, and he to have in every busshell whete a quart for the gryndyng, and if he fett (fetch) itt another quart for the fettyng; and of every busshell malte a pynt for the gryndyng, and if he fett itt anor for the fettyng. . . .'

Monetary payment was substituted by an Act of George III, and now the country miller seldom or never grinds corn at all, though there can be no comparison in nourishment value between the old stone-ground flour and the devitalised white flour produced by the modern roller mill. From the same authority on early mills come these remarks on the process of stone-grinding by a veteran miller.

'In the so-called old-fashioned process,' he says, 'which every miller knows in his heart to be the only real process, the grain is dropped through a hole in the centre of the upper stone. The millstones are dressed diagonally, the effect being to grind the wheat in a circular movement converging towards the centre, and the germ of the grain—a tiny nut which is oily and greasy—is dusted and pulverised by the dry stone into part of the flour from which it cannot be separated.

'This flour, which is swept from the outer side of the stones into a trough which runs round the mill, is the real wholemeal flour. It is afterwards dressed through silks to remove the bran, thus leaving the 'white' flour—in colour a light cream. . . . The old despised windmills and water-mills gave the people the very best flour obtainable, and it is a thousand pities that they are not in use today.'

If ever a revival of public taste demanded stone-ground flour, Minshull Mill could supply it, the redressing and setting of the stones ('French burrs' for corn, 'peaks' for other grains) being the only alteration necessary. At present, however, we give our cattle the benefit of a process we deny to ourselves, and if we do not soon mend our ways there will be no millers left to dress a stone for wheat.

The road down to the mill was set with cobbles so fine that it resembled a shingle beach. Not a great while ago, we were told, these extended the length of the village street, while in the broad space before the smithy, at the meeting of two ways, there was a green where stood a solitary tree, its bole circled by a wooden bench. One can only imagine the children at play and the old men sitting at ease in the evening sun, for now all has been swept away by a tide of black tarmacadam, chequered with painted lines and symbols. To see it made me more than ever thankful that we had chosen to travel the only roads in England which are beyond the power of County Councils to deface.

It was this funereal road alone that brought the twentieth century to Church Minshull, for at night, when the street was dark and still, the village was ageless. Only immemorial country sounds did not break, but contributed to the silence, a cow moving in her stall, the sharp bark of a fox or cry of an owl from the hanging coverts above the river, and the murmur of the weir by the mill— an almost imperceptible rumour of sound. Could he return at such a time, old Thomas Damme would feel no stranger here.

PART THREE

PART THREE

Chapter XXVI

NANTWICH

OUR stay at Church Minshull was so prolonged that when we finally decided to cast off once more, autumn was already far advanced. We had thought of voyaging up the Welsh canal to Llangollen, but the outbreak of war and the prospect of winter's imminence brought about a change of plan, and we decided instead to turn south along a different route, with Oxford our ultimate objective.

Owing to the high cost of petrol and the difficulty of obtaining supplies, I had decided to adapt 'Cressy's' engine to burn paraffin, and our departure was further delayed because the railway company—characteristically—lost the case of vital parts. It should have arrived at Crewe, but after a fortnight of vain telephone conversations with helpless or apathetic clerks it was eventually run to earth at Worleston, a sleepy country station some miles in the opposite direction. We spent three days in fitting the new parts, filling tanks with fuel and laying in copious stores, before, on a Saturday at noon, we slipped our moorings, looking our last on the village we had come to regard with the familiarity of home.

The day was fine and sunny, but a cold westerly breeze was blowing the leaves from the trees and ruffling the surface of the water into wavelets which slapped and gurgled round our bows. Crossing

the exposed bank above the river, it was difficult to prevent
'Cressy' from being blown onto the mud, but we succeeded in
reaching the sheltered cutting under Old Hoolgrave bridge without
having to resort to our shafts. For, in common with the rest of
the Shropshire Union System, the apparent width of the Middlewich canal was very deceptive, the available draught of water
being very small, and any departure from the narrow central
channel scoured by passing boats landed the unwary firmly and
almost inextricably aground.

Because of the low banks and these shallow margins, the canal
was a favoured haunt of herons. Often when walking along the
towing path we had seen them, but could never approach them
closely. Invariably they would wheel away, keeping a distance of
from two to three hundred yards. Soon after we had passed
through Minshull lock and crossed the Weaver by a lofty aqueduct
we sighted a heron, and were surprised to discover that when
approached by water he exhibited no sign of shyness. Instead he
remained motionless on the margin, his long neck craning over the
water until our bows were almost abreast of him, when, quicker
than thought, he struck, the long bill flashing down to emerge
with a writhing silver fish securely held. So close were we by this
time that we could see his neck distend as he swallowed his prey.
When he rose it was only to alight a hundred yards farther ahead
and repeat his tactics. Always he landed some little distance from
the water's edge, approaching to peer over the brink with all the
infinite stealth and concentration of an ardent dry-fly fisherman
stalking his gut-shy quarry on a clear chalk stream. Sometimes he
drew blank and flew ahead without striking, but when he struck
he never failed. This systematic fishing went on for some time, until
we neared the next lock at Cholmondeston, which was evidently
the boundary of his beat, for he winged away over the fields to
alight some distance astern. Though we had seen many herons
on our summer journey, they had always given us a wide berth,
yet this was destined to be only the first of many similar encounters
on our return. We concluded that the reason for this must be that
the fish tend to lie on the bottom as winter approaches, and that the
passage of a boat creates a disturbance among them which the
heron finds very welcome.

Cholmondeston was a good example of the way in which local
place names can defeat the stranger by their unexpected pro-
nunciation. I had felt tolerably certain that it would be ab-

breviated to 'Chumston', until I was enlightened by an old canal lengthman at Nantwich, who not only pronounced it phonetically, but threw in yet another syllable, and stressed the last but one in such a manner that the ponderous word assumed the forcefulness of a rousing mediaeval oath. 'I was born Cholermon*des*ton way' was what he said, and he should know.

Twenty minutes' more running brought us in sight of 'The Jolly Tar' at Barbridge, whose windows command the junction of the Middlewich Branch with the old Chester Canal section of the Shropshire Union 'main line'. Here we turned southward to moor for the night between an old warehouse spanning the waterway from bank to bank and a wooden mission room on the water's edge. We wondered whether the latter was intended for canal boatmen on the lines of a seamen's mission, as its site suggested, but when a service was held there next morning the canal folk were conspicuous by their absence, although several boats passed by.

There is a considerable traffic on this waterway, consisting mainly of Thomas Clayton horse-boats working between Birmingham and Ellesmere Port, and an occasional 'Josher' or Cowburn and Cowpar motor-boat trading from Wolverhampton to Widnes, Runcorn or Manchester via the Middlewich Branch. The latter once travelled via the Staffordshire and Worcestershire Canal to the Trent and Mersey at Great Haywood, but owing to the delay at Harecastle Tunnel and the heavy 'Cheshire locks', the Shropshire route, five miles shorter and considerably easier, came to be adopted.

At Hurleston the mouth of the Welsh Canal climbing westwards towards the Marches was a sore temptation, but we passed it by, and soon came in sight of the fine sandstone tower of Acton church, a prominent landmark on the summit of a gentle slope overlooking Nantwich. An old local saying maintains that 'Acton churchyard is higher than Nantwich steeple'. Whether this be true or not matters little, but it is a recorded fact that Acton was once the mother church of Nantwich, the first place of worship at Wych Malbank, as it was then called, being a diminutive Norman chapel-of-ease.

Until it became part of a through route by the construction of Telford's 'Birmingham and Liverpool Junction Canal', the old Chester Navigation terminated in a broad basin between Acton and Nantwich which is still known locally as 'Basin End'. Wide boats once traded regularly between Ellesmere Port and the basin, but now it has fallen into disuse, the old warehouse having become a store for Cheshire cheeses, a better fate than has befallen most.

Acting upon the advice of a lengthman at Barbridge, we tried to moor in this basin, but soon discovered that he had not taken into account the bar of mud thrown across the entrance by the wash of passing motor-boats. After we had made two abortive attempts we gave it up, mooring outside and walking up the hill to Acton village, where we took a lunch of bread and cheese at 'The Star', a fine old timbered inn with a mounting-block on the cobbles before the door. Because the interstices of the timber framing had been filled with brickwork, it was not a perfect specimen of regional building construction; nevertheless it was an attractive example of the roadside 'hedge-tavern'. The dark, stone-flagged interior was rendered even darker by a typical Victorian 'stuffiness' of wallpaper, aspidistras, lace curtains and coloured lithographs, yet we felt that even this was preferable to exploitation by the builders of Tudor roadhouses and 'olde-worlde' tea-barns to whom it might have fallen an easy prey.

According to Leland there were four hundred salt workings in Nantwich at the time of Henry VIII, but their numbers slowly dwindled until, unlike the neighbouring 'wiches', the trade vanished altogether, its only traces being the brine baths and the way in which the subsidence of old workings has caused many houses to sink below street level. Three times visited by plague, twice laid waste by fire, besieged in the civil war, the old town now faces a new and more insidious peril, the invasion of its upstart neighbour Crewe, which is threatening to engulf it in a spate of 'desirable housing estates'. Though these have encroached perilously near, Nantwich still contrives to preserve the atmosphere of an old market town catering solely for the needs of an agricultural district. The existence of Crewe and of the strangers at the gates is not yet acknowledged, but how much longer will this happy immunity survive? In view of the recent establishment of a vast new factory at Crewe, it would seem all too probable that it will soon be swallowed up by its swollen neighbour of the cinemas, chain stores and sordid streets. Meanwhile the shops of Nantwich reflect the needs and standard of living of the countrymen for whom they cater. This standard, unlike that of Crewe, is high, a fact which refutes the common belief that it is industrialism which has brought about improved living. The grocers, bakers and butchers

of Nantwich made it abundantly clear to us that the countrymen
of Cheshire do not live out of tins and refuse to accept inferior
imported foods. To ask a Nantwich butcher for foreign meat
would constitute a personal insult, and during our stay in Cheshire
we had home-killed joints that in their tenderness and flavour
rivalled the famous roasts of Simpsons in the Strand. We delighted
also in sampling the local delicacies—chorley cakes, a currant-
filled pastry eaten hot with butter, pikelets, a species of crumpet,
great flat oatcakes fried with breakfast bacon, and last but by no
means least, prime Cheshire cheese.

This is the only vigorous survivor of that goodly company of
English cheeses which have been banished to oblivion, or at best
to extreme rarity, by a soap-like factory product wrapped in tin-
foil or a characterless substance fit only to bait mouse-traps. The
fact that the cheese-room still takes its rightful place in the active
life of so many farms in the Vale Royal is the highest tribute to the
tenacity of the tradition of rural life in Cheshire. These are the
same cheese-rooms which, in the seventeenth century, were exempted
from the window tax, and the cheese-markets held weekly in
Nantwich, where the large barrel-shaped cheeses in their cloth
coverings are auctioned, are the direct lineal descendants of the
great cheese-fairs of a more prosperous past.

Originally composed entirely of timber-built houses, it is not
surprising that the town was thrice ravaged by fire. That of 1583
was so devastating that Queen Elizabeth came to the rescue of the
homeless inhabitants with a grant of timber from her royal forest
of Delamere. Her favour is perpetuated to this day by the inscrip-
tion over the gable of a house in the square which runs:

'God grante our ryal Queen
In England long to raign,
For she hath put her helping hand
To bild this towne again.'

There are still many excellent examples of timber-work in
the town, particularly the old Crown Hotel, with its great gallery
window extending the whole length of the upper storey and, most
notable of all, the mansion of Richard Churche in Hospital
Street. Though very different in style and of later date, the latter
shares with Grevel's fourteenth-century house at Campden in
Gloucestershire the distinction of being one of the very few wealthy
merchant houses remaining in England, for the heavy hand of
progress has naturally dealt more hardly with the town house of

the merchant venturer than with the secluded country manor of
squire or yeoman.

Churche's mansion is as fine a flowering of the regional style
as is the Grevel House of Cotswold Gothic. The timberwork
of the long, four-gabled front is most elaborately and finely
wrought in a design of linked Maltese crosses varied by a pattern
of alternately erect and inverted triple branches in the gable-heads.
Within we found a wealth of magnificent panelling and carved
over-mantels, some of which still bear the marks of tallow dips
which have been ruthlessly stuck upon them in the past with singular
disregard for the danger of fire. Although we should otherwise
have been unable to see the interior, we could not help regretting
that the house should have become a tea and antique shop.
Nevertheless we were inclined to a more charitable view when we
learnt that the present owners had not only saved the house from
the fate of being shipped piecemeal to America, like the Snowshill
Smithy, but with their own hands had restored the interior, strip-
ping as many as twenty layers of wallpaper from the panelling.
They had also brought the old rooms to life with many beautiful
and tastefully chosen things, for which, though they were for sale,
they displayed a genuine pride and affection. Notable among
these was a superb refectory table thirty feet long and bearing a
salt mark, which graced the great dining-room. They had refused
a good offer for this table on learning that the prospective purchaser
proposed cutting it in half. The rooms were lit entirely by candles,
and the picture we carried with us from Churche's Mansion
was one of the friendly gloom of the panelled dining-hall starred
with their flickering gracious light shining out from the wall-
sconces and branch candelabra as the dusk fell.

As a permanent dwelling-place I would prefer the stalwart
limestone walls of Grevel's house, for walls of timber, lath and
plaster, no matter how truly built, can never afford the same degree
of warmth, while searching draughts whistle through ill-fitting
casements whose frames inevitably distort with age. Nevertheless,
had I to live in Cheshire I would choose such a house, for I confess
I care little for the local sandstone. Of a blackened, sombre quality
unresponsive to light or shadow, it possesses neither the lightness
nor the durability of oolitic limestone, which, in its subtle range of
colouring, varying from silver to deepest ochre, is the perfect
medium for the soaring grace of Perpendicular Gothic. Because
it is built of this unsympathetic sandstone, which the weather

defaces as effectively as any Puritan, I was little moved by the fabric of Nantwich church, fine though it undoubtedly is. There are some more than usually grotesque gargoyles carved with characteristic vigour and humour, especially one representing a devil of exceptional depravity bearing off a bibulous woman still clinging to her quart pot. There is also a very fine stone pulpit, whose panels and slender pedestal are richly carved in the Perpendicular style of double arcading to harmonise with the low chancel screen from which it springs with the natural exuberance of a flower. Nevertheless I saw nothing to change my view that wood and not stone was the chosen medium of the mediaeval craftsmen of Cheshire. For the glory of this church are the canopied choir stalls of late fifteenth-century workmanship. There are twenty of them, and their delicate openwork canopies, each embracing three image niches, spire to the chancel roof in such a wealth of slender shafts and crocketed pinnacles that it is as though a hundred springing fountain jets had petrified in oak. But it was in the misericords beneath that the craftsman of the Age of Faith had expressed most exuberantly his mediaeval fancy. Their carving spoke with the voice of the singers in the inn at Shardlow, a voice that has been stilled forever by that new spirit of joyless sanctimony which was a product of commercialism. So prodigal is the rich blend of humour, imagination and piety that has found expression here that the mind shrinks from the contrast of our own impoverishment. Here, wrought with infinite toil and cunning, are knights and dragons, monks, nuns and wrestlers, dolphins, mermaids, strange man-headed birds and Reynard the fox setting forth on a hunting foray, a leather bottle slung about his waist. These misericords are poetry in oak, for wood and stone were to the mediaeval craftsman what words are to the poet. When shall we see their like again?

Chapter XXVII

INTO SHROPSHIRE

WE got up at dawn on the day of our departure from Nantwich, to be rewarded by a sunrise of rare splendour. A long, violet-coloured bar of cloud hung in the east, but between it and the horizon there lay a strip of clear sky at first only a silver luminence in a grey half-light, but slowly flushing from palest salmon-pink to a brilliance that fired the fringes of the cloud above. Against this magic backcloth the towers and roofs of the town, wreathed in the smoke of morning fires, looked as blue, remote and unreal as did Camelot to Gareth and his companions when they saw 'the silver misty morn rolling her smoke about the royal mount'. Now, as then, the birds made melody, while a slowly approaching boat travelled on such a path of reflected glory that it might well have been bound for Avilion with the wounded King. When the sun passed behind the bank of cloud, colour ebbed swiftly, prosaic Nantwich reappeared, the water darkened and the boat passed by, a Thomas Clayton with a cargo of oil for Ellesmere Port.

When we had breakfasted and laid in a further stock of provisions from the town, we cast off, crossing the Chester road and the Vale of Nantwich by a cast-iron aqueduct and a mile-long embankment.

Construction of the Birmingham and Liverpool Junction Canal was not commenced until 1826, and so far as I know it was the last important waterway, excluding ship canals, to be built in this country. Its inception was entirely due to the success of George Stephenson's Liverpool and Manchester Railway, for the canal proprietors, alarmed by the threat of their new competitor, desired a quicker and easier route between the two great industrial areas. For this reason it is unequalled by any other waterway in the magnitude of its earthworks and the directness of its course. Across the level pastures from Nantwich, through Hack Green, to Audlem it cuts as straight as a Roman road, and for the first and only time on our travels we found ourselves wishing that 'Cressy' was capable of a little more speed. The older winding waterways fully gratified that chief joy of travel, the expectation of what may lie round the next corner, but here, when our attention became focussed on a bridge perhaps a mile distant, this element was entirely lacking and our progress seemed intolerably slow. By nightfall we reached the end of this monotonous stretch, crossing the Weaver by Hankelow Mill, and mooring below the Audlem flight of fifteen locks by which the canal leaves the plain.

Having worked over a hundred and fifty locks by this time, lockage had become a matter of easy routine, and we made short work of the Audlem flight next morning, although they were all against us. Angela went ahead on her bicycle to set them, closing the top gates and drawing the bottom paddles, so that when they were empty 'Cressy' could push the lower gates open for herself. When I had filled the locks she could open the top gates also, an advantage when working a boat with so small a crew which cannot be enjoyed when locking downhill, as the gates then open against the direction of travel.

Half-way up the locks we paused at Audlem, a sleepy group of old houses, inns and shops clustering about a church perched upon a mound; an agricultural town so small that it might equally well be described as a large village. We found the much-restored interior of the church disappointing, bought some Chorley cakes and home-made treacle toffee at the baker's shop, and continued on our way.

At the summit of the flight we crossed the border of Shropshire, and found the rolling wooded country between this point and the next five locks at Adderley a welcome change after the monotony of the Cheshire levels. By this time the westerly breeze had freshened considerably and a wrack of swift chasing clouds was sweeping like smoke out of Wales. We had climbed to the last of the five locks when a cold rain began to fall, so we lost no time in

tying up, and were soon settling down to tea in the welcome
warmth of the sitting-cabin, eating hot buttered chorley cakes in
the flickering firelight while the rain beat against the windows and
pattered on the deck above.

We were discovering that canal cruising aboard 'Cressy' did not
depend for its fascination upon summer weather. Bare branches
dark against a winter sky, and a flight of rooks beating homeward, wind-tossed like charred scraps of paper; the rich bloom of
new ploughland, great honey-coloured ricks new thatched, and
the stillness of sky-reflecting pools—such pictures can convey but
little of rewards as great as any that summer had brought us. It
was a new and unfailing delight, after standing for hours at the
tiller in the keen air rich with the scents of late autumn, to moor
in some lonely place, close the hatches and retreat to the sitting-
cabin, an island of warmth and comfort in the gathering dark
where familiar objects, the many-coloured bindings of beloved
books, the gleaming copper kettle and outspread tea-things, awoke
to new and gracious life in the lamplight. To lie in bed of a night
or in the drowsy warmth of a hot bath and listen to the wind
rushing overhead was to be reminded of Frances Cornford's poem
'The Country Bedroom':

> 'My room's a square and candle-lighted boat,
> In the surrounding depths of night afloat,
> My windows are the portholes, and the seas
> The sound of rain in the dark apple-trees.'

When curtains were drawn it was often hard to believe that our
room really was 'a square and candle-lighted boat', whose windows
looked out each night upon a strange darkness.

We had almost decided to remain overnight at Adderley when
a boat passed by. After the usual exchange of greetings, 'Why
don't you go on to Drayton Wharf?' her captain suggested. 'It's
only three miles, and it's market day tomorrow.' Though the wind
was still blowing, the rain had ceased and there were patches of
clear evening sky between the flying clouds, so we took his advice
and moved on through the stormy half-light over Betton Moss.

The name of Betton seemed vaguely familiar, but it was not
until we reached Betton Wood, where the trees, pressing close,
made a darkness about us and the water was unruffled by the wind
which tossed their branches, that I recalled the association in the
line: 'Than that which walks in Betton Wood knows why it walks
or why it cries'. Connoisseurs of the ghost story will doubtless

have read 'A Neighbour's Landmark' by the immortal M. R. James, and so remember Betton Wood, where walked the shrieking ghost having 'no language but a cry'. It mattered little to me that the wood in the story was grubbed up owing to its evil reputation, whereas this one was very much alive, for any winter wood on a windy dusk is a haunted place.

When we came into the open again it was to catch the full force of the wind on our long cabin side, and our last mile that night was fraught with difficulty. However, by opening up the engine and driving along crabwise with the bow held well into the wind, we had only one encounter with the mud. Even so it was almost pitch dark by the time we drew alongside Victoria Wharf at Market Drayton, nor could we have gone farther had we wished to, for the wind rose rapidly to gale force, and all night long, great gusts and driving squalls rocked the boat.

From the time of its first publication in December 1944, the text of *Narrow Boat* and the gentle black-and-white illustrations by Denys Watkins-Pitchford have seemed the perfect marriage. Who shall say that the publisher, Douglas Jerrold of Eyre and Spottiswoode, was wrong to refuse to use photographs at that time? The

many times rejected text had lain unvisited for about four years. The publisher, though confident, was taking a chance. However, the effect of the book thus produced, with browning wartime paper and the inherited ancient beauty of Herbert Tooley's decorations for the cover, was not only to make it an instant success, reprinting as soon as paper – better paper – could be obtained, but also to render it at once timeless. *Narrow Boat* has never been out of print.

Those gentle black and whites were in fact made from Angela's photographs and now, with this new edition, we can let them and other of her photographs free into the text. Angela, Tom's first wife, had an eye behind the lens and she was there to record the passing scene with discernment. Alongside Angela's pictures, we also include several surviving photographs from the time by other hands – some famous in their own right. Taken together, these photographs are the best of all accompaniments to this celebratory edition, providing an authentic glimpse of the times, people and places described.

This is the book that inspired the canal preservation movement, making possible, against the odds, the survival of many aspects of the scene it so lovingly depicted. It is to be celebrated that, from that day to this, photographers and artists are able to continue to record their own views and to draw inspiration from the ongoing canal scene.

Sonia and Tim Rolt
April 2014

A misty morning view from the bows of *Cressy* (Rolt Collection)

The author, aged twenty, in 1930 on an early outing on a still steam-powered *Cressy* (Rolt Collection)

October 1936: *Cressy* near Berkhampstead in a photograph taken by the author on a voyage described in part one of his autobiography, *Landscape With Machines* (Author/Rolt Collection)

Cressy undergoing alterations at Tooley's boatyard, Banbury, early in 1939 (Author/Rolt Collection)

The interior of *Cressy*'s main cabin looking aft. The writing flap is closed to make room to entertain visitors (Angela Rolt/Rolt Collection)

An interior detail from the main bedroom on *Cressy* (Angela Rolt/Rolt Collection)

On the move: drawbridge on the Oxford Canal (Angela Rolt/Tim Wilkinson Collection)

A rare snap by the author of Angela fishing from *Cressy*, most probably on the River Soar near Leicester (Author/Rolt

Alfred and Mrs Hone on their boat *Cylgate*, moored alongside Tooley's boatyard at Banbury, 1939 (Angela Rolt/Hugh McKnight Collection)

The Hone family boats *Rose and Betty* and *White City* lying opposite
Tooley's boatyard at Banbury (Angela Rolt/Rolt Collection)

Banbury Wharf: the boatman's mule prepared for the day's work on the towpath (Angela Rolt/Hugh McKnight Collection)

The Samuel Barlow boats, loaded with aluminium from Brentford, in
Cowley Lock, on the Grand Union Canal, at the start of their journey north
(Angela Rolt/Rolt Collection)

Cowley Lock on the Grand Union Canal. The toll clerk checks the tonnage on the boat when the lock is full by measuring the 'dry inches' between the boat's gunwale and the water level (Angela Rolt/Hugh McKnight Collection)

Samuel Barlow's narrow boats *Cairo* and *Warwick* wait below Cowley Lock
(Angela Rolt/Rolt Collection)

Loaded with coal, and working on the tow rope, a pair of Grand Union Canal
Carrying Company boats pass the Samuel Barlow boats from Brentford
(Angela Rolt/Tim Wilkinson Collection)

Loaded narrow boats leave the bottom of Marsworth Locks on the Grand Union Canal (Angela Rolt/Tim Wilkinson Collection)

These working narrow boats, Samuel Barlow's *Cairo* and *Warwick*, are in the top lock of Stoke Bruern. The house on the right was the home of Sister Mary, whose help and care of the boating community are legendary (Angela Rolt/Tim Wilkinson Collection)

The Christopher March boat *Heather Bell*, built by Nurser Bros of Braunston, working down Tardebigge Locks on the Worcester to Birmingham Canal. It was from this boat that the scheme for training women to man narrow boats arose. The first encounter between the work crews and *Cressy* took place in Tardebigge flight (Angela Rolt/Hugh McKnight Collection)

Fellows, Morton and Clayton's motor boat *Briar* (built 1935) with butty on the Grand Union Canal (Angela Rolt/Hugh McKnight Collection)

Foxton flight from below the bottom lock on the Leicester arm of the Grand Union Canal (Angela Rolt/Tim Wilkinson Collection)

Artefacts of the life: a water-can, painted by Frank Nurser of Braunston, sits on the hatch cover (Angela Rolt/Tim Wilkinson Collection)

Ropework on the painted ram's head of Samuel Barlow's narrow boat
The 'ram's head' referred to the plaited crown, and the 'swan's neck' to the
length of fine ropework behind the 'elum' or helm. The whiteness was the result
of hard scrubbing with cut water (Angela Rolt/Tim Wilkinson Collection)

A narrow boat cabin interior. The ticket drawer, which contained the documents for the trip, is screened by a layer of thick hand crochet. Measham pottery jugs hang above the stove (Angela Rolt/Tim Wilkinson Collection)

Where it all began: Herbert and George Tooley at work in Banbury dry dock.
George, left, is caulking seams with oakum and grease, and Herbert, right,
is fitting a new elm bottom. Their yard is once again likely to disappear in a
new shopping development (Angela Rolt/Hugh McKnight Collection)

Herbert Tooley painting roses, Banbury Dock (Angela Rolt/Hugh McKnight Collection)

Lock-gate making at Tardebigge Depot, Worcester & Birmingham Canal. The shell-auger is in use (Angela Rolt/Hugh McKnight Collection)

The rope-worn bollard would become the star of many photographs. This example was taken in the 1940s at Hawkesbury Junction by Robert Longden (Robert Longden Archive)

A new boat under construction at Braunston in the 1940s (Robert Longden/ Robert Longden Archive)

A new boat at Braunston nearing completion (Robert Longden/Robert
Longden Archive)

Renowned canal man: boatbuilder, painter, yard owner Frank Nurser shows off a hand bowl (Robert Longden/Robert Longden Archive)

Two views of the Tardebigge mooring on the Worcester & Birmingham remained here for a total of 1,800 days (Both Eric de Maré/Rolt

The 1947 campaigning days. *Cressy* successfully forces a passage at Lifford Bridge on the Stratford Canal (Rolt Collection)

Shropshire Union Canal, Welsh Section, 1947. 'Tom Rolt at the scene of the bank burst one mile south of Frankton Junction near Oswestry, in 1936. Local maintenance workers assembled materials to repair the breach but were ordered by the Company not to proceed. Trade to Welshpool and Newtown automatically ceased and traders received no compensation. Having defied their legal obligations to maintain this beautiful waterway in good order, the Company obtained abandonment powers in 1943.' (All preceding wording taken from an IWA exhibition print caption of the late 1940s) (Angela Rolt/Hugh McKnight Collection)

Dining al fresco on the fore end. *L–R*: Vanessa de Maré, Angela and Tom Rolt. *Cressy* revisits the same wartime Tardebigge mooring in 1948 or 1949 (Eric de Maré/Hugh McKnight Collection)

Cressy noses into King's Norton Stop Lock (Angela Rolt/Rolt Collection)

The author contemplates an empty pound on the Worcester & Birmingham
Canal at Tardebigge (Eric de Maré/Hugh McKnight Collection)

Publicity photograph taken during the Market Harborough IWA Rally of 1950. The author's third canal book, *Inland Waterways of England*, had just been published. Tom and Angela were told to keep away from the festival by the IWA, but decided to defy the instruction (Rolt Collection)

The author negotiating Hawkesbury Junction in 1949 (Robert Longden/
Robert Longden Archive)

Chapter XXVIII

'DIRTY FAIR'

AFTER our experience of 'Market' Harborough we were prepared to be disillusioned when we walked into the town the next morning. Instead we found ourselves in one of the best open markets we had seen. Market Drayton still lives up to its name, for not only was the square and the long street leading from it thronged with stalls, but countrywomen stood on the kerb-sides with great baskets of eggs, trussed poultry and vegetables which were a joy to behold.

The day, though fine, was very cold, and at noon the old inns round the square were crowded. In the stand-up bars there was much noisy bargaining and talk of feeding-stuffs or fat stock, while in the snug parlours plump farmers' wives exchanged the gossip of the week, topping up their glasses of rum from a steaming kettle on the hearth. From them we learnt that we had been lucky enough to arrive in time for Market Drayton's annual Horse Fair, commonly called 'Dirty Fair', because the weather on that day is proverbially wet. Determined not to miss such an event, we therefore delayed our departure.

The weather on fair day certainly lived up to tradition, but because it was obviously accepted as a time-honoured matter of course, everyone had come prepared for the worst, and the pouring rain made not a jot of difference. The open pens and covered sheds of the big cattle market were packed with horse-flesh of every shape, size and condition, from ponies and fluffy foals to lumbering cart-horses, while the men who moved among them, critically examining teeth or passing a knowledgeable hand over hocks or shoulders, were of even greater interest. Cloth-gaitered, bowler-hatted yeoman farmers whose faces were suffused by the cold rain to a fine mesh of ruddy veins, rubbed shoulders with dark, pale-skinned men from the Welsh mountains, whose soft, lilting speech mingled with the broader tones of the Shropshire dialect. There were many gipsies also, in their strange vivid clothes, the men wearing bright neckerchiefs, and their swarthy women-folk carrying babies wrapped with them in their heavy, check-patterned shawls. No doubt many of them came from Whixall Moss on the Marches near Whitchurch, a desolate tract of heath and bogland which has always been a favourite haunt of the people of Little Egypt. The farm labourers and carters were there too, clumping to and fro in their heavy, clay-caked boots with slow, tireless gait, their legs protected from the wet by improvised puttees made from coils of sacking tied with binder twine.

One old, white-bearded countryman in his best suit of sombre broadcloth was actually wearing an ancient tall hat, a form of headgear I had thought as extinct as the fine, quilted smocks of shepherd or waggoner, and which I may never see again.

But it was in the muddy field adjoining that most of the fun of the fair was taking place, for here there were great droves of unbroken colts and wild-eyed Welsh ponies straight from Clun Forest or the Berwyns. The scene was one of incessant movement and commotion, for one or other of the steaming, closely packed herds was forever stampeding, sending the crowd scattering for safety like a receding wave, while drovers brandishing long whips ran shouting and gesticulating hither and thither, trying to sort out their respective charges from a plunging, kicking and snorting *mêlée*.

We caught sight of a hard-bitten representative of the local county, threading her way through the motley throng, obviously in search of a mount for the small daughter who trailed in her wake. The Welshman in charge of one of the groups of ponies saw her also, and claimed her swiftly before his rivals could get a look in. Thrusting his face within a few inches of her ear, to her manifest discomfiture, he proceeded to beguile her with I know not what plausible confidences, while his assistant seized a halter and plunged among the ponies to emerge miraculously triumphant from a short chaotic struggle with his reluctant choice, shouting: 'Here you are, lady! Real Llangammarch Welsh.' Then, while the dealers sang its praises in glowing terms, curious onlookers formed an impromptu show ring and the pony was put through its paces, shaking its head wickedly, rearing and feinting so that the small boy who clung for dear life to the halter floundered like a fish upon a line. Although in this particular instance there was no sale, we saw a deal of hard bargaining concluded by the ceremonial slapping of palms, and watched the most unlikely and disreputable of customers pay out as much as ten or fifteen pounds in notes before celebrating the closing of the deal in the adjoining inn, whose takings on this occasion must be astronomical.

The horse-dealer is proverbially a plausible rogue, but withal he is a picturesque, characterful figure, and one which his modern counterpart, the down-at-heel second-hand car dealer, in a grease-spotted lounge suit, can never replace. Therefore, as we walked back through the rain to the canal we counted ourselves fortunate indeed to have shared in a scene which rightly belonged to the older England of 'Lavengro' and 'Romany Rye'. When the motor-car has finally routed the last of these old country festivals, when the last gipsy caravan has gone from the camping-place and the Welshmen no longer drive their ponies across the border, we shall still remember 'Dirty Fair'.

Chapter XXIX

CHESWARDINE WHARF

HAVING conveniently replenished our coal-bunkers at Victoria Wharf, we left Market Drayton at noon on a perfect day, crossing the valley of the Tern on a lofty embankment fringed with pine trees, between whose boles we caught glimpses of the wooded slopes and sunlit levels through which the little river wound. On regaining the high ground on the farther side, we almost immediately entered a cutting through bare sandstone so narrow and so arched and overgrown by trees and hazel bushes that it more nearly resembled a flooded Devon lane than a canal. This brought us to the Tyrley flight of five locks, the last for many miles to come, and when we had reached the summit we moored for tea beside a scented pinewood. The evening air was so mild that we sat on the foredeck, enjoying the last of the lowering sunlight. This was our last open-air meal of the year.

Determined to make the most of this fine, still weather, we travelled on afterwards, and soon entered a second cutting of far greater magnitude than that below the locks. Over a mile long, and from fifty to sixty feet deep, it carved a way through the same central ridge which the Trent and Mersey Canal pierces at Harecastle. Though doubtless less costly to construct than a tunnel, it was obvious, from the way in which the crumbling rock had in many places slipped down the almost precipitous sides onto the towing path or into the water, that it was a constant source of trouble and expense to the canal maintenance department. To journey through it as we did in the subdued half-light of dusk brought a strange sense of remoteness and unreality. The narrow ribbon of still water ahead and our slowly gliding boat seemed more than ever to be the stuff of dreams shut away from the world of men, an illusion before closed eyes from which we must soon awake. The trees which interlaced their branches high overhead to cover the water with perpetual shadow leant crazily one upon the other from their crumbling root-holds on the slopes. Like a tropical jungle, their branches trailed heavy curtains of creepers, dark ground ivy and silvery Old Man's Beard. Even the familiar canal bridges had here assumed strange and fanciful proportions, their arches airily heightened in their leap from lip to lip of the gorge.

When we eventually emerged into the open once more it was almost dark, but by the light of a faint emerald afterglow we could just distinguish a slope of common-land clothed with russet bracken, and the trunks of birches, a faint silver luminence, growing down to the water's edge. It was an ideal mooring place, but alas the margins were so shallow that we could not bring 'Cressy' near enough to the bank to be clear of passing boats. Moving slowly ahead in quest of deeper water, we presently saw through the gloom a wharf with a boat moored beside it, but on closer approach found the warehouse in ruins and the boat a rotting hulk lying gunwale awash. The basin, moreover, was so filled with mud that it would scarcely have floated a punt, as a sounding with one of our shafts proved. It was then that we noticed that the solitary cottage beside the wharf bore a sign: 'The Wharf Inn', it read, 'By H. Carpenter'. Assuming that it had not shared the fate of the warehouse, this was the most secluded canal inn we had yet encountered, and we became more than ever determined to moor up somehow, mud or no mud. Feeling certain that where there was an inn there must be a mooring place, we allowed 'Cressy' to drift slowly on through the bridge hole which cut off farther view ahead, and there found a Thomas Clayton horse-boat already tied up, her cabin fire smoking bravely in the clear night air. When we had moored and made all secure for the night, I looked up our position on the map. We were at Goldstone Common, one mile to the west of the village of Cheswardine, in the densely wooded, broken country on the Shropshire–Staffordshire border.

After dinner we walked out into a night starlit but moonless to make the acquaintance of 'The Wharf Inn'. We found a cheerful fire blazing in the little bar parlour, where sat the landlord, his wife and the captain of the horse-boat with a pint glass on the table before him. To come from the darkness of a strange countryside into the warmth and cheer of a simple, friendly house such as this, to take one's place on a rough bench before the fire and be carried easily into the smooth, unhurried flow of country talk as soothing as the murmur of bees, while the firelight glows in the brimming glass, this is to appreciate the true worth of the English inn. As no motorist dashing from one road-house to another in the close confinement of his saloon car can ever do, I found it easy to recapture the feelings of the hard-riding travellers of the past, and there came into my mind the words on the old sign of 'The Plough' at Ford on Cotswold, which so perfectly express that older and richer hospitality:

> 'Ye weary travelers that pass by,
> With dust and scorching sunbeams dry,
> Or be benumb'd with snow and frost,
> With having these bleak cotswolds crosst,
> Step in and quaff my nut-brown ale
> Bright as rubys mild and stale.
> 'Twill make your laging trotters dance
> As nimble as the suns of france.
> Then ye will own, ye men of sense,
> That neare was better spent six pence.'

This was the boatman's second stage on his eighty-mile journey between Oldbury and Ellesmere Port, which he covered in three and a half days, a daily mileage which put us to shame and meant travelling from before dawn until well after dark. The previous night he had spent near Wheaton Aston, the next would find him at Beeston or Chester, and on the mid-day following he would arrive at his destination. Since his liquid cargo took little time to discharge, he made the round trip in a week. He had but lately lost his wife, and now worked his boat with the help of his three small children, the eldest a girl of ten. There had been four, until one was drowned in Tyrley top lock. How they lived and what they ate will forever be a mystery, yet the captain appeared remarkably cheerful and philosophical, despite his bereavement. When he had gone, the landlord, who knew all the passing boatmen intimately, affirmed with a shake of his head that he was 'taking more beer than he used'. One can hardly blame him.

We went on to discuss the illiteracy of the canal folk, which our host considered a scandal 'in these times', citing the fact that most of them were unable even to read the time by his clock. He may be right, but my answer was that education has so far done little for the unemployed townsman except to make his tragic existence more intolerable. I certainly consider that the simple, forthright mother wit of the illiterate boatman is preferable to a 'culture' born of the cinema and Sunday newspaper, and though I could not lose the company of books, I have often envied him his happy immunity from the howling bedlam of the hoarding and the popular Press.

While we were talking the door opened and there entered a very old man whose lean, wizened face was framed in white side-whiskers. Sharp-eyed, but leaning heavily upon his stick, he bade the company good evening and made straight for the seat in the chimney corner which was evidently his by right of long custom, for the landlord immediately vacated it, unbidden and unacknow-ledged. This newcomer, it transpired, was a bachelor, and all the eighty-five years of his life he had spent on the same farm 'up Cheswardine way'. He had never seen the sea, nor travelled in a train, his boldest exploit being a rare excursion to Market Drayton, a venture he had not undertaken of recent years. His elder brother, it seemed, had been of a less conservative temperament, being fond of a ride in a 'moty-car' until his death a while back, when the cottage in which they had lived together had been sold up. Now this surviving veteran lived alone in a caravan which he had 'bought off a diddicoy Whitchurch way'. Every spring he repainted his home inside and out, and when he had a mind to it he would still give a helping hand on the farm. His hobby was collecting birds, and the caravan, we were told, was hung about with many cages, though no one knew, for he would never tell, how he contrived to catch them.

When we left the inn we thought we had been privileged to meet the oldest inhabitant of the district, but it subsequently transpired that we were wrong. We were talking to the canal lengthman the next morning, a burly countryman in the sixties, with a heavy white moustache and round, weatherbeaten face, and had been deploring the decline in the painting of the boats.

"That's just what my dad's always saying,' he agreed. 'I can remember as a boy his boat used to look a treat; you never see the like along here now—all done up with flowers and that.' The way in which he referred to his father in the present tense prompted us to ask whether he was still alive. 'Bless you yes!' he exclaimed. 'Why, he went to Drayton only last week to have a tooth took out.'

'My Dad', we discovered, was over ninety, still active and clear in mind. He had only one idiosyncrasy, which was evidently a source of worry to his son. A great walker all his life, his feet were now troubling him, but he refused to admit the infirmity, shifting the blame on to his boots. 'They can't make boots like they used', he would maintain stoutly, and given the opportunity would throw them on the fire. Woe betide his son if he should let him see a new pair, for: 'That's a nice pair o' boots you got there,

Jim', the veteran would say, eyeing them jealously, and would give him no peace until he had tried them, only to consign them to the same fate in a day or two if he was not carefully watched. Nevertheless it seemed that his feet still managed to carry him as far as 'The Wharf Inn' occasionally.

Such grand old countrymen as these are the living successors of Thomas Parr of Glyn and Damme of Leighton. There may be some particular quality in this rolling countryside of Shropshire which is conducive to long life, but surely the true elixir is the tranquil measure of their days, a natural rhythm of labour and of rest as unhurried yet deliberate as the burgeoning of spring.

GUILLOTINE GATE, OLD SHREWSBURY CANAL

Chapter XXX

NORBURY, NEWPORT AND 'CUT END'

OWING to unfavourable weather, we remained moored for a day at Cheswardine, but the next morning broke fine, and we then made short work of the seven-and-a-half-mile level to Norbury Junction, which we reached soon after noon, in ample time to visit the nearby town of Newport for supplies. We passed through an undulating, sparsely populated countryside, densely wooded cuttings alternating with high embankments—or 'valleys', as the boatmen call them—which afforded us wide views across the plain to westward. Shebdon was the only village we passed, but there were several canal-side inns, a feature with which the Shropshire Union main line seems uncommonly well supplied.

Norbury is the junction of the Newport and Old Shrewsbury Canal Branch, a waterway that is on our list for future exploration, not only because it passes through the heart of a lovely rural district in the Vale of Shrewsbury, but because it is in many ways unique. It is twenty-five miles long, falling to Newport by a flight of eighteen locks, and then proceeding by Wappenshall Junction, through Berwick Tunnel to Shrewsbury Basin. At Wappenshall the disused Shropshire Tub Boat Canal commenced. These tub boats measured about twenty feet in length by six feet two inches

beam, and carried five tons. They were horse-drawn in trains of
as many as twenty at a time, the boatman in charge steering by
the rudimentary method of keeping the leading boat in the centre
of the channel by means of a long shaft from the towing-path. At
Trench, two miles from Wappenshall, they were hauled up one of
the earliest inclined plane lifts in the country. It was two hundred
and twenty-seven yards long, with a vertical rise of seventy-three
feet, the ascending and descending trolleys drawn by wire cables,
each carrying one tub.

According to the dimensions given by Bradshaw's guide, the
nine hundred and seventy-yard tunnel at Berwick must be the
most restricted of any in England, being only seven feet in width
by six feet high. It must also have been the scene of even fiercer
disputes than those which took place in the early days at Harecastle, for Mr. de Salis adds the following note:

'There are no fixed hours for boats to pass through the tunnel.
There is a white mark in the middle of the tunnel, and should two
boats meet, the one who has reached the middle of the tunnel first
has the right of way.'

The two locks at Eyton, a mile or so west of Wappenshall, are
also unique. They have lower gates of the very rare 'Guillotine'
type, which open vertically, and the chambers, though only six feet
four inches wide, were made over eighty feet long, to pass four
tub boats at a time. If these dimensions hold good today, 'Cressy',
with her beam of seven feet, would not pass through, and furthermore we heard reports that the canal beyond Newport was in
a derelict state. On the other hand, a travelling maintenance
engineer whom we met at Basin End told us he had taken his boat
through Berwick Tunnel earlier in the year. We resolved one day
to settle the truth of these conflicting reports.

At Norbury, as at Fradley, the village proper was some little
distance away from the canal, and a second community had
grown up, grouped around the wide basin where a roving bridge
carried the towing-path of the main canal over the mouth of the
branch. These included 'The Junction Inn', several cottages, and
the extensive workshops and yards which form the southern head-
quarters of the canal company. Here were stored all the materials
necessary for canal repairs—piles of bricks, clay puddle and
gravel, ironwork and spare beams for the locks. Here, too, the
captains of maintenance boats reported for orders.

The surrounding country looked prosperous enough, and we

expected to find Newport as flourishing a market town as Market Drayton. At first sight its wide main street of tall and gracious Queen Anne or Georgian houses certainly seemed to confirm this expectation, but on closer acquaintance they revealed an air of slightly faded decadence, like that of an out-at-elbows aristocrat, a melancholy such as pervades the Regency crescents and terraces of Bath. The shop windows looked shoddy and fly-blown, and even the inhabitants seemed to share in the general lassitude. Many healthy country towns may be described as sleepy when their quiet streets drowse in the sun of a summer afternoon, but at Newport this sleep seemed near to death. I know not what the reason for this may be, but I suspect that the younger generation have migrated to the industrial districts of Wolverhampton, Stafford or the Potteries, leaving Newport to the old and their memories.

No matter where you may be in this part of Shropshire, the Wrekin dominates the landscape, for it is to the yeomen of the Shropshire plain what Beeston is to the Cheshire men: a landmark, a beacon, and barometer. One day a dim cloud on the horizon as blue and remote as the skies, the next a stark outline of crystal clarity, at other times capped with cloud or altogether veiled by mist and rain, this solitary mountain is the farmer's unfailing weather prophet. Like all outliers, it has a trick of changing its shape in the most bewildering fashion as one moves about the plain. To some districts it presents a long and irregular whale-back of woods, but crossing the lofty 'valley' beyond Norbury the next morning we sighted it for the first time as it should be seen: a precipitous, perfectly conical shape as forbidding as a solitary volcano. It was indistinct, being covered by a drab grey veil which boded rain later, a forecast that was subsequently fulfilled.

Spending the greater part of our days in the open, we discovered that we were beginning to acquire something of the countryman's sense of the weather, which springs from the almost subconscious observance of subtle changes in the quality of the atmosphere, of cloud formation and movement, and of veering winds. Such a gift is only within the reach of those who lead an open-air life, so that it is yet another heritage of the past which the townsman has lost.

Passing through the village of Gnosall (pronounced Nawzall by the boatmen), we entered another of the chasm-like cuttings which are the dominant feature of this canal. In places the rock sides fell sheer to the water's edge, the streamers of ground ivy a living arras upon them. Here, too, was the short Cowley Tunnel, the only one on the canal.

At Wheaton Aston we came to the solitary lock in an otherwise unbroken level of twenty-five miles, while around Brewood and Deans Hall there were extensive parks of fine timber and dense coverts which crowded close to the water. Notices forbade landing and threatened trespassing boatmen with dire penalties, for the plump, reared pheasants, as tame as chickens, that strutted unconcernedly on the banks were easy and tempting game.

Considering their unrivalled opportunities, it is small wonder that many boat captains are accomplished poachers, and I do not blame them. I know of more than one who habitually carries a gun in his cabin, and nearly all boat-dogs are accomplished hunters and retrievers. Since most horse boatmen carry long whips, which they crack resoundingly as they stand at the tiller if the horse should lag, it is easy enough to cover the report of a small gun such as a four-ten. Fishing with rod and line is usually permissible, provided the boatman remains on his boat, but since few have sufficient leisure to indulge in this pastime, they resort to the less legal methods of the spinner or the night-line.

The only fishermen we met on the Shropshire Canal were herons and kingfishers, especially the latter. Every copse and spinny that we passed seemed to harbour at least one of these vivid birds. The brilliant iridescent blue of their plumage against the russet background of late autumn made a contrast so tropically extravagant that the sight provoked a shock of surprise such as one would feel were some exotic orchid or hibiscus to appear growing by the margin. Like the herons, the kingfishers sometimes fished the water ahead of us, but adopted different tactics, darting low over the surface in mid-stream and falling with a splash upon their prey, like a swallow dipping for a floating fly. One morning early we heard an unfamiliar high-pitched chattering, more like the squeaking of rats than the sound of a bird, and, looking out, saw a pair of them perched upon our bow mooring-line.

As the afternoon wore on the country around us began to assume the desolate, blackened look we had now come to know so well. Sure enough the tall chimney-stacks on the outskirts of Wolverhampton came in sight as we drew clear of the woods of Chillington Park, and the remaining three miles of the 'Shroppie' to Autherley led us into a veritable no-man's-land. The water became black with pollution, there was a desolate swamp upon either hand and, as if this were not enough, it began to rain heavily from a leaden sky.

At Autherley stop lock—or 'Cut End', as the boatmen call it—the Shropshire Canal terminates in a junction with the Staffordshire and Worcestershire, usually more briefly referred to as the 'Stour Cut'. When I walked into the toll office beside the lock to pay my dues, my spirits, somewhat damped by the weather, were revived no little by the toll clerk's greeting. Though I had never set eyes on him in my life, he jumped from his stool with a hearty 'How are you?', clapping me on the shoulder and wringing me by the hand as though I were his prodigal son or had just made a solo crossing of the Atlantic.

When we had obtained the necessary passes we lost no time in mooring up just beyond the mouth of the junction, and were glad to draw curtains and light lamps, shutting out our wet and dreary surroundings. On referring to Bradshaw later that evening, I confirmed the fact that we had made our longest day's run, of fifteen and a half miles.

Chapter XXXI

'THE STOUR CUT'

OUR shortest route southward to Oxford from Wolverhampton would have been to have joined the Birmingham Canal, main line, at Aldersley Junction, half a mile south of Autherley. This would have brought us to the northern terminus of the Grand Union at Digbeth, and so via Warwick to the Oxford Canal at Napton. Not only would this have involved traversing the entire length of the Black Country, however, but the lockage would have been extremely heavy, there being no less than eighty-four in all between Aldersley and Napton. Yet another alternative was to take the Hatherton branch of the Stafford and Worcester, and so by way of the Wyrley and Essington Canal to join the Coventry Canal at Huddlesford Junction near Lichfield. In this case again the lockage over Cannock Chase would be heavy and the region dolorous, so we decided to skirt the fringe of the whole industrial region by turning northwards once more to Great Haywood, and from thence to retrace our tracks as far as Fradley. Though the mileage was greater, the lockage was reduced by half, and the way promised to be of greater interest.

Though it was blowing half a gale the next morning, we decided to struggle on at all costs rather than spend the day in such dismal surroundings. The wind was coming off the tow-path dead on our beam, so Angela walked ahead with a bow-line to keep 'Cressy' from being blown onto the mud until we gained the welcome lee of a cutting so narrow that passing places had been cut into the banks at intervals. Thereafter we travelled better than we had expected, thanks mainly to the shelter afforded by high hedges and to the fact that the canal was much deeper than the muddy waterways of Shropshire. It was a welcome change to be back once more on an old canal with its tantalising twists and turns. A unique feature were the old brick bridges, which were not merely numbered, but bore, on weathered cast-iron plaques, such intriguing names as Mops Farm, Moat House, Long Moll's and Hazlestrine.

We were congratulating ourselves on having successfully shaken off the purlieus of Wolverhampton, having passed the junction of the Hatherton branch five miles from Autherley, when, at an acute turn, a violent gust caught us fairly broadside to sweep us uncontrollably on to the bank, where we landed, not upon mud, but on a rocky bottom with a most alarming series of bumps. It took us an hour of bitter struggling with both bow and stern lines ashore to haul 'Cressy' into the shelter of a bridge-hole a hundred yards ahead. We then tried again, but at Calf Heath Bridge, half a mile beyond, despite all our efforts, the wind, now risen to a gale force, beat us again. It drove us onto the tow-path side, where we should have fouled the navigation, and so great was its force on our cabin side that it was all we could do to shaft across and moor securely on the opposite bank. This we eventually managed, using double lines fore and aft, those aft round the trunk of a convenient thorn bush, the forrard ones to both our mooring spikes. Even so these were nearly torn out of the ground during the night. It had been an unusually hard day, but this only made it more enjoyable to settle down for a comfortable evening by the fireside while the wind boomed impotently outside.

The gale spent itself before dawn, and we awoke to see sunlight patterning our cabin roof with light. The previous day having been a Sunday, we had met no traffic, but now we heard the sound of hooves and creak of tackle from the tow-path. We looked out, to see the first 'Day Boats' we had so far encountered.

These craft, sometimes called 'Open Boats', are used for short-distance traffic, the boatmen who work them plying continuously to and fro, spending no time at the wharves in loading or unloading, but picking up a different boat. They carry no sleeping accommodation, being either quite open or having a diminutive cabin to provide shelter for meals in inclement weather. These particular examples were working between the Wolverhampton area and the Cannock Colliery wharves at Rodbaston near Gailey. Although most of them were extremely dirty, and carried little or no paint-work, their construction was interesting, for, unlike the long-distance narrow boats, they were built with completely square bilges, a taller towing mast and a very primitive type of cut-water bow. They resembled minutely the boats appearing in Percival Skelton's illustrations to the early editions of Smiles' 'Lives of the Engineers', and therefore may well be survivals of the canal boat in its original form.

In view of the perfect morning, we lost no time in getting under way, and were soon taking our turn to lock down through the busy locks at Gailey. A hundred yards or so beyond the tail of Rod-baston Lock we passed the coal wharf where the Day Boats were loading, and entered upon one of the most interesting stages of the whole journey.

One Day Boat still makes a weekly journey with coal to the Stafford Salt Works, but otherwise this northern section of the canal to its terminus at Great Haywood is virtually disused, except on rare occasions when through traffic is diverted owing to a stop-page on the Shropshire Union route. The towing-path, up till now a wide, miry track, suddenly became a field path, narrow and over-grown, while the canal itself underwent a similar transformation, resembling the reedy channel of the Leicester canal. The sides of the locks were matted with weeds and coarse grasses, the paddle-gears on their gates dry and rusty from little use. Willows long unpolled stretched their branches so far and low over the water that Angela's bicycle was swept from the deck to hang precariously by one pedal from the cant rail. It was just after we had retrieved this misfortune that we sighted 'The Cross Keys', a little lost canal inn standing amid the fields beside the tow-path. Its windows seemed to be gazing over the water with pathetic expectancy for boats which never came, so that we had not the heart to pass it by. Sitting on a bench in the sun before the door, we talked with the landlord while we drank a glass of his mild. Trade had been brisk, he recalled wistfully, until the traffic had passed to the Shropshire Canal, and he remembered the time when never a night passed by but several boatmen would moor by the door and lead their horses to his stable. 'A jolly lot they were,' he said, 'and rare times we had when they got in here of an evening a-singing and playing.' Now he had made the best of new manners and changing fortunes by letting out his field to campers from the Black Country during the summer months, but in the winter, he confessed with a shake of his head, he 'kept very quiet'.

Half a mile from 'The Cross Keys', through Filance Lock, we came to the village of Penkridge, where we paused again, this time to lay in stores at the village shop. What we saw of the place from the canal was pleasant enough, but the road traveller sees a very different picture. For it has the misfortune to lie on the main road from Wolverhampton to the Potteries and Manchester. The narrow main street was no match for the great Leylands and Scammels which shook the old houses to their foundations, so progress has blasted a bleak three-track motor road through the heart of Penkridge, and yet another English village has been laid waste to save minutes.

When we were ready to cast off again the sun had gone in, and we travelled on through one of those grey and windless afternoons peculiar to the Indian summer of late autumn, when the richly scented air is still mild and so calm that the eye can detect no movement of faded leaf or reed blade, while even the birds are still and silent. On such a day all Nature, save only restless man, seems to pause from the endless labour of the seasons, as though to gather strength to face the winter.

Though it would have been a lovely journey at any season, the country through which we passed appeared at its best advantage in this calm, sunless weather. Our course lay between the marshes of the little river Penk and the dark woods of Teddesley Park, which swept down from the slopes of Cannock on our right. Nowhere, either upon the long levels of the marsh or in the dense coverts which pressed close to the water's edge, was there sign or movement of any living thing, so that 'Cressy', slowly gliding over the mirror-like surface of the water, seemed an intruder in some forbidden sanctuary, and the road she travelled some forgotten river backwater instead of a man-made canal.

We returned to the workaday world when we cleared the sheltering trees of the park, for at the hamlet of Acton Trussell a woman in a bright printed apron was feeding her chickens, and a cowman was calling his herd to the evening milking with a 'Come hup!' and a melodious 'Hi ho!'

This day's journey came to an end when we moored by the bridge called Roseford under Acton Hill, the sky clearing towards sunset and the night starlit.

The next day proved a contrast, for never before had we seen so many birds as haunted the marshlands between Deptmore Lock and Haywood. Not only were there our old friends kingfisher, heron, swan, coot and moorhen, but snipe darting away in swift, flickering flight, and wild duck breaking suddenly from the reeds by the margin with a startled whirr of wings. We had not gone far before we were joined by an escort of swans, which swam steadily before us for over two miles. If I speeded up 'Cressy' they immediately responded by paddling more furiously, clinging desperately to their precious dignity, but at last they tired of the relentless pursuit and, taking to the air with turbulent commotion, circled over our heads, their great wings making a rhythmic drumming sound.

Having followed the Penk to its confluence with the Sow near Stafford, the canal, which had up to now been heading almost due north, swung abruptly south-eastwards to follow the Sow valley, thus circling the high ground which marched continuously on the right bank. At this turning point was the blocked-up mouth of the old Stafford Branch, and also the Stafford Salt Works, where we saw the solitary Day Boat unloading its weekly cargo, and knew that we were entering deserted waters. Even on the canals where it is a common occurrence to travel all day without meeting another boat there is an added sense of satisfaction to be derived from navigating a disused water-way.

If any proof were needed that we were the first boat to cover the four miles from Baswich to Haywood for many months, it was the dense patch of weed which we struck near Lodgefield Bridge. Fortunately it did not extend very far, for it was a veritable Sargasso, so dense and deep that although we entered it at a good pace, 'Cressy' rapidly lost way, and only just reached clear water without assistance.

At Milford, beneath the shadow of the Milford Hills, we crossed the river by an old stone-built aqueduct of the familiar Brindley construction, and approached the last lock on the canal, Old Hill or Tixall. The lock-keeper was busy on the tow-path trimming the hedge, but as we hove in sight round the bend he dropped his bill and ran back to the lock as fast as his elderly legs would carry him. No wonder the passage of a boat through Tixall Lock was something of a major event, for we were the first, he said, for six months. He insisted upon working the lock for us, which was probably all to the good, since the lower gates were so decrepit that they looked in imminent danger of collapse and leaked so badly that the lock chamber had half emptied before he had had time to draw the paddles. He assured us, not without

'DESERTED WATERS'

pride, that one gate at least was over thirty years old, and we saw no reason to doubt it.

If we had been struck by the beauty of Great Haywood when we came to it by the Trent and Mersey Canal, the approach from this direction surpassed it. Coming round a bend below the tail of the lock the canal broadened unexpectedly, so that we found ourselves sailing out into a long lake fringed by tall flags and dotted with hundreds of coot and moorhen. Though the water was very deep, it was of such remarkable crystal clarity that, looking down from the deck, I could see every pebble on the bottom, and the full shape of our hull. In this way we came to the Junction by the familiar, graceful bridge, drifting slowly across this still expanse of water which might well have been that magic mere whence Bedivere flung Excalibur, the lazy ripples from our screw dying long before they reached its borders.

On the crest of a park-like slope overlooking this lake we had noticed a curious building, which we took to be Tixall Hall, so, as there were some hours of daylight left when we had moored by the Junction, we set out on foot to explore. What we had seen turned out to be merely the enormous gatehouse, a most fearsome example of Strawberry Hill Gothic. Its three-storeyed façade gaped with great stone mullions, while over the archway plump nude figures reclined in voluptuous abandonment. Behind this monstrosity lay a vast barrack of stabling in the shape of a rotunda, but of the house itself not a stone remained. Assuming the gatehouse to have been but an insignificant foretaste of things to come, I shudder to contemplate what the hall must have looked like, for as an example of the grotesque caricatures which resulted from self-conscious architects' attempts to recreate the purity of mediaeval Gothic, the gatehouse of Tixall could scarcely be surpassed. Its floors are missing, and the great open fireplaces, one above the other, yawn into space, but we climbed a spiral stairway in one of the turrets and, standing on the 'battlements' gazed out across the slope of the park, over the canal to the wooded heights of the Satnall Hills, where, sure enough, stood the inevitable 'whimsy' without which no eighteenth-century 'vista' was complete. It also was evident that the canal had been bidden to conceal its commercial origin and masquerade as a lake to placate the vanished lord of Tixall.

Descending, we walked back to the boat, through the gathering dusk. Along the water-side the coot were clucking and calling to each other, setting the tall rushes waving as they scurried to their shelter.

Chapter XXXII

LICHFIELD AND THE COVENTRY CANAL

THE Coventry Canal has had a very chequered history. Its construction was authorised by Parliament in 1768, James Brindley being appointed engineer, but unfortunately the capital of the company proved quite inadequate if the work was to be carried out according to his plans, so, having constructed the first fourteen miles from Coventry to Atherstone, he threw up his appointment, lest it should bring his name into discredit. The canal remained in this unfinished state for many years, until at last, in 1785, the Birmingham and Fazeley and the Grand Trunk Companies between them completed the section from Atherstone to Fradley Junction. The fortunes of the Coventry Company then improved sufficiently to enable them to purchase that portion constructed by the Grand Trunk from Fradley to Whittington Brook near Lichfield, but the remaining five and a half miles from the latter place to Fazeley is still owned by the Birmingham Canal Company, so that through traffic has to pay two tolls. This is only one instance of the complicated toll payments which beset the long-distance canal trader and constitute one of the reasons why canal transport has declined. It is significant that the railway companies, who have long ago set their own house in order by means of the railway clearing house, have done nothing to remedy this state of affairs on the many canals which they own.

Having made our way without incident down the familiar length of the Trent and Mersey from Great Haywood, we moored for a night beside 'The Swan' at Fradley Junction before embarking once more on strange waters. Strange indeed they proved to be, for on the little-used section as far as Fazeley the mud banks on the turns were quite the worst we had encountered. A pair of loaded 'Joshers' travelling south from Manchester which preceded us proved that laden craft can navigate successfully, albeit slowly, but we were lucky not to meet any boats while we were on the way, as in many places passing would have been extremely difficult.

We had not been travelling long before our old enemy the wind got up, making navigation so difficult that by midday we decided to abandon further progress before we became badly stranded, and moored at Huddlesford, the junction of the Wyrley and Essington Canal, in sight of the spires of Lichfield.

Curiously enough, Lichfield was the only cathedral town we visited on our travels, if one excludes Leicester, whose parish church of St. Martin has only been raised to the dignity of a cathedral in recent years. The birthplace of Samuel Johnson, Lichfield is in theory a market town, but the open market which we saw in the square under the statue of the immortal doctor can have been but the poor shadow of its former self. The industrial development of Cannock has taken its inevitable toll of the town and the country around it, nor are matters improved by the heavy traffic of Rykneld Street which thunders by, shaking the old houses to their foundations. Nevertheless a great deal that is old and graceful still survives, while once away from the din of the lorries one is made aware of that particular atmosphere of enduring peace and tranquility which seems to permeate the very stones of a cathedral town. This ageless quality was particularly strong in the cathedral close, reminiscent of Salisbury, where gracious houses of every age overlook the trim grass quadrangle where stands the great church. Places such as this are backwaters in time, surviving in a frenzied age to speak of a more ordered world than ours. Standing upon this green while rooks cawed in the trees and high overhead the bells chimed the quarters in leisured repetition, the mind saw gardeners in green baize aprons pruning roses, the dean at tea upon the lawn, and heard the click of phantom croquet mallets.

The general proportions of the cathedral are magnificent, the triple spires from a distance a beautiful example of the soaring majesty that can be achieved in stone, but on closer approach the eye is distracted from its appreciation of the grace of the general form by the over-elaboration of detail decoration. Particularly is this true of the West Front, where a multiplicity of image niches, many containing inferior reproductions of the original occupants, are reminiscent of an overburdened corner of some museum. Yet when it is realised that Lichfield suffered more than any other church in England at the hands of the Puritans, having already survived the usual vicissitudes at the Dissolution, it must be admitted that the restorers have displayed far more than the average good taste. Cromwell's cannon shot down the central tower, the great bells were broken, even the lead was stripped from the roofs, while large portions of the fabric were pulled down and sold piecemeal. When at the Restoration of Charles II the work of rebuilding was begun, there were only two of the original Cathedral body left to remember its former glory, Canon William Higgins, the Precentor, and the Subchanter, who went by the curious name of Zachariah Turnpenny. Soon after, the celebrated Bishop Hackett joined forces with them, and it is to the energy of this devoted trio that the credit for the reconstruction must largely be due.

Unfortunately, the Victorians, as usual, have had their innings, their most noticeable contribution being the ornate reredos of polished stone behind the high altar, which was the work of Sir Gilbert Scott, and certainly in no way enhances the view of the east end from the nave. The eye is soon lifted up to higher and better things, however, for the great east window and those of the Lady Chapel are aglow with superb sixteenth-century glass which originally graced the Cistercian Abbey at Herckenrode. I have seen no finer glass than this, and to compare it with the modern painted windows in the choir aisles is to realise that the making of coloured glass is yet another of our lost arts.

The other feature of the Cathedral which particularly attracted us was the Chapter House. It is a ten-sided building with a very fine vaulted roof supported by a single central column which reveals in a most striking manner the individuality of the mediaeval stonemason. For it is obviously the work of four men, each of whom adopted a distinctive design for his particular portion of the richly carved abacus from which the ten shafts of the vaulting spring. The result of such independence might well have been chaotic, yet such was the comeliness of their communal thought that the result is perfectly harmonious. Thus this column constitutes a perfect vindication of the infallible 'rightness' of all true craftsmanship.

One of the corbels which support the roof-ribs represents a cowled monk whose features, grinning sardonically, are turned away from the Chapter House table. Thereby hangs a tale, for this stone head, carved with great vigour and skill, commemorates the differences which long existed between the rival chapters, secular and monastic, of Lichfield and Coventry over the right of electing Bishops to the See. So corrupt did the monastic order become that upon one famous occasion when Coventry held the privilege, and a newly elected bishop, who was known to have obtained office by graft, arrived at Lichfield, the dean and chapter exercised their little-known right and closed the great west doors in his face. Today these disputes are long forgotten, and the chapter controls the largest diocese in England, while only a monk of stone averts his ageless face from their council table.

Owing to the continuing high wind we lay for a whole day at Huddlesford before moving on through a dreary country of sodden, neglected pastures in the valley of the river Tame. We were now heading due south, having followed different river valleys round three sides of Cannock. For a short distance our surroundings improved as we passed along the steeply sloping flank of Hopwas Hays wood, with the river directly below us, but the blackened village of Hopwas just beyond proclaimed only too clearly that we were now on the very edge of the Black Country. Half an hour later we sighted the tower of Tamworth church beside the great sandstone block of the de Frevilles' Norman castle, and so came to Fazeley, the junction of the Birmingham Canal, and a drab village on Watling Street, where we made a brief stop to buy supplies. Journeying on again, we soon entered Warwickshire by an aqueduct over the Tame, and worked our way up the two locks at Glascote, where we paid our Birmingham Canal toll. We were now in a dour neighbourhood of chimney-stacks and sprawling tenements, so that the sight of an old friend, the 'Captain Cook', one of the familiar Oxford Canal traders, lying newly painted in Samuel Barlow's dockyard, was as welcome and unexpected as flowers in December. It was good to see once more the bright profusion of roses and castles on her cabin sides, and the vivid diamond work of mast and cratches. Actually it turned out that 'Captain Cook' was only the first of many, in fact the whole of this next and somewhat sombre stage of our journey from Glascote to Hawkesbury was lightened by the beauty and variety of the boats we met.

They were changing shifts at the collieries round Amington and Alvecote above the locks, for we met many pitmen trudging home by twos and threes along the tow-path, their faces so blackened with coal-dust and sweat that as they turned to grin at us teeth and eyeballs flashed like those of a coon at a seaside concert party. We passed through the heart of some of these pits, between barren shale-tips, rows of 'tubs', spinning headgears and basins where boats were loading. On every hand the land had been laid waste by subsidences, pastures had become reedy swamps of stagnant water, while such farm buildings as remained stood empty and were fast falling to ruin. What we could not see, but could picture most vividly, was the inhuman darkness of the narrow galleries below, the heat, the choking dust and the din of the coal-cutting machines, the hell below earth that the demand for power has created.

That night we lay at Pooley Hall, where this new world met the old. They stood side by side on the canal bank, a colliery wreathed in steam and smoke, and the crumbling, battlemented tower of the old hall. The tower returned the blank stare of the tall windows of the winding house from arrow slits that were like eyes veiled with mistrust.

Throughout the next day our course lay along the valley of the Anker to Atherstone, where we stopped to replenish our fuel tanks. Atherstone is an old market town which has suffered inevitably from its situation on the Watling Street and its proximity to Birmingham, or 'Birnigum' as the boat people call the canal centre of England. As a result the town appears to derive more of its revenue from 'commercial gentlemen' than from the farmer, for, as though determined to carve a particular niche for itself in the complex structure of industrial development that was springing up on every side, Atherstone now manufactures bowler hats in prodigious quantities. Peering through the dusty windows of warehouses, we could see enough to supply a generation of salesmen.

The flight of twelve locks here were quite the slowest filling of any we had encountered. We had ascended seven before going into the town, and on our return we decided to push on through the remaining five before dark, so that we would have a clear run before us the next morning. We thought we should accomplish this easily, but by the time we moored at the summit night had fallen, and our tea was therefore somewhat belated.

Later that evening in the inn whose windows overlooked our

moorings we fell into conversation with two boatmen, and the talk turned to the subject of donkeys—or 'animals', as they are called on the canals. Once they were used extensively, a pair to a single boat, but now to the best of my knowledge this practice is extinct. They appear to have been most favoured by boatmen on the Worcester and Birmingham Canal, but since this is a waterway which 'Cressy' has not yet visited, I do not know whether any still survive. There seems to be no good reason for their extinction, as all boatmen agree that they were good workers, long lived, extremely hardy and cheap, because they would eat almost anything. I had previously enquired of canal folk in many parts of the country whether any donkeys were still in use, but received, as on this occasion, a negative reply, followed by a flood of reminiscence. The latter inevitably included reference to a certain boatman who had worked over the 'Stour Cut' with a pair of 'animals', the stories of his exploits being so widespread over the waterways that it seemed he was rapidly becoming a legendary figure. The lockkeeper at Tixall had spoken of him, and now in this inn at Atherstone we heard the same feats recounted.

'A great strong chap he was. Why, when these animals of his got a bit tired like he'd lift 'em aboard and haul the boat hisself for a mile or two.' Or again: 'One winter he was iced up for so long Stourport way he was spent up and had to sell 'em to make out. So he bow hauled for a trip or two that time till he'd made enough to buy 'em back.'

Just before we cast away the next morning one of our friends of the previous night passed us with the most resplendent pair of newly painted boats we had yet seen, the motor 'Forget-me-not' and the butty 'Sarah Jane' of Leighton Buzzard, southward bound with coal. Needless to say, they were 'Number Ones', and it was heartening to see that their captain, who was inordinately proud of them, was a young man still in his twenties.

The steep hill ridge which marches beside the right bank of the canal from Atherstone to Nuneaton has been so eroded by granite quarries that its profile has become a succession of beetling rock faces and towering waste-heaps. Every now and again minute locomotives and rows of tipping wagons appeared in sharp silhouette on their high skyline, and we heard repeatedly the deep, reverberating thud of blasting. So great is the concussion of these blasts, particularly in the neighbourhood of Tuttle Hill, that the quarrying companies are constantly paying compensation to the local inhabitants for broken crockery or window-panes.

Nuneaton, with its adjoining suburb of Chilvers Coton, presented us with the worst example of suburban jerry-building we had seen, a desert of mediocrity which terminated finally in the first canal-side inn, which we had no hesitation whatsoever in passing by. A dingy building of sooty-grey stucco, it announced in gilt letters a foot high that it was 'Ye Olde Wharfe Inne', thus carrying the 'old-world' fetish to the ultimate limit of absurdity.

Continuing without pause until we had left this cheerless region well astern, we passed the junction of the Ashby-de-la-Zouch canal at Marston, and moored for lunch at a more honest inn at Bedworth which overlooked a busy wharf where many boats were loading coal from the neighbouring collieries. Here we found a very patriarch among boatmen. Retired now, he sat yarning with his late companions in the bar, wearing a shiny peaked cap and an old reefer jacket. Though he looked a vigorous sixty, he was actually seventy-nine years old, and since the death of his sister at the age of ninety-eight he had lived quite alone in the cottage next door, where they had both been born. This cottage, it transpired, had been scheduled for demolition under the Slum Clearance Act, for the veteran related with great gusto how he had dealt with the inspector who had visited them. ' "We'll walk straight down into t'cut fust', I told en; "for we was born 'ere, an' we means to die 'ere." That touched en, see,' the old man explained triumphantly, and the upshot was that the cottage was to stand for the remainder of his days. In the course of fifty years a-boating he had 'buried three wives i' different parts o' the country'. This and a deal more he told us, but his speech was so broad that at times it was extremely difficult to follow. It abounded in quaint turns of phrase most apt and rich, such as 'billy-bally work' to describe the arduous yet delicate task of unloading a fragile cargo of bricks, and when he at last rose to go, it was with a 'Good day to you, good people' that he bade us farewell.

Just as we were leaving Bedworth we met the wife of the captain of the 'Franklin', a boat we had last seen at 'The Bull and Butcher' at Napton. From her we learned that a tragedy had taken place on the morning after our last meeting. Her husband had been taken seriously ill while they were ascending Napton Locks, and had died in his cabin before a doctor could reach him. Though we could do no more than express conventional sympathy, it was with a genuine feeling of regret that I learned of his passing, for he was a quiet, kindly man whom I had come to know well during my long stay at Banbury. No doubt he had been born in a boat cabin, lived all his days upon the water, and would have chosen no other place in which to die. There was consolation in the thought of this hard yet simple life ending as it had begun.

Chapter XXXIII

THE OXFORD CANAL AGAIN

THOUGH it continued for a further five and a half miles to its terminus in Coventry basin, we came to the end of our journey over the Coventry Canal when we reached its junction with the Oxford Canal at Hawkesbury. The early engineers seem to have constructed canal junctions with a blissful disregard for the length of the boats which would have to negotiate them, for with a few rare exceptions they are so acute that boats must needs be checked round with lines from the shore. In this respect Hawkesbury Junction was even worse than most, the two canals actually running parallel with each other for a little distance, only a few yards apart, before being connected by an acute hairpin turn beneath a roving bridge. This presented us with a nice little problem in navigation, and as our approach was watched with curiosity by the crews of several moored boats, we were particularly anxious to give a good account of ourselves. The fates usually ordain that such circumstances lead to some humiliating fiasco, but on this occasion we were lucky. By putting 'Cressy' alternately ahead and astern and at the same time using the rudder as a paddle to swing her stern, we came about in fine style, without having to use lines or shafts.

When we had paid our dues to Oxford in the toll office beside the stop lock, it was a relief to find ourselves heading for open country once more, after so many miles on the sooty fringes of the Black Country, and that night we moored at Ansty, the first purely agricultural village we had seen since we left Fradley. There is a considerable traffic over this northern section of the Oxford Canal, so much so that 'Cressy', disturbed by the wash of passing boats, carried away the seemingly substantial fence post to which we had moored her bow and swung broadside across the water during the night. The first we knew of this was when we were awakened in the early hours of the morning by the urgent siren of an approaching Grand Union boat.

The original course of the canal from Hawkesbury to Napton as laid out by Brindley was even more roundabout than the summit section from Marston Doles to Claydon is today, but in 1820 new cuts were made to avoid these detours, with the result that the total length of the canal has been reduced by no less than thirteen miles. So tortuous was the old canal around Brinklow that it was a well-known saying among the boatmen which has come down through successive generations to the present day that 'You could travel all day within sound of Brinklow clock'. As we traversed the 'new' embankments and cuttings, which were reminiscent of the Shropshire Union, the old waterway crossed and re-crossed our course, winding away over the fields, in places a barely discernible depression of the ground, in others still a reedy bed spanned by a crumbling brick bridge.

For some years after the improved canal was cut, sections of the old remained navigable in the guise of short branches to the neighbouring villages, but with the decline of short-distance traffic these, too, have fallen to ruin. One of these was the branch to Brinklow, and just beyond its reed-grown entrance in a wooded cutting by the park of Newbold Revel we moored and walked into the village. Brinklow's single main street of great length, in places bordered by a strip of greensward, is characteristic of the district, and the heterogeneous rank of houses of every style, age and material somehow contrive to mix passably well with one another. This gently sloping street was overlooked at its upper end by one of the largest castle mounds, circled by a double moat, that I have ever seen. Of its history we could discover nothing, but, since it stands on the Fosse Way, the Romans no doubt made use of it. The church at the foot of this mound had image niches let into the angles of the tower, and within the remains of a stone stairway by the chancel arch which evidently once gave access to a vanished rood screen. We subsequently discovered that these two features were to be found in many churches in this neighbourhood. Much more remarkable was the floor of the nave and chancel, which sloped steeply upwards to the altar, to produce an effect that was most curious and, in my experience, unique. No doubt the reason was simply a structural one, although the old lady who was busily dusting the pews had other and more startling ideas. "Twas the battle as done it,' she declared, jerking her head in the direction of the castle mound. 'Back in the old days, so they say.' But how a mediaeval battle achieved this remarkable result, and who 'they' were she did not explain.

A fine rain began to fall as we were walking back to the boat with some jars of honey which we had bought from a bee-keeper in the village, so we decided to journey no farther that day. The next morning dawned fine, however, and the strong wind which had swept away the rain-clouds gave us little trouble, as the canal was for the most part sheltered by tall hedgerows which seemed purposely to have been left unlaid to afford a wind-break. These were covered with a prodigal crop of scarlet hips and haws, on which scores of bullfinches were feeding. We had never before seen so many of these lovely birds. Travelling well, we reached Newbold-upon-Avon by noon, having passed through the short tunnel of that name. Newbold is a pleasant village, but unfortunately it is rapidly becoming a suburb of Rugby, for it stands on high ground overlooking its ugly neighbour, whose outskirts are relentlessly advancing up the slope towards it. We ate a simple lunch of bread and cheese at the sign of 'The Boat' by the canal side, a sign representing a narrow boat on the move which did the brewers concerned, a Leamington firm, great credit. In some quarters there is evidence such as this that the neglected art of the inn sign is being belatedly revived, some more enlightened brewers, notably Messrs. Flowers of Stratford-on-Avon, having accomplished much in recent years. Evidently it is dawning upon the brewers' commercial mind that the average countryman goes to the village inn because he is thirsty and because he wishes to gossip with his neighbours, and therefore that to advertise their beer in foot-high letters across the outside walls is not merely unsightly, but expensive and ineffectual.

The most notable feature of the red sandstone church at Newbold are the memorials of the Boughton family. They are inescapable, because the church is full of them, and they constitute a striking commentary on the transition of style and taste through the ages. The fifteenth-century knight and his lady lie side by side, he in his full plate armour, she in weeds and coif, their simplicity and the calm repose of their features eloquent of dignity. Near by the smaller painted figure of their be-ruffled Tudor descendant kneels with his wife and children, a monument more stylised and naïve, but no less sincere. Finally, occupying a considerable area of the small chancel, there stands the ornate marble memorial to the eighteenth-century scion of the house. This life-size figure, with pupil-less eyes blankly staring, and looking, in its studied pose, lifeless and empty of all feeling, surmounts a plinth whereon his manifold virtues are described at fulsome length. It is a wonder the armoured knight does not arise lance in hand to tumble this pompous popinjay from his pedestal of conceit.

Passing northwards of Rugby and crossing the valleys of the Swift and Avon, we came that afternoon to the three locks at Hillmorton, where stand the tall steel masts of the Post Office transatlantic beam. Dusk found us crossing a wilderness of flat scrub pasture-land, which, on referring to my map, I found to be the edge of Dunsmore Heath, and it was in this desolate place, under the meagre shelter of a row of stunted thorn bushes, that we moored for the night in a rising gale. It blew so hard overnight that 'Cressy' uprooted both her mooring spikes and drifted astern for over two hundred yards, fortunately without swinging across the channel or doing any damage.

We had been travelling for little over two hours the next morning before we sighted the familiar spire of Braunston church perched upon its hill, and so, at the junction of the Grand Union Canal, we completed the second loop of the huge figure of eight in which we had travelled round the Midlands of England. We did not care that from this point onwards as far as Banbury we should be navigating familiar waters, for no matter how many times one may journey over the same canal, its beauty is ever changing according to the season, and the fascinating character of this slow canal travel is sufficient in itself. Nor is this all, as we discovered when we had moored just south of Braunston turn.

No matter how observant a traveller may be, he cannot discover all the interesting things he passes on a single journey, and we had not before noticed the church standing lost in the fields a little distance from the canal, with only a rough track leading to the door. Near by was a substantial farm and a solitary cottage, the total extent, it would seem, of what from the map I concluded was the hamlet of Wolfamcote. We found that the church, which was very large for so small a place, was locked, but, as we hoped, the cottage held the key, which they gave to us willingly, explaining that services were only held during the summer months, owing to the absence of any form of heating system. Even with the help of the key we had a struggle to get in, since the square rod to which the door handle was attached was so worn that it would no longer lift the latch. Within a tragic scene of desolation met our eyes. The stone floor was covered with dust and debris, while damp streamed down the walls from the leaking roof, part of which had been covered with corrugated iron. In the midst of this ruin stood some magnificent oak pews and a fourteenth-century oak screen slowly mouldering into decay. Some of the slender balusters of the latter had already given way, and had been replaced by pitifully poor machine-turned replicas. Of the stonework worthy of mention, there were some corbel heads of true Gothic vigour, and a fine Norman font, while the tower showed signs of very early workmanship. Yet we did not linger long, for there was an indescribable air of melancholy about this forsaken church, standing alone in the fields. Even its dead seemed long forgotten, so overgrown were the drunkenly leaning tombstones by the long rank grass of the churchyard. It was good to be out in the fresh air and the sunlight again, crossing the fields to the boat.

We made 'The Bull and Butcher' that night, and the next, a windy day of bitter cold, the top of Napton Locks at Marston Doles. Despite gloomy forecasts of snow, the wind dropped overnight, and the morning was clear and frosty as we set out over the winding summit level. Every man has some particular part of England that he favours most, so perhaps it was mere prejudice on my part that made this rolling country of the North Oxfordshire border appear softer, kindlier and of more subtle colouring, in its shades of blue and green, than any we had seen to the north. Certainly the day gave of its best, especially towards evening, when we approached Fenny Compton Wharf, and the sun, sinking clear and red, bathed the broad fields and gentle hills in such a magic light that the country looked just as lovely as it had done in the languorous days of high summer.

On the following evening we reached Cropredy, the old cottages of stone and thatch appearing like old and familiar friends. In sharp contrast to that summer evening, the first of our long journey, when we had last passed by, the air was keen with frost as we walked up the street to 'The Red Lion' after dinner, and when we awoke next morning the canal was covered with ice, all the willows glittering with rime.

Ice soon cuts deeply into the timbers of a wooden narrow boat,

but we were particularly anxious to reach Banbury if, as seemed
highly probable, we were destined to be frozen in. The distance to
be covered was short, so we started away, carving through the
seemingly solid surface ahead with a loud grinding noise, and leaving behind us a dark, narrow channel fringed with jutting points.
When we reached the familiar outskirts of Banbury it was to find
that the influx of warm water from factories had prevented the ice
from forming, and so it was through clear water that we reached
familiar moorings at the Banbury Boatyard.

OXFORD CANAL OVER THE RIVER SWIFT (ERIC GASKELL)

WELSH FRANKTON (ERIC GASKELL)

SUTTON STOP (ERIC GASKELL)

GAUXHOLME, TODMORDEN (ERIC GASKELL)

THE THAMES AT RADCOT (ERIC GASKELL)

HATTON FLIGHT, TOP LOCK (ERIC GASKELL)

HALFPENNY BRIDGE AT
LECHLADE (ERIC GASKELL)

CHIRK AQUEDUCT LOOKING
TOWARD ENGLAND (ERIC
GASKELL)

BRAUNSTON DRY DOCKS
(ERIC GASKELL)

AUDLEM MILL,
THE SHROPPIE FLY AND
LOCK 13 (ERIC GASKELL)

Chapter *XXXIV*

FROST

THE threat of frost was fulfilled more thoroughly than ever we had thought possible, and for nearly three months we lay at Banbury, held immovable in the grip of ice six inches thick. It soon became difficult to believe that we had ever been afloat, for the familiar rocking motion with which the boat responded to our movements or to a sudden gust of wind had ceased, and when, after a fortnight of black frost, a heavy fall of snow covered the boat, the canal and the banks in a uniform mantle of white, the illusion of solid foundation was complete. At night the ice creaked and cracked with hollow reverberation or a sharp repetitive knocking, like urgent knuckles rapping against the hull, while sounds from other boats were mysteriously magnified as through some whispering gallery.

Our unorthodox design for living emerged triumphantly from the supreme test of this severe weather, while in the town gas and water supplies were often cut off and many an icicle from sill or down-spout told a sorry tale of burst pipes. Burning night and day with little attention, the stove in our sitting-cabin maintained a constant cheerful warmth, while two small paraffin heaters effectively kept the frost from the drinking-water tank and the independent boiler in the bathroom. Furthermore, the intake of the hand pump supplying the galley sink remained below ice level, and so maintained an uninterrupted water supply.

For company we had the Hone family—father and son—with

their three boats. They, like us, were lucky to have reached a mooring so convenient for supplies, for news slowly filtered over the beleaguered water-way of others less fortunate who, marooned at Claydon Top, 'Fenny', or Marston Doles, were reduced to drinking canal water and walking many miles for bread. The time passed pleasantly enough, for not only were there several minor repairs and improvements which we had in any case intended to carry out at Banbury, but many were the talks we had with old Mr. Alfred Hone and his wife, who had moored 'Cylgate' immediately opposite. We visited each other's cabins, we to marvel at their 'infinite treasure in a little room'—the family photographs, the openwork plates, the knick-knacks, the lace and brass (the latter including a beautifully made pair of miniature lock windlasses), for all of which they contrived to find a place—and they to tip-toe gingerly over our carpet and gaze with polite incredulity at our bath.

Though Mr. Hone was sixty-five years old, it would be grossly unfair to describe him as an old man, for he was as well preserved, as active and tireless as most men of half his age. His bright blue eyes, deep set amid good-humoured wrinkles in his tanned face, twinkled perpetually with the infectious merriment of youth while he related with a wealth of quaintly phrased detail innumerable simple tales of his long life on the canals. He told of his youth, when, with his father, he had worked 'up the West Country by Boblukoi', by which he meant the upper Thames and Bablockhythe. He told, too, of the six years he had spent courting his first wife. Their wooing had perforce been restricted to the rare occasions when their boats met in the short pound between Napton Junction and Braunston, for he was working to Oxford, while she was a boat girl on the London–Birmingham route. It was easy to see that he was proud of those six years, and the faded, old-fashioned photograph which he preserved made such patient tenacity readily understandable. For the first Mrs. Hone must undoubtedly have been a very handsome woman. Her features looked firm and finely moulded, while a pair of dark gipsy eyes gazed with a fixed, proud steadfastness from the tawdry confines of the cheap gilt frame. Her dark hair was braided into plaits coiled about her head, and she wore a massive pair of gold earrings.

His present wife, prior to marriage, had worked at 'The George and Dragon' at Fenny Compton. Courtship this time had been accelerated to twice-weekly visits as he plied to and fro, with the

'WINTER ON THE OXFORD CANAL'

result that it had occupied a mere four years. Thin, energetic, hard-headed Mrs. Hone, though lacking the glamour of her pre-decessor, was an admirable second in command, and an almost unique example of a woman who had in middle age adapted herself to the boatman's way of living with complete success. In fact, she averred stoutly that she would never go back to the land. It would seem the quiet waterways had opened strange doors within her simple mind, to reveal a dimly comprehended beauty which she could ill express, but which far outweighed the synthetic attractions of the cinema, which constitute the usual refuge of her class, for, she explained, 'It's so quiet and peaceful like, nobody don't trouble you and,' she added, 'in the spring up 'leven mile pound you can smell the violets in the banks something lovely as you goes along.'

Being 'off the land', Mrs. Hone was the only member of the family capable of reading or writing, and was regarded with a certain awe in consequence. On Sunday mornings it became customary for her to stand at the cabin hatch of the 'Cylgate' as before a lectern, reading extracts from the Sunday newspaper in a slow, expressionless monotone to a rapt audience, consisting of the rest of the family and any other canal folk who happened to be within earshot. They habitually stood in a silent group on the tow-path, never interrupting, but pondering each word as though it was a pearl of wisdom from some remote and god-like in-telligence.

After the snowfall came signs of a thaw, and the ice-breakers were brought out. These consist of small but stoutly built steel boats varying from thirty to fifty feet long and, unlike most other canal craft, having completely rounded bilges. The larger boats have a single bar mounted waist high amidships, the smaller two bars along the gunwales. To these cling a gang of willing volunteers, who, by swinging their weight to and fro, impart a vigorous rocking motion to the boat as it is drawn along by as many as six horses. This rocking action, which at first sight has something of the absurdity of a child's game being played by grown men, is actually extremely hard physical labour, and essential if the ice is to be broken effectively. For if the boat were allowed to 'swim' upon an even keel, the ice upon either side of her would remain unbroken, with the result that she would soon either become tightly jammed or else be drawn bodily on to the top of the ice.

Two gangs of breakers made a spectacular arrival at Banbury, one from the north and the other from the south. Long before they came in sight their approach was heralded by a grinding and crashing sound that was like the clash of arms, then round the bend came the sweating horses, keeping a fine pace, as though entering into the spirit of the adventure. Finally the boat itself appeared, rolling almost gunwale under from the efforts of her heaving crew, who, ruddy-faced from the cold wind and strenuous labour, seemed oblivious alike to the jets of icy water which spurted from overside and the dirty puddle which slopped to and fro beneath their feet. At the tiller stood an elderly lengthman, balancing first on one leg, then on the other as he endeavoured to keep the bucketing craft upon some semblance of a course.

In the wake of these pioneers came the liberated boats, the ice-floes slithering and grinding round their bows, but Alfred Hone looked at the clearing sky, shook his head significantly, and made no move to be gone. His weather wisdom was confirmed that night, when, under stars of cold brilliance, the frost set in again with redoubled bitterness.

This long period of enforced idleness told heavily upon the slender resources of the boatmen, especially the 'Number Ones'. Those employed by carrying companies had half-pay or the dole to fall back upon, but the 'Number Ones' were reduced to living on their 'docking money'—in other words, the hard-earned savings normally set aside for the periodical overhaul of their boats. At long last, however, the seemingly endless spell of clear weather and biting north-east winds came to an end in a day of mist and grey, scurrying clouds. Simultaneously the wind veered sharply to the south-west, and soon the gurgle of running water from every downspout, ditch and culvert proclaimed the thaw. Next morning the sun rose warm above a steaming haze, and Cherwell, swollen by the melting snowdrifts of the Wolds, overran its broad water-meadows. Even on the canal the flood-water coursed down over the ice, submerging the towing-path and thundering over the lock gates, despite the fact that both paddles had been drawn.

When these floods had abated, the ice-breakers set forth once more, and there was great activity down the long line of moored boats. Brasses were polished, trusses of hay were stowed under fore-hatches, and finally, while the motor-boats were starting their long-silent engines, the horses were brought out, looking plump and sleek after their long rest. Amid this bustle and commotion there was much talk and good-natured banter between boat and boat, for everyone was glad to be on the move again.

Despite its great thickness, the ice thawed with surprising rapidity, and in a day or so all that remained to tell of the great frost were thin, smooth-edged floating fragments which, at the passage of a boat, jostled each other with a musical tinkling sound like that of Japanese windbells. Soon even these vanished, and there was a smell in the air that presaged the turn of the year. A great tit piped his recurrent call from the branch of the apple tree that overhung the boatyard wall. It was time to be gone.

SHIPTON-ON-CHERWELL

Chapter XXXV

SPRING AT HAMPTON GAY

THE sun was shining brightly on the morning we set forth on the last stage of our interrupted journey. Banbury's sordid southern outskirts around the railway station were soon passed by, so that we presently found ourselves winding through the familiar Cherwell meadows, our landmarks the towers of Banbury astern and the tall, remarkably slender spire of Kings Sutton rising above the willows to the south-east.

We had been travelling little more than half an hour when we reached Grants Lock, the first below Banbury, and here we met with an unexpected delay. When we came to swing the lower gate, which, as is the case at all the locks between Banbury and Oxford, was a massive single one, the 'breast', rotted with age, parted from the balance beam. Lacking the counter-balancing effect of the beam, the gate at once dropped in its quoins and refused to open. After several abortive attempts had failed, we hit upon a plan. The spindles operating the paddles were mounted on the beam, so, by disconnecting the pinion of one of them from its rack and by lashing a line between it and the gate below, we were able to use it as a winch to draw the two together. This done, we had no difficulty in locking through, but our repair looked so perilously insecure that we lost no time in reporting the damage to the lock-keeper at King's Sutton wharf.

Apart from this incident the day's journey was uneventful, but doubly enjoyable after so long a spell of enforced idleness. Though not so intricately tortuous as on its course north of Banbury, the canal was never so straight as to become dull, but wound this way and that in a delightfully haphazard fashion as it followed the loops and curves of the river valley, while the characteristic wooden drawbridges were here so numerous that their spreading beams, uplifted over the fields, were the dominant feature of our landscape. Because they were for the most part little used, affording access from field to field, most of them were open to the waterway, though some were unsecured, and rocked in the breeze to give us some uneasy moments when we slid through the narrow channel beneath them.

At Nell Bridge we came in sight of Aynho, a trim cluster of grey cottages on the crest of a hill a mile distant. Though brick was the chosen medium of the canal builders, here even they had used stone for the fixed bridges, for we were now entering the stone country proper, the grey Cotswold oolite that flows over the wolds to spill into the valleys of Evenlode and Cherwell. Somerton was the next village we sighted; like Aynho and the rest of the villages along the river, it is set on high ground above flood level, and the canal wharf lies immediately at the foot of the sloping street. Here we stopped for tea before moving on over Heyford Common, to moor at nightfall in perfect surroundings by Heyford Mill Lock. The evening was brilliantly clear, and the ranks of pollard willows which marched westwards across the meadows were silhouetted with a startling clarity that was almost unreal against the sunset's afterglow. Eastwards we were sheltered by a steep bank, at the top of which, screened by a belt of tall elms, lay the village of Upper Heyford.

The weather was still brilliant the next morning when we cast off and traversed the lovely tree-bordered pound that extends from Heyford Mill through Lower Heyford to Dashwood Lock. At Northbrook, a lonely lock lost amid the trees by the river margin, we paused for a mid-morning cup of coffee before continuing on our way through Kirtlington woods, past the secluded 'Pigeons' inn to Gibraltar Lock, at the tail of which we entered the Cherwell. The ensuing river section is a mile long, and abounds in acute turns; moreover, the current is at all times swift, so that in times of flood it often becomes unnavigable. On this account traffic is frequently held up, so that it would seem that the canal engineers showed some lack of foresight in not cutting an independent course throughout.

We left the river's devious windings at Weir, an unusual type of flood-lock with a diamond-shaped chamber. The precise reason for its odd construction was not clear, nor could the lock-keeper enlighten us, since, for all its apparent size, it could accommodate only one narrow boat at a time. When we had locked through and rounded the bend beyond the lock tail we sighted the grey church and manor house of Shipton-on-Cherwell overpeering the water from their vantage on the high right bank, while across the river not a quarter of a mile away stood the tiny chapel of Hampton Gay, dreaming alone in the fields, with only a grass pathway to its door. In the golden evening light the combination of grey buildings, green meadows, tall trees and still, sky-reflecting water made a picture so entrancing that we forthwith decided to journey no farther, and moored 'Cressy' where the dry-wall of Shipton churchyard sloped down to the water's edge. When I stopped her engine, silence fell swiftly, no breath-bating hush of suspense, but a soundless calm that seemed to lap as closely about us as the water round our hull and which brought with it a sense of peace unassailable and timeless.

The willows were casting long fingers of shadow when we walked across the meadows and over the river footbridge to Hampton Gay. The morrow would bring us within sight of the many spires and towers of Oxford, the end for a time of four hundred miles of this slow voyaging. What could be better, then, I thought, than in this quiet place to bring the story of our journey to a close, since such a wandering tale should have no ending. The many miles we had covered had only served to bring nearer the tempting prospects of new waterways to explore and of others to revisit. The lures of the Welsh Canal, the Kennet and Avon, the Fenlands, and the Rivers Severn, Avon, Nene and Thames, to mention only a few, were all the stronger for the coming of another spring. Yet because the world of men must needs devote themselves to evil things in a senseless struggle for power, all must remain unsure, the future be unknown and beauty go a-begging. It was with these somewhat melancholy thoughts that we passed the chapel and came upon the ruined manor of Hampton Gay, where we found a symbol of new promise.

According to an old countryman whom we met trudging homeward over the fields, the old house was fired by its last unscrupulous occupant with the object of collecting the insurance money, a plot which brought about his downfall. Harsh-crying jackdaws had made their habitation in the towering chimney-stacks, crumbling stone mullions gaped in ruin and the charred fragments of great beams still lay where they had fallen in the nettles that grew thickly within the walls. Yet nature's tireless growth had covered this sorry monument of human greed and violence with a kindly cloak of trees, whose branches swept the walls on every side. As though this were not enough, upon the floor of the wood the unfailing promise of spring had been fulfilled in all its matchless purity, for about the tree-boles and the scarred walls surged a white wave of snowdrops starred with yellow aconite. Ugliness had been defeated by an irrepressible beauty.

As we walked back towards Shipton the last of the sunlight was glowing on the old grey stones of the church tower. Below, a dim blue shape in the deep twilight of the trees, we could see our boat.

CONCLUSION

THE journey which this book describes occupied the fateful summer and winter of 1939–40. Since then the war, which at that time still seemed a nightmare from which we would soon awaken, has spread desolation across the world and has brought many changes to England. For the present, at all events, the neglected fields have come to life because the town has once more been made aware of its ultimate dependence upon the land. The pledge has been given that never again will the country be allowed to fall to ruin, and it is the duty of all who hold the welfare of that country dear to ensure that this pledge is honoured. For all too often in time of tribulation nations, like individuals, are eager to admit past faults and to make good resolutions for the future, but equally ready to forget them when their adversities are over.

If the country is in danger of future neglect on the one hand, it is equally in danger of exploitation on the other. Today the talk is all of planning, and there are many who would plan and control the country from the town. The fact that this is seriously contemplated is a measure of the gulf which divides the countryman from the urban philosopher. For the land is not a food factory, to be exploited by large highly mechanised ranches run by business men and mechanics, and the ruinous effect on fertility of this conception of cash-crop farming is already evident in other countries. The land needs husbandmen, not machines and their slaves; it offers us a way of life, not a source of profit.

There are two courses open to each man in his brief lifetime: either he can seek the good life, or he can struggle for wealth and power; the former emphasises spiritual, the latter material values. After the war the choice will still be ours, and if it be the good life, the land awaits our coming. If, on the other hand, we continue to pursue our material obsession, the urban bureaucrats are ready to plan our lives from cradle to grave and we shall become the slaves of a scientific 'Technocracy'.

Although the war has deepened the conviction that there is something seriously wrong with our civilisation, we have become

so besotted with the idea of the inevitability of scientific progress
that we are contemplating plunging even deeper into the mire of
mechanised living, in the tragic belief that, despite the evidence
of the past one hundred and fifty years, it is still the way to
Utopia. In fact, to follow this road is to sacrifice the individuality
and creative ability of man on the altar of material prosperity.
The factories and mean streets of our industrial cities may represent the wealth of England, but the greatness of the English tradition was born of our fields and villages, and is dying with the
peasant, the yeoman and the craftsman. It was the desire to discover whether this tradition was in fact a living force, or merely
the nostalgic 'remembrance of things past', which led me to build
my home and to travel about England in the way I have tried to
describe. I argued that the canals belonged to a past when that
tradition, though threatened, was still vital, and that it was from
that past that I should view the present in order to see it in its
proper perspective. The result of my experiment has not merely
proved to me the validity of an older way of life, it has left me
appalled at the loss which our civilisation has sustained. The men
I have been privileged to meet, some of whom I have mentioned
in these pages, revealed more eloquently than any words of mine
a way of life, which was the antithesis of the stereotyped and root-
less existence of twentieth-century 'economic man', and it is the
spirit of which these men are the unthinking guardians which must
not be permitted to perish from the earth. The restoration of that
spirit does not involve, as many suppose, a reactionary 'back-to-
nature' process, but simply the adoption of the aim of the good
life. Controlled by such a principle, science, of which the machine
is the symbol, would become a slave instead of a master, a com-
plement to, rather than a substitute for, the creative ability of man.

The future of the English Canals, which are the particular
vehicle of this book, depends no less than that of the countryside
on the order which we build after the war. At present the prospects
are not bright, for despite the fuel and rubber crisis and much
propaganda to the contrary, the waterways are still the victims of
vested interest, some still lying idle, others handling less than their
pre-war traffic. In a society framed to cherish our national heritage
the canals can play their part not only as a means of transport and
employment, but as part of an efficient system of land drainage and
a source of beauty and pleasure. But if the canals are left to the
mercies of economists and scientific planners, before many years

are past the last of them will become a weedy, stagnant ditch, and the bright boats will rot at the wharves, to live on only in old men's memories. It is because I fear that this may happen that I have made this record of them.

Not only have these waterways introduced me to the peasant and the craftsman, but they have recaptured for me that sense of place which swift transport, standardisation and ever more centralised urban government are doing their best to destroy. It is this sense of place or *genius loci*, as it has been called, which is the countryman's birthright, and which was once made manifest by him in his use of local materials, in his speech, song and story, and in countless other intimate ways which faithfully reflected the character of the region of his birth. It is an essence not easy to capture, and still more difficult to translate into words, although I have attempted to convey something of its changing quality which I perceived as we moved through the Midland Shires.

That journey which I have recorded here did not end with this book. From Oxford, 'Cressy' moved down Thames, and so by Kennet into the Wiltshire Downs. Today she lies at the summit of the great flight of locks which climbs from Severn on to the watershed which divides that river from Avon and her tributaries Arrow and Alne. As I write I look from my window across the broad vale of Severn to the Abberley Hills above the Teme, to the dark slopes of Wyre and beyond to the high summits of Titterstone Clee and Abdon Burf. And as I gaze there come into my mind the lines of Sir Arthur Quiller-Couch, who from Eckington Bridge saw this same green heart of England and wrote:—

'Man shall outlast his battles. They have swept
Avon from Naseby Field to Severn Ham;
And Evesham's dedicated stones have stepp'd
Down to the dust with Montfort's oriflamme.
Nor the red tear nor the reflected tower
Abides; but yet these eloquent grooves remain,
Worn in the sandstone parapet hour by hour
By labouring bargemen where they shifted ropes.
E'en so shall man turn back from violent hopes
To Adam's cheer, and toil with spade again.'

'CRESSY'

CABIN PLAN

APPENDIX I

THIS is not a technical book, but for the benefit of those who may have more than a passing interest in the subject these few notes may be of value.

(1) *The Boat.* 'Cressy' is a Shropshire Union Canal narrow boat, 70 ft. in length by 7 ft. beam, with an average draught of 1 ft. 6 ins. Originally a horse-drawn 'fly-boat', when converted she was fitted with a 'Model T' Ford marine conversion which utilises the original epicyclic gearbox as a marine reverse gear. This unit is mounted at deck level, driving the propellor shaft by a double chain, an unusual arrangement which renders the engine very accessible for overhaul, sump draining and similar jobs. An engine-driven pump draws water through a sea-cock for cooling purposes. This is normally discharged overside through the exhaust pipe, but by closing a stop valve it may be diverted into the large roof-tank which supplies bath-water. By means of a two-way tap on the suction side this pump also extracts the bilge-water.

A battery and dynamo supply current for starting, also for lighting throughout the boat. There is a roomy hold under the aft deck where fuel, lubricating oil, tools, etc., are stored, while above deck against the aft cabin bulkhead are mounted petrol and paraffin tanks holding six and twenty-five gallons respectively. In addition to supplying the engine through a vaporiser, the latter fuel was chosen for all cooking, water-heating and additional lighting purposes because it is so readily obtainable even in the most remote village.

The aft doors and sliding hatchway give access by steps to a small workshop and storeroom, where are shelves for sundry stores such as polishes, etc., hanging space for overcoats, and a workbench with vise and tool racks.

Next comes the bathroom. So that the bath waste should drain over-side, it was necessary to mount it somewhat higher than usual, and it has therefore been encased, so that the space beneath it could be utilised to form two roomy cupboards with flush-fitting doors. A wash-basin lets down from the wall to rest on the sides of the bath, and being hinged after the fashion of a farm gate, it can then be slid under the bath-taps. This basin drains via the bath-waste. Copper pipes connect the bath-taps to the roof tank and to an independent boiler, which, fired by a single paraffin burner of Optimus type, provides sufficient hot water for a bath in an hour from lighting up. The tank above has sufficient capacity for five full baths, and its top is detachable for cleaning purposes. Hanging cupboards, a mirror and towel rail complete the bathroom fittings, while the chemical closet adjoins.

The stateroom which next follows has a recessed hanging wardrobe with shoe-racks beneath concealed by a curtain, and a glass-topped dressing-table with shelves below and mirror over. There is also a three-quarter-length mirror on the communicating door to the bathroom. The box-spring double berth has a cupboard mounted on the wall over the head, and space for luggage beneath. There are two roof ventilators, while light is provided by three windows and electric lights over bed and dressing-table. A folding bedside table lets down from the wall.

The sitting-cabin, which is the largest in the boat, is situated amidships and is lighted by six windows, one of these being very large, extending almost from roof to gunwale. This has two casements which open outwards to fold flat against the cabin sides. All the other windows in the boat slide open on runners, otherwise they are liable, when open, to foul lock sides or bridges. The aft bulkhead of this cabin is occupied entirely by bookshelves, with which is incorporated a folding writing-desk. The only other fixtures are a small seat built into the angle of the opposite bulkhead, and the stove, which is of the 'Cozy' open-fire type. The floor is carpeted with dark brown pile, and there are two easy chairs.

The galley adjoining has, upon one side of the central gangway, a two-burner cooking stove with plate-rack and shelving over, and alongside it a kitchen table with three deep drawers below. The sink opposite is fitted with a detachable draining board, which rests on the table top of a large store cupboard. On the wall above hangs a plate drying-rack. Opposite this, with tap projecting over the sink, stands a small round water-tank, which is supplied with water by a semi-rotary hand pump mounted on the bulkhead. A single-burner stove stands on a shelf beneath this tank, and thus conveniently provides hot water for washing up. The sink, of course, drains into the canal. Numerous shelves for saucepans, cannisters and jars of spice or herbs complete the equipment.

Lastly comes the fore-cabin, which serves the dual purpose of dining-saloon and spare twin-berth sleeping-cabin. The two berths are built in the form of chests to contain linen, rugs and blankets. When the cabin is in use for meals the central portion of one berth folds back upon itself, and between the two separate seats thus formed the dining-table folds down from the wall above. Three people can comfortably sit at this table; in the event of a larger party, a folding table is used, set lengthwise between the two berths. At the head of one berth there are shelves for crockery, with a cupboard below for glasses and bottles, by the other a hanging wardrobe, dressing-table and cupboard for the use of guests, these being concealed by flush fitting doors when not in use.

Double doors open on to the fore deck in which are two hatches giving access to the coal bunkers beneath, which hold five hundredweight. A ladder communicates with the cabin roof and a small door opens into the fore peak, which is used as a larder and storeroom. On one side it contains a large meat-safe, on the other a fifteen-gallon drinking-water tank with filler cap projecting through the deck, and tap conveniently set over the well-deck.

The headroom in the cabins is approximately six feet three inches, reduced by eight inches in the bathroom and workshop, owing to the floor being raised to make room for four tons of metal ballast. This is necessary in order to bring propellor and rudder well beneath the surface, an essential point if a boat is to travel and 'swim' well.

The dimensions of the cabins may be said to be the maximum which can confidently be taken anywhere on the canal system without fear of fouling. The 'tumble home' of the cabin walls conforms to the contour of the canal bridges, and only the roof-tank approaches the safe limit of headroom. This latter, however, was purposely made readily detachable.

Speed averages approximately three to three and a half miles per hour in still water, but depends largely on the breadth and depth of the channel. In a very narrow channel it is largely limited by the speed with which the water, forced aside by the bows, can pass the hull. Fuel consumption averages one gallon per hour, but this again varies considerably with conditions encountered.

(2) *Equipment.* We carried with us the following essential equipment: two shafts or boat-hooks on deck, one long and one short. Two thirty-foot cotton mooring lines fore and aft, also additional lines stowed in hold. One single purchase tackle for emergency

use in the event of our running very heavily aground. One ten-foot gang plank—most essential on canals with shallow margins. One rope bow fender to prevent damage when entering locks. Mooring spikes for use when no bollards or convenient tree stumps were available for mooring. Four lock windlasses to suit the different sizes of paddle spindles to be met with on various canal systems. Two large-size funnels for easy filling of paraffin and drinking-water tanks. A hand bilge-pump of the standard pattern found on the canals.

Drums and cans for replenishing fuel and water.

Rag mop for swabbing decks and cabin-work.

'Bradshaw's Guide to the Canals and Navigable Rivers of England and Wales'.

Inch-to-the-Mile Ordnance Survey maps of every district covered.

(3) *Tolls*. These vary to such an extent that it is almost impossible to give any average figure of expense. As an instance of this the following charges may be quoted. Grand Union Canal, Braunston to Trent Junction, seventy miles, £2 10*s*. Trent and Mersey Canal, Derwent Mouth to Middlewich, seventy-six miles, 18*s*. Shropshire Union Canal, Middlewich to Autherley, fifty-two miles, 11*s*. Birmingham Canal (Coventry Canal Section), Whittington Brook to Fazeley, five miles, 10*s*. 6*d*.

In theory a boat pays principally for the single lock of water which it uses on its passage through a canal, irrespective of the number of locks encountered. When it is pointed out, however, that the five miles on the Birmingham Canal mentioned above include no locks, it will be realised that it is impossible for the stranger to assess what any given toll is likely to be.

No specific time limit is laid down for a given journey, and charges for prolonged mooring are usually negligible and fixed by annual agreement with the company concerned. Locks must almost invariably be worked by the boat's crew, but the canal folk are unfailingly helpful in case of difficulty, provided full credit is given to them for knowledge and experience. Rightly, they have little time for the amateur boatman who airs his knowledge, since they realise full well that the experience of a life-time cannot be acquired in a few weeks' pleasure cruising.

GLOSSARY

(For the definition of many of the terms given below I am indebted to 'Bradshaw's Guide to the Canals and Navigable Rivers of England and Wales' by the late Mr. Rodolph de Salis.)

Animals.—A boatman's name for donkeys, which until recently were much in use for towing purposes, particularly on the canals tributary to the River Severn, a pair of them taking the place of one horse.

Balance Beam or Balance.—The beam projecting from a lock gate which balances its weight, and by pushing against which the gate is opened or closed.

Barge.—A term including a variety of vessels, both sailing and non-sailing, in use for canal or river traffic, whose beam is approximately twice that of a narrow boat. The name 'barge' is often applied erroneously to all vessels carrying goods on a canal or river, whether barge, wide boat, narrow boat, lighter or any other vessel.

Blow, to.—To give warning when approaching a bridge-hole or other narrow place where the view ahead is restricted and there is therefore a danger of collision. Motor-boats sound sirens of different types, while captains of horse-boats either crack their whips or blow a horn of polished brass which is kept in the cabin within reach of the steerer.

Bobbins.—Short, hollow wooden rollers, several of which are usually threaded on each of the traces of horses engaged in towing, to prevent the traces chafing. They are often painted in bright colours.

Bow Hauling.—Hauling by men, in distinction from the more usual method of hauling by horses. When a motor-boat and butty are working through a flight of narrow locks, the tow-line is usually detached and the butty bow hauled.

Breast or Mitre Post.—Of a lock gate, the vertical post of the gate farthest from its hanging; where the gates are in pairs, the two breasts are usually mitred to bed against each other when shut.

Bridge Hole.—The narrow channel beneath an over-bridge.

Butty Boat.—A boat working in company with another boat. The term is generally applied to a boat towed by a motor-boat.

Bye Trader.—A term used to designate any trader on a canal other than the canal company itself when carriers. All canal companies are not carriers themselves, some merely providing the water-way and taking toll for its use.

Chalico.—A mixture of tar, cow-hair and horse-dung made hot, used for dressing the timbers of wooden boats.

Compartment Boat.—Commonly called a 'Tom Pudding', a type of boat in use on the Aire and Calder Navigation, which is worked in trains with other similar boats.

Cratches.—The supports of the gang-planks of a narrow boat at the fore end of the boat. The deck cratch is placed at the point where the fore deck terminates and the cargo space begins, the false cratch being situated a short distance abaft the deck cratch.

Cut.—A boatman's name for canal, so applied on account of its artificially cut channel, as distinguished from the natural channel of a river.

Day Boats.—Boats without cabins, used in working short-distance traffic and on which there is no sleeping accommodation. Also called open boats.

Doors.—A Fen term for gates; in the Fens all lock gates are called sluice doors.

Draw.—To draw a paddle, slacker, slat, weir or staunch is to open it in order to allow the water to escape. The reverse is to 'lower', 'drop' or 'shut in', or in the case of a staunch to 'set'.

Dydle (Norfolk).—To dredge, to clean out.

Flash or Flush.—A body of accumulated water suddenly released, used for the purpose of assisting navigation on river.

Flash (Cheshire).—An inland lake caused by subsidence of the ground due to salt-mining.

Flat.—A Mersey flat is a type of vessel which conducts the bulk of the traffic on that river and neighbouring canals. A black flat is a larger vessel trading between Liverpool and the River Weaver. The term 'flat' is also used to describe the shallow punts or rafts used by lock-keepers or lengthmen for canal maintenance.

Fly Boat.—Originally described a horse-boat which, using relays of horses, travelled day and night. The term now applies to any type of boat so travelling. A boatman so engaged is said to be 'working fly'.

Freshet.—An increase in the flow of a river due to rain.

Gang.—The number of Fen lighters or River Stour (Suffolk) lighters chained together for travelling. In the case of Fen lighters the number in a gang is five, on the River Stour always two.

Gang Planks.—Removable planks used to afford a means of passing from one end of a narrow boat to the other; when in place they run from the top of the cabin aft to the deck cratch forward, being supported in between by upright supports called stands. These stands, which are also removable, fit into mortices in the stretchers and boat's floor, and have the gang-planks tightly lashed down to them.

Gauging.—The means of ascertaining by the draught of a vessel the weight of cargo on board for the purpose of taking tolls. The first gauging of canal boats is carried out at a weigh-dock, where particulars of the boat's draught are taken when empty, and when fully loaded, and at intermediate points, such as at every ton of loading. The boat is loaded with weights kept for the purpose, which are lifted in and out by cranes; the result arrived at is then either transferred to graduated scales fixed to the boat's sides, which can be read at any time, or the particulars of each vessel are furnished to each toll office in a book, from which, on gauging the immersion of the boat, the number of tons on board can be at once ascertained. The usual method of gauging a boat for immersion is to take what is called the 'dry inches'—that is, the freeboard, at four points, at one point each side near the bow and at one point each side near the stern. This is done by an instrument consisting of a float in a tube, having a bracket projecting from the side of the tube. The bracket is rested on the boat's gunwale, and the float indicates the number of inches between that and the level of the water in the canal.

Give Way, to.—To concede the right of passage to another boat—*e.g.*, empty boats usually give way to loaded, motors to horse-boats. The actual passing rule varies on different water-ways, keeping to the right being now most general, but a motor-boat always gives a horse-boat the tow-path side, for obvious reasons.

Gongoozler.—An idle and inquisitive person who stands staring for prolonged periods at anything out of the common. This word is believed to have its origin in the Lake District.

Handspike.—A bar of wood used as a lever; one some of the old-fashioned locks a handspike was required for working the lock paddles instead of rack and pinion gears. It is also used for working the anchor chain roller on river barges.

Hane (Norfolk) Higher.—'The water is hane today.' That is: The water is higher today.

Haling Way.—A Fen term; a towing-path.

Heel Post.—The vertical post of a lock gate nearest to its hanging, and the axis on which the gate turns, being rounded at the back to fit into the hollow quoin, in which it partially revolves.

Hold in, Hold out.—Boatmen's terms used as directions for steering, having reference to the position of the towing-path. 'Hold in' means hold the boat in to the towing-path side of the canal, and vice versa.

Hollow Quoin.—The recess into which the heel post of a lock gate is fitted, and in which it partially revolves when being opened and closed.

Horse Boat.—Strictly speaking, a small open boat for ferrying over towing horses from one side of a river to the other where no bridge is available. In common use in the Fen district, where it is towed astern of a gang of lighters. One is also kept for use at Trent Junction to ferry horses from the mouth of the River Soar over the Trent to the junction of the Erewash Canal. Of recent years the term has come to be loosely used to describe any horse-drawn narrow boat, as distinct from motor craft.

Horse Marines (Yorkshire).—Men who contract for the haulage of vessels by horses on the canals.

House Lighter.—A Fen term, used to denote a lighter provided with a cabin.

Invert.—An inverted arch of brickwork or masonry, used chiefly as regards canal work to form the bottom of locks and tunnels in cases where lateral or upward pressure has to be sustained.

Josher.—A term used by boatmen to signify a boat belonging to Fellows Morton and Clayton, Ltd., Canal Carriers, the Christian name of the late Mr. Fellows having been Joshua.

Keb.—An iron rake used for fishing up coal or other articles from the bottom of a canal. Boatmen may often be seen fishing for coal in this way at coal wharves.

Keel.—A type of boat in extensive use on the Yorkshire rivers and canals, they measure approximately 58 ft. long by 14 ft. beam.

Land Water.—A term used to denote the water in a river brought down from up country, in distinction from the water set up by the flood-tide from seawards.

Legging.—A method used to propel horse-drawn boats through tunnels which have no towing-path, the boatman pushing with his feet against the tunnel walls. At one time leggers could be hired at most of the longer tunnels, notably Standedge on the Huddersfield Narrow Canal, 5,456 yds. long, which is the longest in England, and Sapperton on the old Thames and Severn Canal, 3,808 yds.

Lengthman.—A canal company's employee in charge of a particular section or length of water-way.

Let Off.—An appliance for getting rid of some of the water from a canal in rainy weather so that it may not overflow its banks. Originally a trap-door sluice set in the bottom of the canal and worked by a chain, but now resembling the ordinary lock paddle.

Level.—When two reaches of water, one on each side of a lock or weir, from the flow of the tide or other cause become level, a level is said to be made.

Lighter.—A term including a variety of vessels in use on the Fens, the Thames, the River Stour (Suffolk) and the Bridgwater Canal. On an average they measure 42 ft. in length by 10 ft. beam, but Thames Lighters equal barges in size, differing from them in the respect that they have 'swim ends'—*i.e.*, flat, sloping ends like a punt.

Lock, to.—To work a vessel through a lock.

Loodel.—A staff used to form a vertical extension of the tiller of a barge for the purpose of steering when loaded with high loads, such as hay or straw. The loodel, when required, is inserted in a mortice in the fore end of the tiller.

Narrow Boat.—A craft measuring approximately 70 ft. long by 7 ft. beam, extensively used throughout the Midland canal system. Sometimes also referred to as a *Monkey Boat* or *Long Boat*.

Nip (River Trent).—A narrow place.

Number Ones.—Boats owned by the boatmen who work them, and who are consequently their own masters, in distinction from boats owned by a firm or company.

Paddle.—A sluice valve, by opening or closing which the water can either be allowed to pass or be retained.
 Sometimes also called a *slacker* or *clough*. Ground paddles or jack cloughs are those that admit water to the lock by culverts built in the ground, as distinct from the Fly Paddles, Ranters or Flashers, which are fitted to the gates themselves.

Pen (a Lock Pen).—A Fen term; a lock chamber. Also 'to pen', to lock a vessel—*e.g.*, 'A narrow boat is too long to pen at Stanground'.

Pound.—The stretch of water on a canal between two locks.

Quant (Norfolk).—A pole or shaft.

Ram's Head.—The boatman's name for the wooden rudder post of a narrow boat; usually it is bound with pipe-clayed Turk's-head knots, and occasionally decorated with a horse's tail.

Rimers.—The posts in the removable portions of weirs on the Upper Thames against which the weir paddles are placed.

Roding.—A Fen term; cutting rushes or reeds in a river, or cotting if they are uprooted.

Roving Bridge or Turnover Bridge.—A bridge carrying a towing-path from one side of a canal to the other.

Screw.—A boatman's term for any boat driven by a screw pro-peller.

Set, to.—To set a staunch is to close it so that the water may accumulate.

Shaft, to.—To propel a boat through a tunnel with a long shaft as an alternative to legging.

Sill.—Of a lock. The bar of masonry below water against which the bottom of the lock gates rests when closed.

Staircase Locks.—Also called *risers*. A flight or series of locks so arranged that the top gate or gates of each lock except the highest also form the bottom gate or gates of the lock above. The best example of a staircase in England is the flight of five at Bingley on the Leeds and Liverpool Canal.

Staith (*Midlands and North*).—A coal-loading wharf. In Norfolk the word refers to a general wharf.

Stands.—The intermediate supports for the gang-planks of a narrow boat.

Stank.—A temporary water-tight dam constructed of piling from which the water can be pumped to enable below-water repairs to be carried out. The word is also used as a verb—*e.g.*, 'to stank off'.

Staunch or Navigation Weir.—An appliance for overcoming change of level in a navigable river. It consists of a weir provided with a gate through which vessels may pass, and which is equipped with paddles like a lock gate. When proceeding upstream, vessels close the gate behind them and wait until sufficient depth of water has accumulated in the reach above the gate to allow them to proceed. Travelling downstream the procedure is re-versed. This is naturally a very slow business, but examples are still in use in the Fen district and at Pershore and Crop-thorne on the Warwickshire Avon.

Stemmed, Stemmed up.—The boatman's term for running aground on a mud-bank.

Stop.—A *stop* or *stop lock* is generally a gate or a lock erected at the junction of one canal with another, to prevent loss of water from one to the other if necessary, normally there being little or no change of level. There is generally a toll office at a stop lock where cargoes are declared and gauged and tolls paid.

Stop Gates.—They answer the same purpose as stop grooves and planks, but are made in the form of lock gates, and are always kept open except when required for use. In long canal pounds it is usual for stop gates to be fitted at intervals, so that in the event of a leak or burst the escape of water may be confined to that portion of the pound between two gates.

Stop Grooves.—Vertical grooves, usually provided at the head and tail of a lock and in other situations where under-water repairs may have to be carried out, into which stop planks can be inserted to form a temporary dam or stank.

Stoppage.—A temporary closing of a waterway for repairs.

Stud.—The tee-headed pin fitted on bow and stern of a narrow boat to which mooring lines are attached. The towing stud of a narrow boat is C-shaped, and is fitted to the top of a tall post called the mast.

Summit Level.—The highest pound of water in a canal, and therefore the pound into which the main supply of water for working the locks has to be delivered. Consequently, in dry weather it is the first to be affected as regards deficiency of navigable depth. The highest summit level in England is that of the Huddersfield Narrow Canal, which is 4½ miles long from Diggle to Marsden, and is 644 ft. 9 ins. above Ordnance Datum. For 3¼ miles of this summit level the course of the canal is through Standedge Tunnel.

Sweep.—A large oar.

Swim, to.—A boat light in draught and which answers readily to the helm is described by boatmen as 'a good swimmer', or may be said to 'swim well'.

Tackle.—A boatman's name for the harness of a boat horse.

Tail (of a lock).—That portion immediately below the bottom gates. The equivalent portion above the top gates is called the *head*.

Toll.—The charge payable by a trader for the use of a canal.

Towing Path.—The path beside a canal for the use of towing horses, also called in different districts *haling path* or *haling way*.

Trow.—A type of vessel in use on the River Severn; they measure approximately 70 ft. long by 17 ft. beam.

Tub Boats.—Small box boats carrying from three to five tons, once used in Shropshire and on the Bude canal in Cornwall.

Turns, Waiting Turns or Working Turns.—A system often adopted in dry weather in order to make the utmost use of the water. At any lock a boat must wait for the arrival of another coming in the opposite direction, thus making sure that the maximum of traffic is passed for the water consumed.

Tying Point.—The shallowest point in a navigation. For instance, the bottom sill of Cranfleet Lock, better known to boatmen as Old Sal's Lock, was at one time the tying point on the river Trent between Nottingham and the junction of the Erewash Canal; that is to say, any vessel that could float over this sill could find enough water everywhere else between these places.

Wash Lands or Washes.—Lands adjoining a river, so embanked that the river can overflow on to them when in flood.

Wherry.—The name given to the sailing vessels which trade over the rivers Bure, Yare and Waveney and their connecting dykes and broads; they vary considerably, from a 12-ton boat about 35 ft. long by 9 ft. beam to the 'Wonder' of Norwich, 65 ft. long by 19 ft. beam.

Wide Boat.—A type of boat in use on canals having wide locks. It is of a size between the narrow boat and the barge, 70 ft. long by 10 to 11 ft. beam. Such craft navigate the Grand Union Canal from London as far north as Berkhampstead. They are not used for longer distances, since they do not travel so well as a narrow motor boat and butty, on account of their broader beam.

Wind, to.—To wind a boat is to turn a boat round.

Winding Place, Winding Hole, Winning Place or Winning Hole.—A wide place in a canal provided for the purpose of turning a boat round.

Windlass.—Also called in some districts a *crank*, is a handle or key for opening and closing lock paddles, shaped in the form of the letter L, and having a square socket at one end to fit on the square of the spindle operating the paddle gear.

Wings.—Flat pieces of board rigged for the purpose of legging in tunnels when the tunnel is too wide to permit of the leggers reaching the side walls with their feet from the boat's deck. A fully equipped narrow boat would carry two pairs of wings, a pair of 'narrow-cut wings' and a pair of 'broad-cut wings'—that is, a pair of wings suitable for the full-size tunnels of narrow boat canals, and also a pair suitable for the tunnels of barge canals.

INDEX OF NAMES AND PLACES